Strategic Information Systems for Strategic, Manufacturing, Operations, Marketing, Sales, Financial and Human Resources Management

MONOGRAPHS IN ORGANIZATIONAL BEHAVIOR AND INDUSTRIAL RELATIONS, VOLUME 16

Editor: Samuel B. Bacharach, *Department of Organizational Behavior, New York State School of Industrial and Labor Relations, Cornell University*

MONOGRAPHS IN ORGANIZATIONAL BEHAVIOR AND INDUSTRIAL RELATIONS

Edited by
Samuel B. Bacharach
Department of Organizational Behavior
New York State School of Industrial and Labor Relations
Cornell University

Strategic Information Systems for Strategic, Manufacturing, Operations, Marketing, Sales, Financial and Human Resources Management

Edited by **ROBERT P. CERVENY**
Florida Atlantic University
C. CARL PEGELS
G. LAWRENCE SANDERS
State University of New York at Buffalo

 JAI PRESS INC.

Greenwich, Connecticut　　　　　　　*London, England*

658.4038
S898

Library of Congress Cataloging-in-Publication Data

Strategic information systems for strategic, manufacturing,
   operations, marketing, sales, financial and human resources
   management / edited by Robert P. Cerveny, C. Carl Pegels,
G. Lawrence Sanders.
       p.   cm. — (Monographs in organizational behavior and
   industrial relations; v. 16)
       Includes bibliographical references and index.
       ISBN 1-55938-716-5
       1. Management information systems. 2. Strategic planning.
I. Cerveny, Robert P. II. Pegels, C. Carl. III. Sanders,
G. Lawrence. IV. Series.
T58.5.S757   1993
658.4'038—dc20

                                                    93-33185
                                                    CIP

Copyright © 1993 JAI Press Inc.
55 Old Post Road No. 2
Greenwich, Connecticut 06830

JAI Press Ltd.
The Courtyard
28 High Street
Hampton Hill
Middlesex TW12 1PD
England

ISBN: 1-55938-716-5
Library of Congress Catalog Card Number: 93-33185
Manufactured in the United States of America

ACKNOWLEDGMENTS

The authors acknowledge the financial support of the Japanese External Trade Organization (JETRO) during the development of the original ideas contained in this monograph.

The authors dedicate this book to their respective families in gratitude for their support.

CONTENTS

LIST OF CONTRIBUTORS

Ranga Anbil   American Airlines
                         Decision Services

Bruce Andrews   School of Business, Economics,
                           and Management
                         University of Southern Maine

Gordon Armstrong   Ocean Spray Cranberries

Robert P. Cerveny   College of Business
                         Florida Atlantic University

Barry Cox   ICI Pharmaceuticals

Donald Davis   University of Mississippi

Eric Gelman   American Airlines
                         Decision Services

Steve Gisbourne   ICI Corporate Management Services

Gerd Islei   Manchester School of Business
                         University of Manchester

Frank M. Lin   School of Business and Public
                           Administration
                         California State University
                           at San Bernardino

John D.C. Little   Massachusetts Institute of Technology

Geoff Lockett   Manchester School of Business
                         University of Manchester

Larry Meile   School of Business
                         Bentley College

David Meinert   University of Mississippi

Henry Parsons   School of Business, Economics,
                                          and Management
                                        University of Southern Maine

Bruce Patty   Aerican Airlines
                                        Decision Services

C. Carl Pegels   School of Management
                                        State University of New York
                                          at Buffalo

Phil Quinn   Strategic Planning Department
                                        L.L. Bean, Inc.

H.R. Rao   School of Management
                                        State University of New York
                                          at Buffalo

G. Lawrence Sanders   School of Management
                                        State University of New York
                                          at Buffalo

John D. Schmitz   Information Resources

Vijay Sethi   College of Business Administration
                                        University of Oklahoma

Vikram Sethi   Katz Graduate School
                                          of Business
                                        University of Pittsburgh

Mike Stratford   ICI Corporate Management Services

Rajan Tanga   American Airlines
                                        Decision Technologies

PREFACE

The notion of a strategic information system has been around for a while but it has never been satisfactorily defined. It is not the intent of this book to explicitly define strategic information systems. However, by describing, evaluating and analyzing strategic information systems we implicitly provide a definition for them.

The question of whether strategic information systems are designed for the purpose of following a specific strategy is a difficult one. It appears that many strategic information systems have evolved over time, frequently from an information support system to a full-fledged strategic information system. The evolution can span a considerable period of time and many strategic benefits of information systems are frequently by-products or bonuses to the original purposes of the information system.

It is clear, however, that functioning strategic information systems as described in this book are providing an important and critical service to the firms employing them and also provide a strong competitive advantage. Without these strategic tools most firms would not be able to function in today's competitive world.

The three editors want to thank the five contributors of their original work to this publication. We specifically want to thank Professor Frank M. Lin for "Frameworks for Developing Strategic Information Systems," and Professors Vijay Sethi, H. R. Rao and Vikram Sethi for "Strategic Management of Information Technology." We also want to thank Professor

Larry Meile for "The Role of End-User Computing in Strategic Information Systems."

Three journal publications authorized the use of six prior-published articles, five of which are used as appendices to the chapters, and one is used as the second to the last chapter in the volume. The three journals are *Interfaces* published by the Institute of Management Sciences, *Information Resources Management Journal*, published by IDEA Group Publishing, and *IEEE Expert*, published by The Institute of Electrical and Electronic Engineers.

Finally, we want to thank a true professional, Valerie Limpert, who provided superb support in transforming messy drafts and numerous rewrites into a professional document.

Robert P. Cerveny
C. Carl Pegels
G. Lawrence Sanders
Volume Editors

INTRODUCTION TO STRATEGIC INFORMATION SYSTEMS

Robert P. Cerveny, C. Carl Pegels, and
G. Lawrence Sanders

INTRODUCTION

Many definitions have been proposed for strategic information systems (SIS) as shown on Exhibit 1. What emerges from these definitions of SIS is a complex concept which can benefit organizations and especially business corporations in many ways. SIS may be viewed as a philosophy, a philosophy which emphasizes planning, managing and utilizing information technology to solve problems and to take advantage of business opportunities. Strategic Information Systems have become a primary focal point for developing and implementing corporate strategy. But in addition, SIS is taking on a new role to shape corporate strategy and to determine the ways companies will be doing business in the future.

For example, American Airlines' and United Airlines'core business operations in the 1970s were centered on transporting people and cargo, but today, because of the Sabre and Covia reservation systems, the arlines are more than simply transportation systems. The airline reservation systems and their related functions offer a range of profitable services from air, automobile and hotel reservations to vacation packages. For instance, in 1987 American Airlines' Sabre Reservation System had a 39 percent

---

Strategic Information Systems can emerge in two ways. They can be part of the organization's **strategic purposes** and assist in product or service differentiation, cost reductions, and new market niches. Strategic information systems can also be derived from systems for operational and managerial support. This is an instance where operational and managerial systems have **strategic potential** [King and Kraemer, 1989].

Strategic Information Systems are information systems that support or shape a business unit's competitive strategy [Wiseman, 1988].

Strategic Information Systems are information systems that are used to support or shape an organization's competitive strategy, its plan for gaining and/or maintaining advantage [Rackoff, Wiseman, and Ullrich, 1985].

Strategic Information Systems are information systems that are developed in response to corporate business initiative. They link business and computer strategies to gain competitive advantage. They apply Information Service resources in such a way that they have an impact on organizational products and business operations [Buckland and O'Brien, 1989, p.7].

Strategic Information Systems are information Systems that are designed to change the goals, products, services or environmental relationships of organizations [Laudon and Laudon, 1988, p. 62].

Exhibit 1.   Definitions of Strategic Information Systems

profit margin and United Airlines' Covia had a 38 percent profit margin (Wheeler 1987).

Strategic Information systems offer more than just means to implement corporate objectives, they provide new opportunities for products and services and new ways to produce and distribute those products and services. Information technology can become a tool not only for solving problems but also for identifying new business opportunities and horizons.

There are two super strategies (sometimes referred to as generic or meta-strategies) that a firm can embrace to gain a competitive advantage over competitors (Porter and Millar, 1985). A firm can become the low cost producer and/or seek to differentiate its products and services from those offered by competitors. The role of Strategic Information Systems is to assist management in realizing these goals by developing greater operational efficiency and providing information to develop unique, or differentiated, products and services.

The key question is: Who or what function will be developing Strategic Information Systems within organizations? This question is not easy to answer. One could argue that the functional area in an organization should bear responsibility. But the more successful strategic information systems overlap several functional areas such as marketing, operations, finance, accounting, and so forth. Hence, strategic information system development becomes a multi-functional activity which requires considerable coordination. For the time being we shall skip the difficult issue on how to structure these multi-functional activities. We shall assume that strategic information system development occurs and that it is coordinated by a project manager or a project management team.

Next we shall present the job description of the SIS Project Manager whose primary responsibility is to help develop Strategic Information Systems applications. Before we do this we shall first outline the current state of SIS in the United States and identify core knowledge areas necessary for proficiency in SIS Project Management.

SIS PROJECT MANAGEMENT

The major responsibilities of SIS Project Management and the SIS Project Manager are to identify and explore how information technology can be utilized to develop strategic opportunities. The major responsibilities of the SIS Project Manager then are:

- to analyze business operations across functional area boundaries in order to discover opportunities for increasing operational efficiencies and improve managerial decision making through the development and application of information technology. The emphasis here is on the internal support of business operations.
- to investigate intercompany relationships and competitive forces, such as the threat of new competitors, the threat of substitute products and services, and the bargaining power of suppliers. The emphasis here is on the external and especially competitive environment.
- to identify potential applications of information technology that have the potential to result in new and or differentiated products and services.
- to monitor and assess developments in information technology and to identify those emerging information technologies with the potential for solving corporate problems and to identify potential new opportunities from the emerging information technologies.

The above description of SIS Project Management suggests a very broad portfolio of skills necessary for the effective development of SIS. Individuals working as SIS Project Managers will play a new role in the firm. The role is similar to the description of an effective senior information executive in the 1980s, including being a consultant, a business partner, and planner whose focus is on sharing knowledge (Dixon and Darwin, 1989). Such an individual will posses knowledge and skills in the following areas:

- Knowledge of strategic planning and information systems planning.
- Broad-based knowledge of functional areas such as accounting, finance, human resources, marketing, and operations management.
- Knowledge of project management and control concepts.
- Knowledge of modern systems analysis and design practices, and fourth generation language environments.
- Knowledge of information engineering, database design, and relational database technology.
- Knowledge of data communications technologies including local area and wide area networks and an understanding of the managerial issues surrounding these technologies.
- The ability to write effectively and to make oral presentations.

In the next section, the above content areas will be addressed in greater detail.

PRINCIPAL KNOWLEDGE AREAS FOR DETERMINING SIS PROJECT MANAGER QUALIFICATIONS

The knowledge necessary for an individual to be become proficient as a SIS Project Manager can be segmented into information technology knowledge, knowledge of management concepts in functional areas, and systems planning knowledge. Education and training or mastery in three specific areas is necessary for the individual who wishes to become a Strategic Information Systems (SIS) project manager. The three specific areas are:

1. Knowledge of the strategic information systems area and of case studies describing what has been accomplished so far. We shall identify this area as Strategic Information Systems (SIS).
2. Knowledge of the development, building and management of large scale information systems including all issues associated with software/hardware as well as information telecommunications. We shall identify this area as Information Technology (IT).

3. Knowledge of the management techniques, concepts and practices leading to the capstone area of strategic management. Knowledge areas include financial management and control, marketing management, manufacturing, technology and operations management, and human resources management. We shall identify this area as Management (MGT).

Although the SIS area is the focus of this book and it receives an in-depth review of the critical concepts and relevant literature of the SIS area, the areas of IT and MGT will also be covered in detail. The information technology (IT) and functional management content areas (MGT) are the foundations upon which strategic information systems (SIS) are developed as shown graphically in Exhibit 2. That is, the SIS project manager should have knowledge of all functional areas of managerial expertise including general and strategic management as well as a good grasp of information technology (systems development, telecommunications, database, etc.). Information Technology (IT) and Management (MGT) are the pillars supporting Strategic Information Systems (SIS).

The SIS area will be covered in depth below. The information technology (IT) area and the management (MGT) area will be covered by specifying knowledge area modules. Each of the modules will require mastery by the SIS project manager. Although, it is possible to obtain mastery in these areas by self study plus work experience, it is probably desirable that SIS project managers take a series of courses in the knowledge areas covered by the modules.

TYPES OF STRATEGIC INFORMATION SYSTEMS

Within an organization or corporation there is not just one type of strategic information system but there is in fact a portfolio of strategic information systems which can be developed. At the executive level there can be a strategic information system to assist in strategic planning, a strategic information system to assist organizations in becoming the low cost producer, an emerging interorganizational system which takes advantage of electronic data interchange (EDI) technology, and intraorganizational systems which increase the effectiveness of intraorganizational communication. These types of strategic information systems are described.

Strategic Information Systems for Strategic Planning

The purpose of information systems for strategic planning is to provide information in support of decision making processes that arise in strategic

Strategic Information Systems

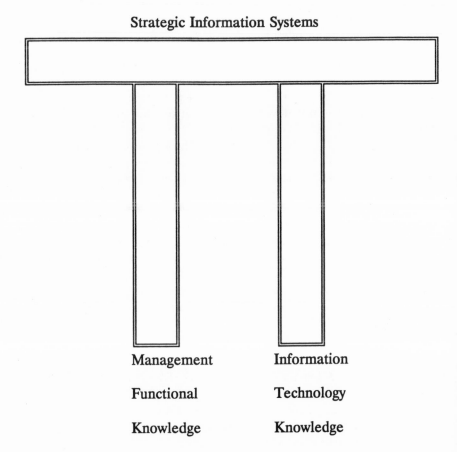

Management   Information

Functional   Technology

Knowledge   Knowledge

Exhibit 2.   The Foundation of Strategic Information systems

planning and, to some extent, in management control. Much of the information in this type of system originates in the external environment of the organization. The major functions of these systems are acquisition, interpretation, storage and retrieval, and presentation of information. A strategic planner uses an information system to learn about the business environment and takes action with respect to it.

Competitive Information System for Low Cost, Differentiated Products

Companies that succeed in an industry in the long run need to out-perform the competitors by either achieving lower costs or by differentiating themselves in the view of the customer, thus enabling them to obtain a premium price for their products or services. The essential emphasis of cost leadership strategies is on operations process efficiency and tight management control systems. The firm is then able to take advantage of technology to increase profitability through more efficient operations than its competitors. The essential emphases of a differential product strategy are on innovation and creativity, on market orientation, and on people-driven rather than systems-driven management controls. Parsons (1983) and others have identified ways in which information systems/information technology can be utilized to deliver these benefits to the various direct and indirect activities of the organization.

Interorganizational Systems

Interorganizational information systems (IOIS) are defined as automated information systems shared by two or more companies (Cash and Konsynski, 1985). Electronic data interchange (EDI), the electronic transmission of standard transaction packets such as orders and invoices, and the sharing of product and other information has begun to blur organizational boundaries. Electronic data interchange found in IOIS can contribute to enhanced productivity, flexibility, and competitiveness of many companies. A classic example of an IOIS is a system named ASAP developed and utilized by American Hospital Supply to communicate with its customers. The literature has shown that IOIS can provide competitive advantage by building barriers to entry and creating switching costs (Cash and Konsynski, 1985); and change the balance of power in buyer-supplier relationships (McFarlan, 1984; Porter and Millar, 1985); and provide substantial first mover advantages (Petre, 1985).

Intraorganizational Systems

Several years ago, Digital Equipment Corporation (DEC) began using corporate videotex to electronically distribute document-based information throughout its many worldwide locations. Videotex is a generic term for an easy-to-use, consistent approach to locating and selectively viewing information on a terminal screen. Content is organized into a tree structure of pages that are selected from a series of menus.

The main benefit of implementing corporate videotex is the reduction of internal operation cost. As Kusekoski (1989) states:

The use of corporate videotex at DEC is producing significant cost savings and increased operating efficiencies. Employees around the world use videotex to quickly and easily access up-to-date information that allows them to make better business decisions. There are numerous groups within DEC that prepare and distribute information to internal audiences. Many of these groups are using videotex to save thousands of dollars in document production and distribution costs while eliminating months of labor from their administrative processes. Aggregated across the corporation, this results in yearly saving of millions of dollars. The use of videotex within the sales force extends well beyond cost savings. It is helping DEC maintain its competitive edge in today's dynamic marketplace.

The key question is how can the development of Strategic Information Systems become institutionalized and thereby become integrated in the corporate planning process? Part of the answer lies in developing organizational structures and processes that promote the philosophy of SIS.

We shall present illustrations of several successful and large-scale strategic information systems. Keep in mind, however, that not all strategic information systems are large scale. Many start out as small systems and evolve into large scale strategic information systems.

The overview consists of six systems which play key strategic roles. Some of these systems have evolved into SIS, perhaps as a result of fortuitous foresight, but they have also been designed surreptitiously as part of the centerpiece of corporate strategy. The important point is that they are central to the strategic positioning of these organizations.

AMERICAN HOSPITAL SUPPLY (AHS)

A leading manufacturer and distributor of a very broad line of products for physicians, laboratories, and hospitals, began development in 1976 of an order-entry distribution system which directly links the majority of its customers electronically to AHS computers. Over 4000 customer terminals at various locations were linked to the American Hospital Supply system. As well as providing the customer with direct access to the AHS order-distribution process, the system also allows customers to perform functions, such as inventory control, for themselves, thereby generating incremental revenues and goodwill for AHS. The American Hospital Supply system has been successful because it simplifies ordering processes for customers, reduces costs for both AHS and the customer, and allows AHS to develop and manage pricing incentives to the customer across all product lines. As a result, customer loyalty is high, and AHS market share has been increasing.

AHS's initial move to electronic ordering was begun by the manager of a regional distribution center working to fill the needs of a single customer. Far-sighted senior management has continually supported the system "with management attention and development funds (Benjamin, Rockart, Scott Morton, and Wyman, 1984)."

MERRILL LYNCH & CO.

In 1977, Merrill Lynch & Co. established the cash management account (CMA) system and shattered the traditional boundaries between the banking and securities industries. The CMA is a combination of charge card, checking account, and brokerage service all rolled into one product. Implementation required a complex information interface of communications and data processing between the Merrill Lynch brokerage offices and Bank One, which acts as the check and direct-card processing center for the CMA accounts. By February 1983, more than 915,000 accounts were in place. Accounts were being added at a rate of 5,000 a week. Other financial institutions such as Shearson and American Express have introduced competitive offerings and are fighting vigorously to gain a share of this newly created market made possible by information technology.

The cash management account's origin was derived from a 1975 study by Stanford Research Institute for the then chairman Donald Regan. The planning organization at Merrill Lynch developed the initial vision into today's highly successful CMA system (Benjamin, Rockart, Scott Morton, and Wyman, 1984).

MCKESSON CORPORATION

McKesson Corporation is a value-added distributor of pharmaceuticals, foods, chemicals and alcoholic beverages. In the mid-1970s, McKesson began to develop its information system called the *Economist*. This system has proved to be very effective for increasing and protecting the company's market share. Since the mid-1970s, McKesson has continued to enhance the system. For instance, McKesson provides pharmacies and other customers with a variety of documents and management reports which have proven to be very useful to their customers. McKesson also offers a claims service for pharmacy customers who have their prescriptions covered by health insurance programs such as Medicare. Customers receive plastic identification cards, similar to credit cards as part of the service. This card is then presented by the customer to the pharmacy when they have a prescription filled. The customer pays a nominal amount toward the price of the prescription. The card is then used to prepare a claims form by which the pharmacy receives the remainder of the payment. Because the processing service is provided free of charge, customers tend to come back to the same pharmacy. On the supply side, McKesson has tied its purchasing system into the order entry systems of its 40 largest suppliers, so that replenishment orders can be entered directly. This has not only speeded up reordering but has greatly increased productivity. Before the system was introduced the company had 85 different pharmaceutical distribution centers and 120 buyers. McKesson was able to reduce the number of distribution centers to fifty five and the number of buyers to fourteen, and the buyers now handle twice the volume of the old system.

The success of McKesson illustrates how management can use information systems to provide new and valuable services to customers and suppliers simultaneously.

AMERICAN AND UNITED AIRLINES

The Sabre and Apollo reservation systems enabled American Airlines and United Air Lines to virtually monopolize the major channel of ticket distribution. By the early 1980s, they formed a powerful duopoly in the computerized travel agency market, with shares of 41 percent and 39 percent, respectively. Within a few years, over 80 percent of the nation's 20,000 travel agencies, accounting for 90 percent of airline ticket sales, had been computerized. But Sabre and Apollo provide their owners with far more than increased ticket revenue. Both systems are substantial profit centers for the respective corporations. In 1985, for example, Sabre produced $143 million in profit on revenues of $336 million. For the first quarter of that year, Sabre contributed more to American Airlines' $93.3 million profit before taxes than did its airline business. The Sabre database provides American Airlines with additional competitive advantages, such as employee reports for travel agencies, and other client reports. These reports, which are generated from Sabre in their dealings with Sabre-using travel agents, permit American Airlines to pressure travel agencies who write too many tickets on other airlines, and to reward travel agencies who utilize American Airlines. (This did lead to litigation against the airline.) Sabre also helps American Airlines manage its seat inventory, and support the American Advantage frequent-flyer program. In addition, Sabre has become American Airlines vehicle for diversification and growth, propelling it into new lines of business and expanding its traditional customer base (Wiseman, 1988).

SEARS ROEBUCK AND COMPANY

Sears Roebuck and Company is using a variety of information systems as the backbone of a strategy to become the leader in American retailing and consumer financial services. The Sears system started with a huge customer database, the largest in the United States, containing 40 million retail customers. Sears collects, stores, and continually utilizes its database to reach home appliance buyers, gardening enthusiasts, and mothers-to-be. Sears uses the same data to provide sales leads to subsidiaries such as Allstate Insurance, brokerage house Dean Witter Reynolds, and real estate brokers Coldwell-Banker. Sears also uses its customer information database to track the purchases made by credit card customers. This information is then used to target direct mail inserts that accompany the monthly credit card bill. In addition, information obtained on the initial credit card application, as well as the history of credit purchases can be used by the marketing staff to target specific subgroups (Laudon and Laudon, 1988).

The development of this large integrated system has prompted counterstrike efforts by their competitors such as the J.C. Penney Company, K-Mart, and Walmart. Sophisticated information technologies by themselves will, however, not overcome other organizational problems. Sears retailing division underwent drastic restructuring early in 1993 despite their sophisticated information technology.

AVIS

The Wizard system developed by Avis car rental company, keeps track of the location, cost, and performance of Avis's rental car fleet. This capability has permitted Avis to bargain more effectively with its suppliers. It has also given Avis an advantage over Hertz, National, and other car rental firms by optimizing the distribution of its rental car fleet to ensure that cars are available at locations where there is a demand for them (Laudon and Laudon, 1988). The Wizard system is an example of a SIS designed to improve the overall productivity.

COMMENTS ON STRATEGIC INFORMATION SYSTEMS

The preceding scenarios illustrate that Strategic Information Systems have become an integral and necessary part of operating a business. These systems directly influence market share, effectiveness, efficiency and resultant earnings in wholesale and retail trade, banking and commerce, the transportation industry and so on. SIS permit companies to compete as the low cost producer, but they also define new products and new markets and have the potential to establish market barriers for competitors.

It has been suggested by some practitioners and academicians that Strategic Information Systems is a misconceptualization. They believe many of the so-called systems developed for competitive advantage were not installed out of strategic necessity (Emery, 1990; Hopper, 1990) but were rather the product of evolution within the firm. However, according to a recent *ComputerWorld* poll of 100 top IS executives this is not the case

(Sullivan-Trainor and Maglitta, 1990). Nearly three-quarters of the respondents indicated that their organizations had implemented information systems during the last year with the single intention of getting ahead of the competition. The *ComputerWorld* survey underscores the critical role of information technology in the strategic planning and operation planning processes. However, technology is never a cure-all for problems with organizational infrastructure. The organization that is able to adapt to new environmental situations and the organization that focuses on customers, employees, and technology will be the one that remains competitive.

REFERENCES

Benjamin, R., J. F. Rockart, M. S. Scott Morton, and J. Wyman. 1984. "Information Technology: A Strategic Opportunity." *Sloan Management Review* 25(3): 3-9.

Buckland, J. A. and R. P. O'Brien. 1989. "Strategic Information Systems." In *Critical Issues in Information Processing Management and Technology* edited by J. W. Masterson. Wellesley, MA: QED Information Services, Inc.

Cash, Jr., J.I. and B.R. Konsynski. 1985. "IS Redraws competitive Boundaries." *Harvard Business Review*, 62(2): 134-142.

Dixon, P. J. and A. J. Darwin. 1989. "Technology Issues Facing Corporate Management in the 1990s." *MIS Quarterly*, 13(2): 247-255.

Emery, J. C. 1990. "Editor's Comments", *MIS Quarterly* 14(2): vii-viii.

Hopper, M. D. 1990. "Rattling SABRE—New Ways to Compete on Information." *Harvard Business Review*, 68(3): 118-129.

King, J. L. and K. L. Kraemer. 1989."Implementation of Strategic Information Systems." Pp. 78-91. In *Information Technology and Management Strategy*, edited by K. Laudon, and J. A. Turner. Englewood Cliffs, NJ: Prentice Hall.

Kusekoski, G. 1989. "Corporate Videotex: A Strategic Business Information Systems." *MIS Quarterly* 13(4): 447-456.

Laudon, K. C. and J. P. Laudon. 1988. *Management Information Systems: A Contemporary Perspective*. NY: Macmillan Publishing

McFarlan, F.W. 1984. "Information Technology Changes the Way You Compete." *Harvard Business Review*, 62(3): 98-103.

Parsons, G. L. 1983. "Information Technology: A New Competitive Weapon." *Sloan Management Review* 25(1): 3-14.

Petre, P. 1985. "How to Keep Customers Happy Captives." *Fortune*, 42-46.

Porter, M. and V. E., Millar. 1985. "How Information Gives You Competitive Advantage." *Harvard Business Review*, 63(4): 149-160.

Rackoff, N., C. Wiseman, and W. A., Ullrich. 1985. "Information Systems for Competitive Advantage: Implementation of a Planning Process." *MIS Quarterly* 9(4): 285-294.

Sullivan-Traynor, M. L. and J., Maglitta. 1990. "Competitive Advantage Fleeting." *ComputerWorld* 24(41): 1,4.

Wheeler, H. 1987. "Air Reservations: New Savvy In the Skies." *High Technology Business*.

Wiseman, C. 1988. *Strategic Information Systems*, Homewood, IL: Richard D. Irwin.

FRAMEWORKS FOR DEVELOPING STRATEGIC INFORMATION SYSTEMS

Frank M. Lin

INTRODUCTION

Several frameworks have been proposed to classify the development of strategic information systems (SIS). The strategic application of information technology can be internally focused or externally focused (Benjamin, Rockart, Morton, and Wyman, 1984; Clemons, 1986; Wyman, 1985). Externally focused applications target customers, suppliers, or competitors (Clemons, 1986). Internally focused applications, on the other hand, target internal operations in the value-added chain such as improving production efficiency, higher product and service quality, reduced product development time, and improved delivery mechanisms for products and services (Porter and Millar, 1985). Selected approaches to developing SIS are discussed below.

STRATEGIC OPPORTUNITIES FRAMEWORK

Benjamin et al. (1984) utilize a 2x2 matrix framework as shown in Exhibit 1. The horizontal axis is divided into internal operations and external operations such as the competitive market place. The vertical axis is

	Competitive Marketplace	Internal Operations
Significant Structural Change	Merrill Lynch Cash Management Account	Digital Equipment Corp. Expert Systems of Configuration Design
Traditional Products and Processes	American Hospital Supply Customer Order Supply	United Airlines Teleconferencing in Operations Control

Source Adapted from Benjamin, Rockart, Scott Morton, and Wyman (1984).

Exhibit 1.   The Foundation of Strategic Information systems

divided into no or little change as found in traditional products and operations processes and major changes such as significant structural changes. This matrix framework is used to raise senior executives' awareness of the strategic potential of strategic information systems.

COMPETITIVE ADVANTAGE FRAMEWORK

Porter and Millar (1985) use the Value- Added Chain as a tool for strategic analysis. Exhibit 2 shows an overview of the Value-Added Chain. It emphasizes cost leadership, product or service differentiation, and focused strategies. A central component of this framework is the linkage between strategic business unit activity and the competitive environment. The key factors that characterize the linkages are: the bargaining power of buyers, the bargaining power of suppliers, the threat of new entrants, the threat of substitute products, and the rivalry among existing competitors (Porter, 1980, 1985; Porter and Millar, 1985).

The basis of the Porter model is that an enterprise exists within an industry and to succeed, it must effectively deal with the competitive forces which exist within the particular industry. Porter's model helps executives clarify their business strategy and identify where information systems potentially may yield competitive advantage in terms of defending the firm against these forces or influencing them in its favor. Thus this framework is useful in helping business managers think strategically and in analyzing the competitive context in which information systems can be exploited.

However, it is also important to note that this framework is less useful to pinpoint specific information systems applications. It is usually necessary to conduct detailed investigations to further understand the sources and nature of the significant forces, what strategic actions are possible and what industry reactions are likely.

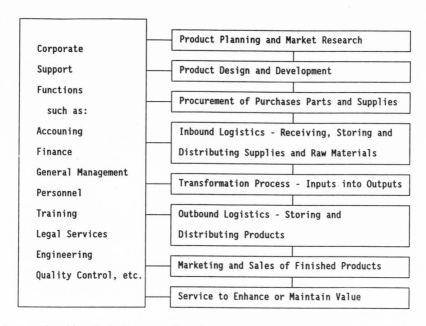

Corporate	Product Planning and Market Research
Support	Product Design and Development
Functions	
such as:	Procurement of Purchases Parts and Supplies
Accouning	Inbound Logistics - Receiving, Storing and
Finance	Distributing Supplies and Raw Materials
General Management	
Personnel	Transformation Process - Inputs into Outputs
Training	Outbound Logistics - Storing and
Legal Services	Distributing Products
Engineering	
Quality Control, etc.	Marketing and Sales of Finished Products
	Service to Enhance or Maintain Value

Source   Adapted from Benjamin, Rockart, Scott Morton, and Wyman (1984).

Exhibit 2.   Information Technology and the Value-Added Chain

STRATEGIC PERSPECTIVE FRAMEWORK (STRATEGIC OPTION GENERATOR)

Based on the logic of Chandler's (1962) growth strategies and Porter's competitive strategic framework, Wiseman points out that competitive advantage related to information systems results from strategic thrusts (Wiseman, 1988). The strategic targets are (1) suppliers which supply essential resources; (2) customers; and (3) competitors which sell similar or substitute products or services. With these strategic targets identified, the firm may choose a number of alternative strategic thrusts including product differentiation, cost leadership, innovation, growth and alliances to attack (offensive) or defend itself (defensive) in the competitive arena. The strategic information systems may be used by the firm itself or provided for the strategic target's use. Effective utilization of this approach relies on a thorough understanding of the state of the industry, the firm's competitive position, the determining factors for success and the industry's value-added system plus a clearly understood business strategy. Like Porter's framework, it is less likely to pinpoint specific information systems applications.

COMPETITIVE STRATEGY FRAMEWORK

McFarlan has conceptualized the ideas of competitive strategy using computer systems to build structural barriers. The concept of the value-added chain can be used to determine where a company can exploit information technology to realize competitive opportunities (Cash, McFarlan, McKenney, and Vitale, 1988). McFarlan and McKenney (1983) have also proposed a framework. The strategic grid, which helps a firm to position itself strategically is shown on Exhibit 3. Where information systems are seen as having little impact at present or in the future, they can be seen as *support* activities which are used to improve management and performance but not critical to the business. Where information systems are critical to current operations but not the heart of the company's strategic development, they may be seen as a *routine* activity which is critical to sustaining existing business. Where information systems are always crucial to the company's operation and the future is dependent on them, they may be seen as a *strategic* activity which is critical for the company's future success. Where information systems have little impact at present, but newly developed or planned to develop information systems will be critical to the company's survival and success, they can be seen as a turnaround activity which may be of future strategic importance. This framework can be useful for assessing the strategic importance of information systems for business unit.

STRATEGIC INFORMATION TECHNOLOGY MANAGEMENT FRAMEWORK

Parsons found that information technology can provide competitive advantages at the industry level, the firm level, and the strategic level (Parsons, 1983). Earl (1989) classified this approach as an impact model where the basis is a recognition and analysis of the competitive environment and strategies of business. This approach focuses on the possible opportunities of firms to exploit information systems for strategic advantage. At the industry level, information technology can change an entire industry by changing the nature of its products and services, markets, and the economies of production. At the firm level, information technology can be used to leverage a particular position to combat competitors who

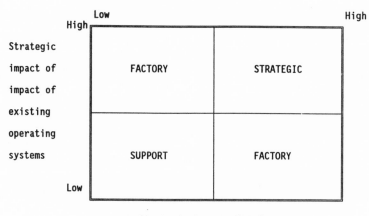

Source Adapted from McFarlan and McKenney (1983).

Exhibit 3. Information Technology Strategic Grid

are establishing entry barriers and switching costs, and who are engaged in product differentiation strategies. The basis for the analysis of the firm level's impacts is Porter's five competitive forces model of competitive strategy (Porter, 1980). At the strategy level, the firm can focus on being a lower cost producer, on overall product differentiation, or on a niche market. The basis for the analysis at the strategy level is again Porter's three generic strategies (Porter, 1980).

INFORMATION ENGINEERING AND STRATEGIC DATA PLANNING

The Information Engineering and Strategic Data Planning approaches (Hackathorn and Karimi, 1988; Sanders, 1990) recognize that most of the so-called systems for "competitive advantage" are built on production databases. Online reservation systems, order entry systems, and customer support systems use wide- band transmission lines, high performance hardware, and sophisticated interface technologies to communicate with these databases. The results are increased efficiency and unique products and services. The information engineering approaches attempt to link corporate strategy concepts with database design concepts to develop systems with strategic potential and purposes.

OVERVIEW OF STRATEGIC INFORMATION SYSTEMS DEVELOPMENT APPROACHES

As illustrated from the above discussion there are several approaches that organizations can utilize for developing strategic information systems. Regardless of the model selected all of the approaches help organizations to focus on the strategic potential of information technology. They provide managers with a structure, or an architecture to assist them to assess the potential impact of information systems on their businesses. They also cause organizations to reevaluate old assumptions and biases and to embrace alternative conceptualizations for the technology-strategy connection. We have adapted a framework developed by Earl (1989) to categorize strategic approaches along two dimensions. Approaches which focus on *strategic opportunities* are useful in identifying strategic possibilities of information systems, by causing organizations to develop an awareness and vision in executives, firms and industries, and in helping to reorient thinking. These approaches can also be used to assist in identifying competitive threats and new opportunities for using information systems strategically. Examples include Benjamin, (1984) strategic opportunities framework, Parson's (1983) strategic information technology management, Porter's (1980) competitive advantage, Wiseman's (1988) strategic option generator and information engineering and strategic data planning approaches. *Position frameworks* are useful in helping executives assess the strategic importance, the particular situation and the inherited situation of information systems for their enterprises. The aim is to improve managerial understanding of the information systems functions and how they should be managed in their particular organization. McFarlan and McKenney's (1983) Strategic Grid is an example of positioning approaches.

In the next section of this paper a fundamental aspect of strategic information systems planning, that is how should the organization determine if the planning meets the requirements of the organization, will be discussed. In the following section the actual contents of the strategic information systems plan is reviewed as well as the evaluation of the planning process.

DESCRIPTION OF SIS PLAN DEVELOPMENT

The planning outcomes may be broadly divided into the development of strategic objectives, and the development of strategies for aligning information systems with organizational strategic plans. The products stemming from the planning process are a mixture of hard and soft outputs. The hard outputs are documents defining strategic plans and tactical plans.

Soft outputs consist of human factors, such as skills, knowledge, awareness and motivation. The details of plans can vary across organizations and may include the following: information systems (IS) mission, objectives, policies, strategies, infrastructure description, priorities of the IS application portfolio, resource requirements for implementation and organizational change requirements to carry out the plan (King, 1978; McLean and Soden, 1977).

EVALUATION OF STRATEGIC INFORMATION SYSTEMS PLAN

Evaluating the effectiveness of the Strategic Information Systems Plan (SISP) involves two measures, measuring the process and measuring the ultimate outcome. Measuring the process involves the assessment of the quality of the system and related support. Measuring the ultimate outcome involves the determination of whether or not the planning system has accomplished its objectives. This distinction between the evaluation of process and outcome is analogous to the evaluation of means versus ends discussed both in the strategic management and information systems literature (Hamilton and Chervany, 1981; Hofer and Schendel, 1978; Mintzberg and Waters, 1985; Schendel and Hofer, 1979).

Evaluation of SISP can be classified into three groups: System Evaluation, Problem-Oriented Evaluation and SISP Methodology (Cerveny, Lin, Sanders, and Sethi). Each approach is summarized in Exhibit 4 in terms of the approach used, the type of evaluation and the criteria proposed for evaluating SISP.

The first approach—System Evaluation—is focused explicitly on developing evaluation criteria related to various components of SISP systems; salient ones being goal congruence, internal consistency and external validity (Henderson and Sifonis, 1988; King, 1988). Goal congruence assesses the degree of integration between information systems strategy and business strategy. Internal consistency refers to the extent to which actions envisioned at a higher level in planning are correctly operationalized at lower levels. External validity refers to the extent of appropriateness of the resulting plan as compared to an external standard.

The second approach—Problem-Oriented Evaluation—identifies problems which impede SISP and evaluate SISP by the avoidance of such problems or threats. Hoffer, Michael, and Carroll (1989) identified five potential threats to the success of SISP: organizational; commitments/ contractual; outcomes/expectations; expertise/technical; and implementation. Lederer and Sethi (1988) identified three additional factors: database; hardware; and cost. The emphasis here is on potential problem areas and how to minimize their effects.

Authors & References	Evaluation Approach	Research Typed	Description of Evaluation Criteria
King (1988)	System Approach	Theoretical	. Effectiveness of ISP . Relative worth of the ISP system . Role and impact of the ISP system . Relative efficiency of the ISP system . Performance of the IS plan . Strategic congruence . Adequacy of ISP resources . Relative worth of IS strategy
Henderson & Sifonis (1988)	System Approach	Theoretical	. External validity . Internal consistency
Lederer & Sethi (1988)	Problem-Oriented Approach	Empirical	. The organization . Database . Implementation . Hardware . Cost
Hoffer, et al. (1989)	Problem-Oriented Approach	Theoretical	. Organization . Outcome/expectation . Commitments/contractual . Implementation . Expertise/technical
Kottermann & Konsynski (1984)	ISP Methodology Approach	Theoretical	. Strategic level addresses . Participation level . Strategic scope addressed . Phase of the planning process

Authors & References	Evaluation Approach	Research Typed	Description of Evaluation Criteria
Sullivan (1985)	ISP Methodology Approach	Empirical	. Diffussion of IS . Infusion of IS
Karimi (1988)	ISP Methodology Approach	Theoretical	. Breadth dimension which consists of organizational analysis to systems implementation . Depth dimension which encompasses methodologies, techniques and tools

Exhibit 4. Criteria for Determining the Effectiveness of Information Systems Planning

The third stream of research—SISP Methodology Evaluation—identifies contingency factors for selecting specific SISP methodologies and uses these factors as evaluation criteria. For instance, Karimi (1988) proposed two contingency factors: the level of systems analysis, design and implementation, and the method used to identify the required processes for promoting the interactions necessary between organizational entities. Kottemann and Konsynski (1984) emphasized the importance of a functional unit's strategic posture. Sullivan (1985) proposed infusion and diffusion of information systems as determinants of the appropriate SISP methodology.

REFERENCES

Benjamin, R., J. F. Rockart, M. S. Scott Morton, and J. Wyman. 1984. "Information Technology: A Strategic Opportunity." *Sloan Management Review* 25(3): 3-9.

Cash, J.I., F.W. McFarlan, J.L. McKenney, and M.R. Vitale. 1985. Corporate Information Systems Management. Homewood, IL: Irwin.

Cerveny, R.P., F. M. Lin, G.L. Sanders, and V. Sethi. 1990. "Modeling the Information Systems Planning Process: Organizational Support and Strategic Weapon." Working Paper, School of Management, SUNY at Buffalo.

Chandler, A. D. 1962. *Strategy and Structure.* Cambridge, MA: MIT Press.

Clemons, E. K. 1986. "Information Systems for Sustainable Competitive Advantage." *Information and Management* 11(3): 131-136.

Earl, M.J. 1989. *Management Strategies for Information Technology.* United Kingdom: Prentice Hall.

Hackathorn, R.D. and J. Karimi. 1988. "A Framework for Comparing Information Engineering Methods." *MIS Quarterly* 12(2): 203-202.

Hamilton, S. and N. L. Chervany. 1981. "Evaluating Information System Effectiveness, Part I: Comparing Evaluation Approaches." *MIS Quarterly* 5(3): 55-69.

Henderson, J. C. and J. G. Sifonis, 1988. "The Values of Strategic IS Planning: Understanding Consistency, Validity, and IS Markets." *MIS Quarterly* 12(2): 187-200.

Hofer, C. W. and D. E. Schendel. 1978. *Strategic Formulation: Analytical Concepts.* New York: West Publishing Co.

Hoffer, J. A., S. J. Michael, and J. J. Carroll. 1989. "The Pitfalls of Strategic Data and Systems Planning: A Research Agenda." *Proceedings of the Twenty-second Annual Hawaii International Conference on Systems Science,* 348-356.

Karimi, J. 1988. "Strategic Planning for Information Systems: Requirements and Information Engineering Methods." *Journal of Management Information Systems* 4(4): 5-24.

King, W. R. 1988. "Strategic Planning for Management Information Systems." *MIS Quarterly* 2(1): 27-37.

King, W. R. 1988. "How Effective is Your Information Systems Planning?" *Long Range Planning* 21(5): 103-112.

Kottemann, J. E. and B. R. Konsynski. 1984. "Information Systems Planning and Development: Strategic Postures and Methodologies." *Journal of Management Information Systems* 1(2): 45-63.

Lederer, A.L. and V. Sethi. 1988. "The Implementation of Strategic Information Systems Planning Methodologies." *MIS Quarterly,* 12(3): 444-461.

McFarlan, F.W. and J.L. McKenney. 1983. *Corporate Information Systems Management: The Issues Facing Senior Executives.* Homewood, IL: Irwin.

McLean, E. R. and J. V. Soden, 1977. *Strategic Planning for MIS.* New York: John Wiley.

Mintzberg, H. and J. A. Waters. 1985. "Of Strategies, Deliberate and Emergent." *Strategic Management Journal* 6(3): 257-272.

Parsons, G. L. 1983. "Information Technology: A New Competitive Weapon." *Sloan Management Review* 25(1): 3-14.

Porter, M. 1980. *Competitive Strategy.* New York: Free Press.

Porter, M. 1985. *Competitive Advantage.* New York: Free Press.

Porter, M. and V. E. Millar. 1985. "How Information Gives You Competitive Advantage." *Harvard Business Review,* 63(4): 149-160.

Sanders, G. L. 1990. "Strategic Database Planning," *Database Programming and Design* (11): 52-56.

Schendel, D. E. and C. W. Hofer. 1985. *Strategic Management: A New View of Business Policy and Planning.* Boston: Little, Brown.

Sullivan, C. H. 1985. "Systems Planning in the Information Age." *Sloan Management Review* 26(2): 3-12.

Wiseman, C. 1988. *Strategic Information Systems.* Homewood, IL: Richard D. Irwin.

Wyman, J. 1985. "Technological Myopia: The Need to Think Strategically about Technology." *Sloan Management Review* 26(3): 59-64.

STRATEGIC MANAGEMENT OF INFORMATION TECHNOLOGY:
A REVIEW AND SOME EMPIRICAL OBSERVATIONS

Vijay Sethi, H.R. Rao and Vikram Sethi

INTRODUCTION

The last decade has seen a tremendous change in the perspective of researchers and practitioners regarding the strategic uses of information technology (IT). This is reflected by the change in the ranking of major issues facing information systems (IS) professionals. The issue, translating IS into Competitive Advantage (CA), ranked second in 1987 (Brancheau and Wetherbe, 1987) is currently ranked third in one survey (Ryan, 1989a) and even lower in another (Ryan, 1989b). On the other hand, major concerns today include communications with top management, line functions, end-users (Ryan 1989a), efficient operations of the IS department, and meeting employees' needs (Ryan 1989b).

These findings reflect a growing realization on the part of organizations that managing IT strategically is difficult, complex and risky, and can potentially become a costly source of mismanagement. As one of the findings of a multi-year MIT study notes, new IT will never be a "quick fix" for strategic or competitive problems. Complex multi-year implementations require sustained commitment from management and employees to reap the benefits (Arthur Young, 1989). The importance of issues such as communications and IS operations indicate that IS managers are seeking to gain long-term organizational commitment as well as attempting to make organizational changes that would enable effective IT management.

A variety of findings can be culled from past studies which provide some guidelines for managing IT. However, most recommendations lack empirical validation. Based upon multiple case studies, this research describes some successful organizational practices for IT management. These strategies encompass management of the IS function, integration of business strategy and IS strategy, and the role of top management, users and IS in IT management. The paper first reviews the literature on strategic IT deployment, then describes its research method and results, and concludes with some implications of the findings.

MANAGING INFORMATION TECHNOLOGY FOR STRATEGIC USE: A REVIEW OF THE LITERATURE

Previous literature forms the basis for a multitude of guidelines regarding managing IT for strategic use. The recommendations are diverse and pertain to a variety of different organizational and IS facets. Presented below is taxonomy in which the guidelines are categorized based upon the focus of their recommendations: the IT application, the firm's overall IT architecture, IT planning, the roles of different participants, or the impact of the environment.

Characteristics of Information Technology Applications

One of the common prescriptions for strategic applications is that they should affect a firm's competitive environment, determined by five key forces according to Porter (1980, 1985): the bargaining power of buyers, the bargaining power of suppliers, the threat of new entrants, the threat of substitute products, and the rivalry among existing competitors (McFarlan, 1984; Porter and Millar, 1985). This guideline calls for an impact at the firm-level (Parsons, 1983) or on competitive strategy (Bakos and Treacy, 1986).

It is also important for an IT application to support business strategy (King, Grover, and Hufnagel, 1986; Clemons and Row, 1987) which may be low-cost leadership, product differentiation, or concentration on market/product niche (Porter, 1980). This impact at the strategy level (Parsons, 1983) or on internal strategy (Bakos and Treacy, 1986) is concerned with IT applications assisting in the development of efficient and effective organizational structures and processes for achieving goals and objectives (Wyman, 1985).

In order to achieve the above objectives, it is recommended that IT applications focus on the following targets: customers, internal operations, suppliers, and competitors (Wyman, 1985; Benjamin, Rockart, Scott Morton, and Wyman, 1984; Wiseman and MacMillan, 1984). According to Clemons (1986), applications targeted towards customers, suppliers, or competitors are externally focussed whereas those targeted towards internal operations are internally focussed.

A successful approach for developing externally focussed applications is to create inter-organizational systems in which information is exchanged across organizational boundaries (Johnston and Vitale, 1988; Cash and Konsynski, 1985). Other recommendations for externally focussed applications call for customer-oriented applications to attend to some aspect of a customer's resource life cycle (Ives and Learmonth, 1984).

Internally-focussed applications should affect a firm's value chain (Porter and Millar, 1985), a collection of activities a firm performs to design, market, deliver, and support its products (Porter, 1985). Improving the efficiency of the value chain using IT is recommended as a powerful source of CA (Bakos and Treacy, 1986).

IT applications may be employed offensively or defensively (Wiseman and MacMillan, 1984). The former, also called a preemptive strike (MacMillan, 1983), is recommended because it enables the firm to enjoy first-mover advantages (Porter, 1980) which are subsequently unavailable to competition. IT applications used defensively reduce the advantage held by the firm's competitors. Such applications should be developed when customers' switching costs are insignificant, innovators are unable to defend their gains, or the ratio of customer adoption time to competitor copy time is large (Clemons and Kimbrough, 1986).

The final guideline relates to the technology underlying strategic systems; it is recommended that the following skills be employed to gain competitive advantage: storage, processing, and communication (Wiseman and MacMillan, 1984; Bakos and Treacy, 1986).

It is important to note that the studies which form the basis of the above recommendations are mainly descriptive or analytical in nature. This is perhaps because these were early studies focussed on developing awareness and opportunities' frameworks only (Earl, 1987). Therefore their recommendations are very general and broad.

The results of a few, empirical studies, however, help to focus and narrow the previous guidelines. King et. al., (1986) found that organizations are predominantly developing applications focussed on customers. This indicates a tremendous opportunity in focussing on other targets. Even customer-oriented applications would become more effective, recommends

Runge (1985), if they would reach further into their customers' value chains and provide lock-in capabilities rather than only link-up or internal support. Finally, IT applications used offensively should be so employed such that they do not become the target of law or regulation (Vitale, 1986).

Characteristics of the Organization's Technological Environment

Strategic IT applications require a systems architecture that is capable of supporting their development and functionality (Grossman and Packer, 1989). A platform for the future is needed that will not restrict the strategic options available to the firm. Firms are thus recommended to undertake core architectural reconfigurations or systems renovation projects (Grossman and Packer, 1989) that will reconcile incompatible business procedures and existing company systems and developing communications links as well as integrating databases among a number of departments. Such programs involve high risks because they require large investments, are very broad in scope, and have to incorporate uncertainty. While there is no single "best" approach for managing these programs, Goodhue, Quillard, and Rockart (1988) recommend considering 80/20 solutions for upgrading while quick rapid gains are sought through limited efforts.

Another related capability is strong technical support and expertise within the firm, found to be an important facilitator of strategic IT use (King et. al., 1986). However, it seems that most firms possess such expertise because limited IT initiatives have not been found attributable to a lack of technical capability. Nevertheless, the importance of this factor should not be overlooked.

Information Technology Planning

Linking the IT plan with the firm's business plan is a guideline which is repeatedly emphasized in the literature. IT applications which are a key, integral part of a firm's business are likely to provide sustained advantage (King et. al., 1986) because competitors would not benefit from copying them (Clemons and Row, 1987). The linkage between IT and business has two distinct aspects: alignment and impact (Vitale, Ives, and Beath, 1986). The former refers to conforming IT with the organization's mission and objectives while the latter, also called exploit (Karimi, 1988), derives new organizational goals based on technological possibilities (Lederer and Sethi, 1988).

In order to establish the above linkages, IT planning should address nine critical issues or planning agendas (Boynton and Zmud, 1987): intra-organizational political analysis, intra-organizational market analysis, business strategy analysis, business market analysis, technology analysis, organizational learning analysis, organizational culture, IT infrastructure analysis, and IT risk-taking analysis. It is further recommended that the following eleven behaviors or processes should be followed during planning (Boynton and Zmud, 1987): an interactive process, a hierarchical process, multiple time horizons, a focus on action, participants "buy in" to the planning process, an informal network of planners, an organizational IT mission, a sense of the organization's pulse, identify strategic opportunities, surface strategic assumptions, and prioritize strategic options.

Empirical evidence indicates that these planning agendas and behaviors are incorporated into two basic planning approaches (Vitale et. al., 1986): top down and adaptive. The top-down process, similar to Huff and Munro's (1985) issues-driven model, starts with the delineation and prioritization of issues at the corporate level and then proceeds to identify IS issues and technology. On the other hand, the adaptive process views IT planning not as a one-time process, but as a continuous program of IT innovation and creativity fostered through changes in organization structure and climate. This model incorporates features of the technology-driven and the opportunistic models described by Huff and Munro, (1985) because of its emphasis on the identification and learning of new technologies and its cautious, step-at-a-time approach towards IT adoption. Firms could also follow an integrated approach, called the normative ideal (Huff and Munro, 1985) by combining features of the top-down and the adaptive processes.

Policies Regarding Information Technology

It is critical that firms employ appropriate criteria for evaluating strategic IT applications. The rationale for this popular recommendation is that traditional measures, financial indicators such as return on investment or assets, have a number of limitations (Crowston and Treacy, 1986). Financial measures are very aggregate and not closely tied to IT. They would therefore show a measurable change only when the impact of an IT application is very large and significant. In some cases, financial measures may be totally irrelevant because "IT applications are not guaranteed to improve return on investment, productivity, or operational efficiency demonstrably. The impact of such systems may be more subtle" (Cash and Konsynski, 1985, p. 138).

However, while there is agreement that financial measures are inappropriate, there is also a consensus that the field lacks any alternative measurement criteria (Parsons, 1983; McFarlan, 1984; Geise, 1984; Rackoff, Wiseman, and Ullrick, 1985, Vitale, 1986; Treacy, 1986; Wiseman, 1988). This dilemma has prompted recommendations endorsing a limited use of financial indicators. According to Weill and Olson (1989), it is appropriate to use sales growth rate to evaluate strategic IT applications. Johnston and

Vitale (1988) recommend following a hierarchical evaluation approach where an attempt is made to justify the system by first considering its quantifiable benefits such as cost reduction for revenue and increased sales. If necessary, an estimate of the "non-quantifiable" benefits, such as increased entry barriers or increased product differentiation, is then included in the analysis.

Not only is it critical for firms to employ appropriate criteria for evaluating individual IT applications, it is also essential for them to adopt an appropriate view of overall expenditure on IT. Viewing IT expenditure as necessary for attaining CA or for experimenting with new technology will ensure that these investments are not inadvisably evaluated using financial measures (McFarlan, 1984). Thus, Wyman (1985) recommends that IT expenditure should be viewed as a priority investment rather than as a necessary investment, a necessary expense, or as an expense to control.

Another policy consideration is whether the firm should follow an independent strategy for IT applications or become a member of a consortium (Clemons and Knez, 1988). A serious consideration of the latter option is recommended because it reduces unit costs and development costs, protects against the high cost of failure, and avoids the difficulties involved in protecting an innovation.

Role of Organizational Participants

It is clear that top management support and involvement are prerequisites to the deployment of strategic IT applications. As one review of the top ten most well-known IT applications noted "There is a direct correlation, however, between the level of a strategic system's success and the level of top-management support for creative information systems development" (*Information Week* 1986, p. 27). Similarly, one of the results of a multi-year MIT study is that the tone at the top matters" (*Arthur Young*, 1989). Gaining top management support and commitment for strategic IT applications may, however, be difficult because of six major reasons (Lederer and Mendelow, 1987): top management lacks awareness of IT, it sees strictly operational uses of computers, it perceives a credibility gap with regard to proposals from the IS department, it does not view information as a resource, it demands financial justification, and it is action-oriented with a focus on short-term benefits. Active engagement of top management may be sought using a three-phase process that is based on the concepts of critical success factors, decision scenarios, and prototyping (Rockart and Crescenzi, 1984). Specific techniques that may help in convincing top management regarding the strategic potential of IT include education, marketing past IT application successes, letting users champion IT applications, promoting a business image for the IS department, responding to outside forces, capitalizing on changes in management, and performing IS planning (Lederer and Mendelow, 1987).

The presence of certain individuals, called champions, has also been found to be vital to the adaption of new IT. The champion often conceives as well as defends new IT initiatives (*Arthur Young*, 1989). A champion is often characterized by a high level of authority and responsibility and by a general business background (Runge, 1985). The power, prestige, and knowledge of such individuals enable them to understand, promote and support new IT endeavors. Organizations are thus recommended to cultivate champions by support and training or by recruiting professionals who demonstrate a grasp of business and IT strategy.

Strategic IT utilization also calls for a major change in the role of line managers and business executives. Executives in general management should be encouraged to propose IT innovations based upon their contact with the marketplace and customer (*Arthur Young*, 1989). Similarly, line managers must assume greater control over IT management. This may be accomplished by instituting mechanisms such as IT reporting to line management rather than a staff-function (Johnston and Carrico, 1988). Thus, the responsibility for budgeting, priority setting, and resource planning for IT must be with line and business managers.

The role and skills of IS executives also requires a major transformation. All executives, starting from the chief information officer, have to emphasize business needs over technology. Such a focus is already prevalent in most leading organizations (Emery, 1989).

In addition to technical skills, it would be useful for IS executives to have strong business background or experience in some functional or business unit *of* the organization (Johnston and Carrico, 1988). Thus, IS executives must become competent managers in addition to competent technicians (Emery, 1989).

Overall, organizations must ensure that the following roles are fulfilled by organizational participants (Vitale, et al., 1986; Huff and Munro, 1985): Wizards, also called gatekeepers, are experts in IT that are judged to be strategic; marriage-broker, or an intermediary between users and wizards; rich-uncle, or a provider of funds for potentially strategic IT; weed-puller, or an evaluator of IT application projects, and; teacher, who educates users regarding IT and IS regarding the organization.

Impact of the Environment

A number of studies have recommended that the nature and pace of IT deployment must be governed by a firm's environment. A variety of conditions are purported to favor the development of strategic IT applications. These conditions are determined by the characteristics of the industry, the market, the products and the value-chain.

IT has a high strategic potential in industries which have recently undergone radical, disruptive change that has altered its structure, its customers' purchasing patterns, and its competitors' power. Further, the practice in the industry should be characterized by complexity, the need for speed, and the presence of repetitive high-volume transaction processing (Clemons, 1986).

Another favorable industry condition is competitive pressure. Pressure from competition has been found to be a major facilitator of strategic IT use (King et. al., 1986). Other evidence also indicates that firms use IT as a means of responding to increased competitive pressure in the industry resulting from sources such as deregulation, foreign competition, new competitors, change in industry technology, or competitors' initiatives (Johnston and Carrico, 1988).

Factors related to the market that are important include market share and position in the product life cycle. King et. al. (1986) had found that a strong market position facilitates the strategic use of IT. However, another framework (Mason, 1984) suggests that strategic opportunities arise only if a firm has a high market share early in the product life cycle and a low share later.

Another important determinant is the information content in a product, also called product information intensity (Porter and Millar, 1985). It refers to everything that a buyer needs to know to obtain the product and use it to achieve the desired result. While some believe that high information intensity provides IT opportunities (Porter and Millar, 1985), others believe that IT should be used to support products low in information intensity (Runge, 1985).

However, there is no dispute regarding the potential of IT to support products and services that have a limited life. Johnston and Carrico (1988) found that products and services that have high market values prior to some movement or period of time and little or no value afterwards are effective candidates for IT applications. Thus, IT has a high potential when products to be managed are valuable and perishable.

Another favorable condition is high information intensity of the value chain, activities that a firm performs to do business (Porter and Millar, 1985). The value chain is a system of interdependent activities which are connected by linkages. Every value activity creates and uses information. Maintaining and coordinating linkages also requires information. Information intensity is thus a function of the steps required to capture, manipulate, and channel the data necessary to perform value-chain activities and to maintain linkages between them.

Empirical results show that businesses that have a high volume of transactions within and between organizations in their value chain usually lead in the development of competitive uses of IT (Johnston and Carrico, 1988).

RESEARCH METHOD AND SOME EMPIRICAL OBSERVATIONS

Research Method

The observations have been culled from research reports prepared by graduate (MBA) students in a Management Information Systems Course at a major public university in the northeast. In spring 1989, students were asked to analyze companies in the region that were large and with a significant investment in information technology. A detailed 5-page questionnaire developed by the authors posed the following primary question: *What is the nature of specific ongoing organizational activities intended to manage (identify, develop, implement, and maintain) information systems that provide competitive advantage?* The questionnaire was used by the students as a guideline for interviews with various top executives in the organization, primarily top IS executives, as well as in some cases, top executives from other functional areas that had close interactions with the IS area.

Some Empirical Observations

An in-depth analysis of the 18 case studies that were finally selected allows us to make the following observations:

Strategic benefits result from using IT to change and improve business processes rather than from the technology itself.

The management of IT was found to be based on the premise that competitive advantage results from using IT innovatively rather than from the technology itself. Thus, the emphasis in firms was on applying and using IT; for instance, the objective of one organization was to use IT to improve customer service, of another two to support "mission critical" company areas, and of another to transform and fundamentally change business processes rather than automate them. Similar objectives reflected in one company's underlying philosophy for developing IT applications: "The impetus for systems is not so much a preemptive strike but a desire to complement, enhance, and improve existing organization structure and operations." Likewise, another's IT management rationale was "You could be the best technology company in the world, but you need clear business management to make an impact."

These findings indicate a growing belief in the resource based model of the firm hypothesis (Clemons, 1989) which maintains that "firms gain advantage by using IT to leverage an intrinsic strength of the firm. Competitive advantage rarely comes from information systems alone, since software can be duplicated and the underlying technology is available to all" (p. 181). The literature provides further evidence that firms have started to view IT as a means rather than an end. For example, according to Rifkin (1989), chief information systems officers are being asked to innovate, to find new ways to compete, to erect barriers to competition, and to make technology a systemic part of the company. A recent survey of 243 senior IS executives similarly showed that the issue of highest concern is reshaping business processes through IT (Wilder, 1990).

Thus, there seems to be a realistic view of the potential of IT, with firms searching for ways to use IT to reengineer (Bozman and Ryan, 1989) or to exploit unique structural advantages of their firms (Clemons and Row, 1987).

Most companies desire to let somebody else take the risk of innovation and want to be a close second in adopting the technology once it has proven to be successful. They believe that competitive advantage is a "fleeting advantage."

Most companies did not want to be pioneers in the use of IT. Their strategy was to continuously monitor new technology developments and rapidly adopt successful applications. For instance, one company's objective is to observe the pioneers and then apply the new, tested, and researched technologies. Another's aim is to be a "second innovator," and thus it implements a system only after waiting for adoption by a major competitor. Similarly, another is a "close second" who is quick to adopt new technologies that have proven to be successful. The literature provides additional examples of this strategy. For instance, 3M wants to be six months behind the leading edge in technology. It does not rush in to buy the newest technology but tries instead to move ahead with it after careful examination. Likewise, a progressive "IT shop" takes pride in being a "fast second." It waits for competitors to initiate new practices, and for practices that seem promising, it commits enough resources so as to attain parity rapidly (Johnston and Carrico, 1988).

The organizations' rationale behind the above conservative approach was that it reduces risk and expense; in fact, they referred to IT pioneers as being on the "bleeding edge." According to Diebold (1990), the assumption that pioneers do not always profit from their innovations is validated by an entire series of events. This includes Chemical Bank which pioneered the use of ATMs in the United States while rival New York Citibank watched and learned before adopting them widely to benefit customers and the banking industry.

Vendors are becoming an important source of ideas about competitors' use of IT and for new ideas regarding technology.

It was found that many organizations view vendors as an important source of ideas regarding new IT as well as competitive products. One company reviews its IT applications portfolio with its vendor to assess whether the capabilities that it offers are comparable with competitors. Another professes that about 15 percent of new IT ideas come from its technology vendor's sales representatives who suggest new innovations based on what they have seen or supplied to competitors. Another company consciously adopts a multi-vendor policy in order to encourage competition between different vendors. The company strongly believes that vendors are the best source of information regarding competitors.

During IT assessment and adoption, users play a significant role in identification and development with the IS department in assessment and design.

In most companies, users and IS were found to participate equally in the process of IT assessment and adoption. Users were the primary source of new ideas. They also assumed responsibility for application development. On the other hand, the IS department undertook detailed examinations and assessments of proposed IT alternatives. The final selection was made mostly by the top IS executive or a steering committee, and, in some cases, top management upon the recommendations of the IS department. An example is a company where users propose a majority of the new ideas for IT applications. The proposals are evaluated by the IS department which selects only those applications that "satisfy company and not only user goals." The company believes that there are "too many low return projects to satisfy all users." Projects are developed jointly by users and IS; all projects have two leaders, a client or end-user and an IS executive. In another company, assessment and evaluation is the responsibility of a steering committee composed of functional area executives. On the other hand, at another organization the IS department is very proactive. It increases awareness of functional area users regarding potentially useful technologies. At times, the IS group may even formulate a trial system to enable users to test new technology.

It thus seems that the IS department is playing an active role in the selection and adoption of new IT. In fact, the IS department seems to have moved from a customer service approach to a partnership approach. In the former, according to Freund and Schlier (1989), the IS department responds to the fragmented tactical requirements of other departments. The focus is therefore on being responsive to the short-term requirements of a user or a set of users, rather than the strategic objectives of the organization. The emphasis is on local rather than global needs. In contrast, in the partnership approach, the IS function treats the organization as its primary customer and its main purpose is to meet strategic business goals.

Efficiency of IS spending is an important organizational concern. Companies are taking a closer look at their IS spending and evaluating the efficiency and the appropriateness of their spending level. They wanted to spend the "right" amount, not more not less. One company tracks its expenditure and takes pride in the fact that its IS spending is 1 percent of sales whereas the industry norm is about 1.4 percent. Another organization's IS spending is at the 1984 level but it feels that this is sufficient for its needs. Another believes that most companies spend significant amounts on projects which yield only marginal advantages and thus it "is not likely to spend money unless there is a compelling reason to do so."

The concern over IS spending and its effectiveness seems to be a global phenomena. It is reflected in the strategy of Pennwalt Corp. which has reduced its IS spending each of the past four years while keeping pace with its competitors' uses of technology (Sullivan-Trainor, 1989). In one survey IS managers ranked the cost of operating their department to be the top issue (Ryan, 1989). The attention to IS expenditures may be mounting because of cost pressure within the corporation and the fact that IS budgets have become significant items on the balance sheet (Sullivan-Trainor, 1989). Another contributing factor may be top management's perceptions of IS; a survey found that about two-thirds of responding CEOs of Fortune 100 companies agreed that their organization was not getting the most for its IS investment and that IS was only partially meeting expectations (Rifkin, 1989).

CONCLUSION

This research has described some successful practices for IT management as well as outlined overall IT strategies that organizations have adopted. These overall strategies encompass management of the IS function, integration of business and IS strategy, the role of top management, the role of users, and the role of information systems in information technology management. It was found that strategic benefits result from using IT to change and improve business processes rather than from the technology itself. Quite significantly, most companies desire to let somebody else take the risk of innovation and want to be a close second in adopting the technology once it has proven to be successful. Many firms believe that competitive advantage is fleeting and demands constant attention in order to reap sustained benefits. Increasingly, vendors are becoming an important source of ideas about competitors' use of IT and for new ideas regarding technology. Users as well as the IS department play a major role in assessment, adoption, development, and design. Finally, organizations are concerned with the level of IS expenditures and want accountability as well as exploitation of IS to leverage organizational strengths.

REFERENCES

Arthur Young. 1989. "The Landmark MIT Study: Management in the 1990s." # M189-1733 189-QG-1868-30M.

Bakos, Y.J. and M.E. Treacy. 1986. "Information Technology and Corporate Strategy: A Research Perspective." *MIS Quarterly* 10(2): 107-119.

Benjamin, R.I., J.F. Rockart, M.S., Scott Morton, and J. Wyman. 1984. "Information Technology: A Strategic Opportunity." *Sloan Management Review* 25(3): 3-10.

Boynton, A.C. and R.W. Zmud. 1987. "Information Technology Planning in the 1990s: Directions for Practice and Research." MIS Quarterly 11(1): 59-71.

Bozman. J.S. and A.J. Ryan. 1989. "Rethink before Automating." *Computerworld* (June 26): 6.

Brancheau, J.C. and J.C. Wetherbe, 1987. "Key Issues in Information Systems Management." *MIS Quarterly* 11(1): 23-45.

Cash, J.I., Jr. and B.R. Konsynski. 1985. "IS Redraws Competitive Boundaries." *Harvard Business Review* 63(2): 134-142.

Clemons, E.K. 1989. "Information Systems and Business Strategy: Minitrack on Current Research." *Proceedings of the Hawaii International Conference on System Sciences* 181-183.

Clemons, E.K. 1986. "Information Systems for Sustainable Competitive Advantage." *Information and Management* 11(3): 131-136.

Clemons, E.K. and S.O. Kimbrough. 1986. "Information Systems, Telecommunications and their Effects on Industrial Organizations." *Seventh Annual International Conference on Information Systems,* (December): 99-108.

Clemons, E.K. and M. Knez. 1988. "Competition and Cooperation in Information Systems Innovation." *Information and Management* 15: 25-35.

Clemons, E.K. and M. Row. 1987. "Structural Differences Among Firms: A Potential Source of Competitive Advantage in the Application of Information Technology." *Eighth Annual International Conference on Information Systems* (December): 1-9.

Crowston, K. and M.E. Treacy. 1986. "Assessing the Impact of Information Technology on Enterprise Level Performance." *Seventh Annual International Conference on Information Systems* (December): 299-310.

Diebold, J. 1990. "John Diebold on Innovation." *Computerworld* (January 22): 108.

Earl, M. 1987. "Formulating Information Technology Strategies," pp. 296-311 in *Management Information Systems: The Technology Challenge,* edited by N. Piercy. East Brunswick, NJ: Nichols Publishing Company.

Emery, J.C. 1989. "Editor's Comments: What Does the CIO Needs to Know About Information Technology?" *MIS Quarterly* 13(4): xv-xvi.

Freund, E. and F. Schlier. 1989. "Changing the IS Mission." *Computerworld* (July 3): 45.

Geise, P.E. 1984. "Using Information Technology to Capture Strategic Position." *Management Review* (September): 8.

Goodhue, D.L., J.A. Quillard, and J.F. Rockart. 1984. "Managing the Data Resource: A Contingency Perspective," *MIS Quarterly* 12(3): 373-394.

Grossman, R.B. and M.B. Packer. 1989. 'Betting the Business:' Strategic Programs to Rebuild Core Information Systems." *Proceedings of the Hawaii International Conference on System Sciences* 184-187.

Huff, S.L. and M.C. Munro. 1985. "Information Technology Assessment and Adoption: A Field Study" *MIS Quarterly* 9(4): 327-339.

Information Week. 1986. "The Strategic Use of Information: Seizing the Competitive Edge." (May 26): 26-62.

Ives, B. and G.P. Learmonth. 1984. "The Information System as a Competitive Weapon." *Communications of the ACM* 27(12): 1193-1201.

Johnston, R.H. and S.R. Carrico. 1988. "Developing Capabilities to Use Information Strategically." *MIS Quarterly* 12(1): 37-50.

Johnston, R.H. and M.R. Vitale. 1988. "Creating Competitive Advantage with Interorganizational Systems" *MIS Quarterly* 12(2): 152-165.

Karimi, J. 1988. "Strategic Planning for Information Systems: Requirements and Information Engineering Methods" *Journal of Management Information Systems* 4(4): 5-24.

King, W.R., V. Grover, and E. Hufnagel. 1986. "Seeking Competitive Advantage Using Information-intensive Strategies: Facilitators and Inhibitors." *The 1986 NYU Symposium on Strategic Uses of Information Technology*.

Lederer, A.L. and A.L. Mendelow. 1987. "Information Resource Planning: Overcoming Difficulties in Identifying Top Management's Objectives." *MIS Quarterly* 11(3): 215-232.

Lederer, A.L., and V. Sethi. 1988. "The Implementation of Strategic Information Systems Planning Methodologies." *MIS Quarterly* 12(3): 209-228.

Mason, R.O. 1984. "IS Technology and Corporate Strategy: Current Research Issues." Pp. 279-307 in *The IS Research Challenge*, edited by W.F. McFarlan. Boston, MA: Harvard Business School Press.

MacMillan, I.C. 1983. "Preemptive Strategies." *Journal of Business Strategy* (Fall): 16-26.

MacMillan, I., M.L. McCaffery, and G.V. Wijk, 1985 "Competitors Response to Easily Imitated New Products — Exploring Commercial Banking Product Introductions." *Strategic Management Journal* 6: 75-86.

McFarlan, W.F. 1984. "Information Technology Changes the Way You Compete." *Harvard Business Review* 62(3): 98-103.

Mason, R.O. 1984. "Conclusion to Part II." Pp. 183-188 in *The Information Systems Research Challenge*, edited by W. F. McFarlan. Boston, MA: Harvard Business School Press.

Parsons, G.L. 1983. "Information Technology: A New Competitive Weapon." *Sloan Management Review*, 24(1): 3-14.

Porter, M. 1980. *Competitive Strategy*. New York: Free Press.

Porter, M. 1985. *Competitive Advantage*. New York: Free Press.

Porter, M. and V.E. Millar. 1985. "How Information Gives You Competitive Advantage." *Harvard Business Review* 62(4): 149-160.

Rackoff, N., C. Wiseman, and W.A. Ullrich, 1985 "Information Systems for Competitive Advantage: Implementation of a Planning Process." *MIS Quarterly*. 9(4): 309-321.

Rifkin, G. 1989. "CEOs Give Credit for Today but Expect More for Tomorrow." *Computerworld* (April 17): 75-82.

Rockart, J.F. and A.D. Crescenzi. 1984. "Engaging Top Management in Information Technology." *Sloan Management Review* 25(1): 3-16.

Runge, D.A. 1985. *Using Telecommunications for Competitive Advantage* Ph.D. Dissertation, Oxford University.

Ryan. A.J. 1989a. "IS Execs' Attention Turns to Business Issues." *Computerworld* (March 20): 61

Ryan. A.J. 1989b. "Utility firms' No. 1 Concern: Systems Costs." *Computerworld* (July 3): 41.

Sullivan-Trainor, M. 1989. "Building Competitive Advantage by Extending Information Systems." *Computerworld* (October 9): SR/19.

Treacy, M.E. 1986. "Towards a Cumulative Tradition of Research on Information Technology as Strategic Business Factor." Center for Information Systems Research, Sloan School of Management, MIT.

Vitale, M.R. 1986. "The Growing Risks of Information Systems Success." *MIS Quarterly* 10(4): 326-334.

Vitale, M.R., B. Ives, and C. Beath. 1986. "Identifying Strategic Information Systems: Finding a Process or Building an Organization." *Proceedings of the Seventh International Conference on Information Systems*, December 1986, San Diego, California.

Weill, P. and M.H. Olson. 1989. "Managing Investment in Information Technology: Mini Case Examples and Implications." *MIS Quarterly* 13(1): 3-18.

Wilder C. 1990. "Re-engineering is IS Priority." *Computerworld* (Febuary 5): 6.

Wiseman, C. 1988. *Strategic Information Systems*. Homewood, Ill: Dow Jones Irwin.

Wiseman, C. 1985. *Strategy and Computers: Information Systems as Competitive Weapons*. Homewood, Ill: Dow Jones Irwin.

Wiseman C. and I. MacMillan. 1984. "Creating Competitive Weapons from Information Systems." *Journal of Business Strategy* (Fall): 42-49.

Wyman, J. 1985. "Technological Myopia — The Need to Think Strategically about Technology." *Sloan Management Review* 26(4): 59-64.

INFORMATION TECHNOLOGY BACKGROUND AREAS

Robert P. Cerveny, C. Carl Pegels, and
G. Lawrence Sanders

INTRODUCTION

Information Technology forms the technical foundation of Strategic Information Systems. The developer of or the participant in developing these systems must have a familiarity with the main technological background areas. Areas which must be considered are:

- Introduction to Management Information Systems
- Information Technology — Hardware/Software
- Telecommunications, including Local Area Networks
- Database Management
- Systems Analysis and Design
- Decision Support Systems

The purpose of this chapter is not to present a detailed description of these areas, but to give a summary description of each subject followed by a list of recommended textbooks which can provide the knowledge background in each subject module. Industry analyses of the use of information technology (IT) in the supermarket and air cargo industries are then developed to show the importance of understanding the underlying issues.

39

INTRODUCTION TO MANAGEMENT
INFORMATION SYSTEMS

This background area provides the setting for management information systems in the business environment. The primary focus is on the relationship of information technology to organizational processes. Concepts include: (1) delineating the role of transaction processing systems in maintaining a foundation for organizational communication; (2) control systems in tracking the effective utilization; and (3) decision support systems for providing organizational direction. Strategies for identifying and building these systems in terms of conceiving, developing, and implementing them must also be reviewed. The challenge of the next decade will be in the functional management areas where systems will be developed by the users. The area of end-user computing requires that information systems managers have both a global and micro vision on how end-user developed systems will be integrated with the other organizational information systems. These concepts, tools, and techniques will provide the foundation for facilitating information processing in complex organizations.

Background References

1. Cash, J.I., F.W. McFarlan, J.L. McKenney, M.R. and Vitale. 1992. Corporate Information Systems Management: Text and Cases, 3rd edition. Homewood, IL: Irwin.
2. Kanter, J. 1986. Computer Essays for Management. Englewood Cliffs, NJ: Prentice-Hall.
3. Laudon, K.C. and J.P. Laudon. 1993. Management Information Systems: A Contemporary Perspective, 2nd edition. New York, NY: Macmillan Publishing.
4. McNurlin, B.C. and R.H. Jr. Sprague. 1989. Information Systems Management in Practice, 2nd edition. Englewood Cliffs, NJ: Prentice-Hall.

INFORMATION TECHNOLOGY

A knowledge of various types of microcomputer, minicomputer, and mainframe computing environments is fundamental to making effective use of IT. Operating systems concepts such as multitasking, multiprocessing, memory management, graphical user interfaces, and resource management also underlie a thorough understanding of IT. The hardware component also includes descriptions of microcomputer through mainframe architecture, communications bus management, peripheral interconnectivity, and topics in graphics. Emerging technologies such as RISC architecture and hyper-processors are also important. This area must also illustrate how the hardware/software requirements of an MIS design proposal are evaluated.

Background References

1. Curtin, D.P. 1990. Application Software, 2nd edition. Englewood Cliffs, NJ: Prentice-Hall Inc.
2. White, R. 1993. How Computers Work. Emeryville, CA: Ziff-Davis Press.
3. Zorkoczy, P. 1993. Information Technology: An Introduction, 3rd edition. London, UK: Pitman.

TELECOMMUNICATIONS

Knowledge of telecommunications is becoming a requirement for organizations wishing to maintain a competitive edge. This is particularly true today as video, voice, electronic data interchange, imaging and electronic mail are providing organizations with advanced methods for inter and extra-organizational communication. There are a variety of technical issues including transmission protocols, characteristics of different methods of data transmission, concentrators and multiplexors, and local and wide area network hardware and software There are also several important managerial issues which complement the technical material. For example identifying opportunities in the firm where telecommunications technology can provide a competitive opportunity, evaluating telecommunications technology, developing and implementing a plan for integrating telecommunications technology, and the ongoing management of telecommunications systems. This area also includes an extensive coverage of business telecommunications including data, voice, and video approaches to telecommunications. A final area to be considered here is the importance of information systems security since telecommunications technology put computer systems at greater risk to intrusion.

As an example of one area where telecommunications is having a significant impact as a competitive tool, consider Electronic Data Interchange (EDI). In its most refined form, a company allows its computer to call other computers to order parts, pay bills and inquire about service information, all without human intervention. This scenario is slightly futuristic, but much of it exists today thanks to EDI.

EDI facilitates computer to computer communications of standardized electronic transactions between sites initiated by human entry of data into a terminal. The roots of these systems may be traced to a system introduced by Texas Instruments early in the 1970s. Widespread implementation really began during the 1980s. The EDI market consisting of EDI networks, software and professional services has been growing some 44 percent annually since 1989. In 1991, 75 percent of all Fortune 100 companies and 39 percent of all Fortune 500 companies employed EDI systems (Snopp, 1991).

EDI allows a company to exchange inventory transactions in a pre-defined format which allows the complete transaction to take place electronically. These systems are also used to exchange shipping schedules, budgets, memos about orders/shipments, financial information and actual exchange of money. The primary benefits include elimination of time spent in the mail system, errors in rekeying data and time spent in internal transfers of information within the companies involved.

Under the traditional approach, using a manual system, if a firm wished to purchase components from a supplier, it had to go through a multistep procedure involving internal departments in the purchasing firm as well as several departments in the supplying firm. Looking at the process from the purchasing firm's point of view, it might look something like this. First the purchasing firm's manufacturing area triggers a purchase request which is sent to the purchasing department. The purchasing department then verifies that the material is definitely needed. Once that is determined, the purchasing department prepares multiple copies of a purchase order (PO). Copies of the PO are then sent to the vendor of the material, to the accounting and to the receiving departments, and perhaps to the Inventory department or manufacturing group. Upon receipt of the material at the purchasing firm's receiving dock, a receiving report is initiated and distributed to the various departments involved. Finally, the accounting department receives an invoice from the supplier of the material asking for payment. The accounting department must then verify with the receiving department that the material was indeed received and was in the amount ordered and in good condition. Only then may the accounting department issue a check to pay for the material. This system involves a lot of paper being sent to a variety of departments and to the supplier. All these movements take time, are prone to various errors and are fraught with opportunities for the necessary information to get lost. EDI removes much of the delay and reconciliation problems. All departments and the supplier are notified within a few hours of the initiation of the request and the necessary "paperwork" is now kept in machine readable form so it is easier to find. Additionally, the information is only keyed in one time, reducing the likelihood of error.

This reduction in delay due to transmission of the order allows a firm to move closer to a Just-In-Time inventory mode. This results in significant reduction in inventories, thus freeing up both the money which was invested in the inventory and the space the inventory took in the plant.

The benefits of EDI are so great that many firms are forcing their suppliers to install EDI systems. For example, Chrysler, Ford and General Motors have all warned suppliers that if they are not equipped with EDI capability, their business will no longer be welcome in Detroit (Nagle, 1989). However, most large firms do not just mandate the use of EDI. They also work with their suppliers to insure that comparable systems are installed. According to Jerome Dreyer, executive director of the Electronic Data Interchange Association (EDIA), most larger companies prefer agreements whereby they educate the smaller firms with which they do business to understand EDI's benefits and help them use the technology (Curran, 1988).

Another example of EDI's use is Hallmark's use of EDI with its retailers. This has the advantage to Hallmark of allowing the orders to be received error free and has advantages to the retailers in that they can get rapid confirmation of their order with a shipping date and they achieve faster turn around time. For example,

> At Lynns Hallmark card store in Pasadena, California, manager Marian Robbins takes inventory with a hand held terminal that, through the use of a modem, also transmits data to Hallmark's company headquarters in Kansas City, Missouri. There, computer operator Demise Asbury supervises the printing of the card order forms transmitted by EDI from retailers such as Lynns' in Pasadena. The printouts are mailed to the retailers and the orders are filled by employees at Hallmark's distribution center in Liberty, Missouri. In buying its own supplies, Hallmark also uses computer technology. For instance, Hallmark's orders for graphic-arts material are received and filed through the EDI system. Through EDI, Hallmark can receive orders the same day they are placed. This process greatly diminishes the amount of labor that would have previously been required without the use of an EDI system" (Childs 1991).

There is considerable cost associated with the implementation of EDI systems. However, there is considerable cost reduction experienced by firms in other parts of the ordering system which typically allows the cost of installation to be recovered within one year. Research estimates that a final purchase order may cost $49 to process manually while EDI processing cuts this to $4.70. In the automobile industry, ... the cost of processing a purchase order (has dropped) from $55 to $18 (Leong 1988).

Background References

1. Bartee, T.C. 1992. Data Communications, Networks, and Systems. Englewood Cliffs, NJ: Prentice Hall,
2. Caelli, W., D. Longley, and M. Shain. 1989. Information Security for Managers. New York: Stockton Press.

3. Green, J.H. 1989. The Dow Jones-Irwin Handbook of Telecommunications Management. Homewood, Ill: Dow Jones-Irwin.
4. Stallings, W. 1990. Business Data Communications New York, NY: Macmillan Publishing.

DATABASE MANAGEMENT

In order to be useful in an information system, data must be organized and stored in a manner which allows effective retrieval and analysis. Data Base Management Systems (DBMS) is the name given to the area of information technology which deals with the organizing and storing data in a manner which allows effective retrieval, updating and analysis. Management of the data resource is fundamental to the use of information systems and underlies areas such as decision support systems and expert systems.

Current technology supports the development and implementation of relational data bases such as IBM's DB2, which runs Structured Query Language (SQL). However, there are many commercial uses of data base technology which lend themselves well to earlier forms of data base languages and so, network and hierarchal languages are still in fairly wide spread use. To be current in this field still requires a knowledge of all three approaches.

This area also encompasses issues in distributed data base technology. The fundamental question to be answered for distributed applications is where the data should reside if the application is run in more than one location. There are conflicting issues of efficiency of data processing and control of the data resource which must be addressed and resolved.

Another area of concern is the issue of data security. In general, the greater the degree of data security, the more difficult it becomes to retrieve, update data, and develop competitive applications. In an age where access to information technology and data bases is spreading and becoming easier, this is a real issue.

Background References

1. Ageloff, R. 1988. A Primer on SQL. New York, NY: Times Mirror/Mosby.
2. Date, C.J. 1990. An Introduction to Database Systems, 5th edition. Boston, MA: Addison-Wesley.
3. Nickerson, R.C. 1987. Fundamentals of Structured COBOL. Boston, MA: Little Brown & Co.

SYSTEMS ANALYSIS AND DESIGN

In order for a computer system to become functional within an organization, it must be conceptualized, determined to be feasible, created, tested and debugged, installed and maintained. Quite often computer professionals and computer users are involved in this activity. Systems analysis and design is the name given to the process of bringing an idea from inception to a functioning computer application. Knowledge of the methodologies and tools is important to controlling both the systems development process and the implementation and maintenance of a computer application. Issues such as the traditional systems development life cycle as well as the use of prototyping are fundamental to an understanding of modern software development practices.

Systems analysis and design techniques are used to communicate system specifications between users and designers. They are used to control the development and installation process and, they provide documentation of systems so that they may be maintained throughout their life. A thorough knowledge of appropriate software engineering techniques such as computer-aided software engineering (CASE), project cost and planning, software quality metrics, structured analysis and design, systems testing and systems conversion are necessary for the professional development of a systems analyst.

There is a healthy tension between techniques designed to control the development process and those designed to ensure that the resultant systems actually meet the users needs. Managers involved with the process need to understand these tensions and the tradeoffs they cause.

In organizations where there is a traditional structure of an MIS group serving a user community, the detailed knowledge of the techniques will reside in the MIS group. In those organizations which have distributed the bulk of their computing activity to the user community, it is incumbent on that community to acquire the necessary knowledge to properly manage the system development process.

Background References

1. Jordan, E.W., J.J. Machesky, and J.B. Matkowski. 1990. Systems Development: Requirements, Evaluation, Design and Implementation. Boston, MA: PWS-Kent Publishing Co.
2. McDermid, D.C. 1990. Software Engineering for Information Systems. Cambridge, MA: Blackwell Scientific Publications.
3. Ng, P.A. and R.T. Yeh, (ed.). 1990. Modern Software Engineering: Foundations and Current Perspectives. New York: Nostrand Reinhold.

4. Olle, T.W., J. Hagelstein, I.G. Mcdonald, C. Rolland, H.G. Sol, F.J.M. Van Assche, and A.A. Varrijn-Stuart. 1991. Information Systems Methodologies: A Framework for Understanding, 2nd edition. Reading, MA: Addison-Wesley.
5. Von Mayrhauser, A. 1990. Software Engineering: Methods and Management. Boston, MA: Academic Press.
6. Whitten, J.L., L.D. Bentley, and V.M. Barlow. 1989. Systems Analysis and Design Methods. 2nd edition. Homewood, IL: Irwin.

DECISION SUPPORT SYSTEMS

Information technology can be used to support decision making in a variety of modes. One of these is the use of models and simulations to allow a decision maker to explore alternative scenarios before deciding on a course of action. Decision Support Systems (DSS) is the name given to this use of information technology to support managerial judgement in specific decision and organizational contexts.

In order to develop systems in this area, an individual should be knowledgeable in data base design, statistical and mathematical modeling and the use of a nonprocedural (fourth generation) language. DSS "planning languages" fall into two broad categories, those that are designed to be used as DSS generators by end-users and those that are designed to be used as applications generators by MIS staff. Languages such as FOCUS (Information Builders, Inc., New York, NY) and RAMIS (On-Line Software International, Fort Lee, NJ) fall into the first category while IDEAL (ADR, East Syracuse, NY) and NATURAL (Software A& G, Reston, VA) are examples of the latter category.

A related area is that of Expert Systems (ES). Decision Support Systems permit a decision maker to explore various alternative courses of action whereas Expert Systems are used to bring the expertise of the best decision makers in a field to bear on a problem. An expert system will elicit information from the decision maker about the problem and then use its reasoning capability to make a decision. The expert systems field is a new and growing field and one decision makers should keep current in so that they can take advantage of the rapid advances in the field.

Background References

1. Alan, P. 1990. *The EIS Book: Information Systems for Top Managers.* Homewood, IL: Dow Jones-Irwin.
2. Lotfi, V. and C. C. Pegels. 1991. *Decision Support Systems for Production and Operations Management, 2nd edition.* Homewood, IL: Dow Jones - Irwin.

3. Sprague, Jr., R.H. and H.J. Watson, (ed.) 1989. *Decision Support Systems: Putting Theory into Practice, 2nd edition.* Englewood Cliffs, NY: Prentice-Hall.
4. Turban, E. 1993. *Decision Support and Expert Systems: Managerial Perspectives, 3rd edition.* New York, NY: Macmillan Publishing, Co.

To illustrate the necessity of a clear undertaking of how these technology issues affect a firm's use of information technology for competition, we present two industry analyses. The first industry study covers the supermarket industry, while the second study covers the air cargo industry.

THE SUPERMARKET INDUSTRY

The supermarket industry in the United States has become increasingly competitive. Factors that have driven this phenomena include changes in regional economies, demographics, and industry overcapacity. These differences have not only helped define new trends in food retailing, but have transformed the nature of the business. Low profit margins and high fixed overhead expenses have forced companies to aggressively pursue programs for managing and controlling operating costs. Moreover, the mature nature of the industry limits growth opportunities to taking market share from rival firms. Nevertheless, non-traditional competitors such as K-Mart and Wal-Mart have recently targeted food retailing for expansion. All of these factors are insuring a role for advanced technology in the grocery business. These technologies improve service, reduce costs, and enhance decision making by providing managers with information in "real time." This situation is exemplified by the $2 billion spent annually on electronic scanning equipment alone (Shulman, 1988). Advanced systems for electronic shelf labeling, computer assisted inventory reordering, direct store delivery management, and even self service checkout now characterize the food business. Satellite technology will also be introduced to food retailing as Wal-Mart expands operations in this relatively demand inelastic business (Tosh, 1992).

According to industry statistics, approximately 145,000 retail food stores accrued sales of $368.5 billion in 1990 (Standard and Poors Survey, 1992). Amazingly, this sales figure actually represents a decline in real terms as compared to the previous year. Current economic conditions have abated the tendency to eat-out which began in 1980, leading analysts to forecast improved supermarket sales volumes in the next 3-5 years. Retailers should be ready for this surge considering the move to larger stores which offer one-stop shopping. These markets have largely been the result of attempts to both increase operating margins in the grocery business and satisfy customer demands. Many stores now include bakeries, delicatessens, butcher shops, pharmacies, and even gourmet cooking facilities. Non-food products and prepared foods have also become popular items, often commanding considerable floor space. While these changes are being made to gain the favor of today's value-minded shopper, they require effective inventory control and space management. Moreover, improving marketing effectiveness has led many chains to adopt a multi-format approach to retailing. This can be challenging for management in that product inventories, in-store services, and building design may vary considerably across the outlets of a particular company. Vons Stores of California has gone so far as to target the Hispanic population of Los Angeles with the "El Tiangus" theme. These stores feature Hispanic foods, traditional Latin American decor, and are staffed by Spanish speaking employees. Similar stores have been opened to serve the Chinese and Korean communities as well (Standard and Poors Survey, 1992).

Information technology also plays a vital role in dealing with changes in the labor pool. Although many stores are unionized, the majority of food market employees work part-time for low wages. As such, this industry has traditionally attracted a large contingency of high school age individuals and other first-time job seekers. Since 1980, however, the population of 14-17 year odds has dropped by more than twenty percent (Standard and Poors Survey, 1992). At the same time, the emergence of larger and more service oriented supermarkets has increased the demand for labor. Not only do these stores employ more people than the traditional grocery store, but competition necessitates that these employees be of a higher caliber. Supermarket operations have become more sophisticated with the introduction of specialty sections and various in-store services. The success of these ventures is largely dependent on a well trained staff of customer and career oriented employees. Supermarket concerns are experiencing the need to invest more money in the areas of training, compensation, and human resource management. Although these efforts should help reduce the high rates of turnover which have typically depicted the industry, food retailers are also taking actions to reduce their dependence on human labor. Once again, technology promises to play a greater role in food store management in the future as applications increase and the supply of labor contracts.

Electronic Scanning

Electronic scanning technology has had a dramatic impact on the supermarket industry. This technology has become so popular that it is no longer considered a differentiating factor, but a necessity. Wegman's Food Markets, Inc. of Rochester, New York, has pioneered the use of these systems in the supermarket industry. Chairman Robert Wegman is not only highly regarded as an outstanding supermarket operator and businessman, but as an outspoken advocate of technology as well. It is no surprise that his organization was one of the first three food retailers in the entire United States to install these innovative checkout devices (Personal Interview, 1992). Mr. Wegman is also credited for his crucial role in the successful development, legalization, and popularization of universal price codes (UPC's). These electronically readable information bars make scanning technology possible.

The supermarket business has long been characterized by relatively low margins and the accompanying need to achieve high volume sales. The general trend toward larger stores with high fixed costs places additional pressures on store management to improve sales. In fact, some "superstores" require weekly sales in the $1 million range just to stay afloat. As such, electronic scanning technology plays an important strategic role in managing today's food market. Industry estimates show that the cost of front-end labor accounts for 25-30 percent of total store sales annually (Shulman, 1987). Scanning not only improves checkout times and productivity, but also reduces the total number of front-end employees needed to process orders. This translates into major cost savings for those chains which employ the technology effectively. These savings can be passed on to consumers in the form of featured sale items, promotional campaigns, and added services. Additionally, less waiting time, more accurate processing, and a modern atmosphere can improve sales and customer relations.

Realizing the need to continually expand existing technologies, Wegman's Food Markets, Inc. has extended the uses of electronic scanning considerably. This regional firm became the first in the United States to print scannable coupons, which further reduced processing times and improved accuracy. Recently, the company completely eliminated the need to print coupons with the introduction of the "Shopper's Club" program. Club members are provided an electronically readable plastic card which automatically affords them any discounts that would have otherwise been offered via coupons. Moreover, important marketing data is collected each time a customer uses the card to make a purchase. This has allowed Wegman's to improve marketing effectiveness and direct particular specials to those customers most likely to respond. The "Shopper's Club" card also offers customers the added convenience of pre-approved check writing and/ or direct account debit.

Electronic scanning is also used to provide management with important sales data in "real time." This current information is used to manage shelf space, establish floor space allocations, place inventory orders, and even set trucking schedules. While it assists management in maximizing store productivity per square foot, it also enables the company to better operating margins and inventory turnover. Finally, effective in-store inventory management is vital to the efficiency of distribution operations and overall firm performance.

Direct Product Profitability (DPP)

Direct Product Profitability (DDP) is being used by Super Valu Stores, Inc. and to increase gross profit margin. It monitors the costs incurred by products as they move through a distribution system and provides information for decision making. The DPP system combines computer and scanning technologies. The system uses scanned data to calculate the profit of individual retail items and generates data that make the calculations of each product's cost and profit possible.

Because DDP leads to a much more accurate measure of retail profit it is replacing gross margin in making merchandising and distribution decisions (Gordon 1986).

The concept of DPP is shown in Exhibit 1. The first step in the DDP process is the identification of the gross margin of one particular product. The calculation of the gross margin also takes into account other factors such as prompt payment discounts. The final direct product profitability is computed by deducting the direct product costs (DPCs) from adjusted gross margin. The direct product costs are generally classified by the major distribution channel activities including warehouse direct costs, transportation direct costs, and store direct costs. All other fixed costs, such as head office costs, are not included. The key concept in determining the allocation of direct product costs is the product causality. Only those costs which are directly incurred by the product are taken into account.

Based on the DPP analysis, managers can classify products into four categories: winners, under-achievers, sleepers and losers as shown on Exhibit 2. According to the classification, managers can easily take proper action on a particular product. For example, when a product is categorized as a sleeper with a high DPP but low volume, managers can lower the price of the product to increase the volume (Pinnock 1989).

Benefits of Direct Product Profitability

There are at least three major benefits provided by DPP. These benefits are briefly described as follows:

1. DPP provides detailed information to help managers make faster and more precise product decisions.
2. DPP can improve overall store profitability. Store managers can discontinue and remove low profitability products and refill the space previously allocated to these products with more profitable products.

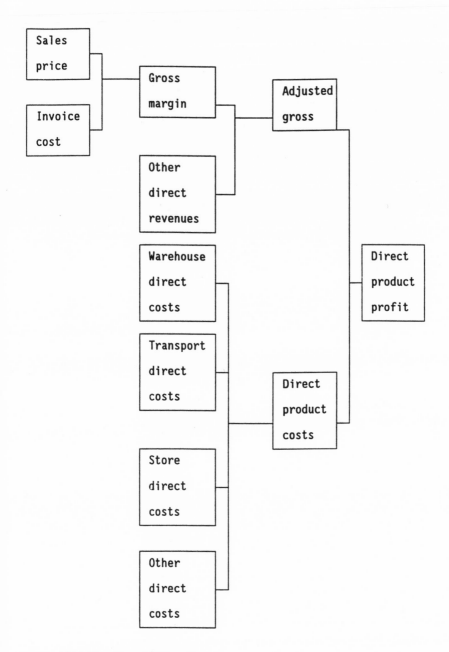

Source: Adapted from Pinnock (1989, p. 18).

Exhibit 1. Conceptual Model of Direct Product Profitability

3. When store managers decide to discontinue some low contribution
    products they can provide suppliers with concrete evidence regarding
    the profitability of their products thus decreasing the conflicts that
    store management has with suppliers.

Further applications of DPP focus on integrating the system with other
decision-support tools such as computerized space management, display and
store layout, and promotion planning models.

HIGH DPP

☐ SLEEPER Increase movement Lower price Increase space	☐ WINNER Promote and display
☐ LOSER Discontinue Change price Change handling	☐ UNDER-ACHIEVER Raise price Reduce space Change handling

LOW   HIGH

VOLUME   VOLUME

LOW DPP

Source: Adapted from Pinnock (1989, p. 19).

Exhibit 2.   Classification Schema of Direct Product Profitability

Direct Store Delivery (DSD)

Another important retail technology is direct store delivery (DSD)
transactions. Certain items sold at the supermarket have such a short life
span that they require direct delivery from vendors as opposed to being
replenished from the retailer's warehouse. From a logistics management

perspective, DSD items have distinctly different characteristics than the ordinary items that are delivered from the retailer's warehouse. One of the major hurdles involving DSD items is that vendors' territories seldom match with regional market areas in which supermarkets are organized. This can result in store-level discrepancies in price discounting, promotion, and delivery date thus making the DSD transaction between the store and supplier more complicated and difficult to control (Shulman 1991). However, the increasing number of DSD between suppliers and retailers is playing an increasingly important role in the supermarket cost control process. According to an article in *Chain Store Age Executive*, industry-wide DSD transactions have surpassed $9 billion a year (Chain Store Age Executive 1990). Information technology has been employed to process these transactions more efficiently. Unfortunately many DSD systems lack interface capabilities thus hindering their integration into a total logistics management system.

An industry-wide data standard called DEX/UCS (Direct Exchange/ Uniform Communication Standard) was introduced in the late 1980s to solve communication problems among the DSD applications and to enhance logistics management. Although the use of DEX/UCS in DSD transactions is still in its infancy, supermarkets are very active players in this arena. Among the chains that use DEX/UCS chain-wide are Price Chopper, Quality Food Centers, Schnuck Markets, and Shaw's Super-markets. Some supermarkets including Furr's, Von Cos., and Ralph's Grocery Co. are using DEX/UCS at their pilot stores. On the vendor side, Frito-Lay, Coca-Cola, Pepsi, L'eggs, Pepperidge Farms, Keebler, and Nabisco are the major players. The tricky part of the DEX/UCS standard is that its success depends on cooperation between the retailer and its vendors. Although there are potential benefits of DEX/UCS to both sides, the benefits cannot be realized until all parties invest in the DEX/UCS standard. If vendors are not ready for the DEX/UCS, the supermarket which is fully DEX-equipped cannot enjoy the advantage of its investment. In the area of interorganizational cooperation in the use of direct store delivery information technology, Price Chopper is the pioneer (Garry 1992).

New Innovations

Vons is a 385 store retail chain based in Arcadia, California that is equipped with "talking" aisles with computerized voices that describe products to shoppers (McCarol 1992). As customers walk between the different aisles, the talking aisles describe feature items and display product names on video screens. Some customers were initially threatened by the system but it has since become a very popular attraction of the stores.

One feature that has given Vons a considerable advantage over its competitors has been Vide-Ocart (Fox 1991). This is a modified shopping cart which has a liquid crystal display mounted on the handle. Besides advertisements, Vide-Ocart displays up-to-date features like sale prices and item location, in-store specials, and a listing of the prepared foods which are "ready" in the food department. The system is also used to inform particular customers that film left to be developed is ready for pick-up. Finally, customers waiting in the check-out lane can play games provided by the Vide-Ocart system.

One of the most important innovations adopted by Vons has been its database marketing (Allan 1991). This system collects data about the preferences, tastes, addresses, and buying habits of individual consumers and households. Vons' goal with its database marketing has been to group various product brands around a common theme and to appeal to the appropriate customer group with the value added promotion. The system is also used to build long-term relationships with selected customers through personalized mailings. The system used by Vons in its stores is called Vision, and it was developed by IBM (Pike, 1989). This sophisticated program combines frequent shopper programs, electronic discounts, electronic payment options and interactive video screens at the point of sale.

Another area in which Vons has shown technological leadership is in space management (Sherrets 1992). Depending on the level of store volume and level of sophistication, Vons may use Accuspace by SAGE Worldwide or Spacemaster from Strategic Merchandiser Applications. Accuspace allows stores to allocate shelf space based on customer demand and profitability and Spacemaster evaluates all categories of products across the entire chain. With this information, the system produces what are referred to as strategic "plan-o-grams," which indicate how many products are going to be needed for each Vons store during a certain time period. An important feature of Spaceman is that it produces plan-o-grams with photo images. With these important informational tools, Vons' management is provided with clear ideas as to the most convenient way to shelf products by location and quantity. This not only increases marketing effectiveness but it also improves inventory control.

In other applications, electronic price tags have replaced paper shelf labels in Vons stores (Brumemback 1988). These new digital labels are linked to a central computer that changes shelf prices and coordinates them with check-out registers. Vons is also using information technology behind the scenes. In warehouses, merchandise is scanned and the inventories are updated by means of a special computer programs. Every Vons store is connected through data communications networks with distribution centers (Moore 1989). In some cases, store shelves are directly linked with warehouses thus allowing merchandise to automatically be dispatched from distribution centers to the store when stock levels are low.

Vons has also instituted a system which allows customers to purchase groceries from home. Because a great percentage of Vons' customers actually have access to a personal computer, Vons has established a system which customers can use to order items from home (Pike 1989). Shoppers can transmit an order, use their credit cards, and get the merchandise delivered to their front door without having to personally contact anyone in the store.

Information technologies have revolutionized the United States supermarket industry. Today, virtually every food store uses one form of technology or another. In fact, some of the most sophisticated systems are so strategically significant they are now considered necessities and not just differentiating factors. The need to improve sales, reduce costs, and improve service have all been important factors in the development of the technologies which appear today. Current trends in the industry promise to continue this move to more advanced technology applications in the future. Industry maturation, changing demographics, new competition and a host of other factors will continually challenge supermarket operators. As they have in the past, this group will turn to information technologies to help them manage the dynamics of their industry.

THE AIR CARGO INDUSTRY

The air cargo industry makes extensive use of information systems. This topic is of current interest because of the turmoil caused by deregulation in 1977. This event sparked the entrance of several new competitors who saw the opportunity to gain market share.

The 1980s witnessed a large shakeout in the air cargo industry when some companies went bankrupt and others merged with competitors. In 1987, Emery Air Flight acquired Purolator Courier and in 1989 Consolidated Freightways (CF) swallowed Emery. However, Emery today operates as an independent subsidiary of CF. Airborne Express, while not as large as Federal Express (FedEx) or United Parcel Service (UPS), has held its own and remained competitive. Exhibit 3 displays the major competitors in the industry and their services.

The Role of Information Technology

Although no longer expanding at the heady 40 percent compound rate which characterized much of the 1980s, the air express industry is still growing at a 20 percent pace. Factors defining this substantial expansion include reliability, speed, price, and, increasingly more important, value-added customer services.

Carriers	Delivery Time	Discounts	Weekends
Airborne Express	Noon, or your money back.	Save $3 off overnight cost by taking your letter or package to a service center or drop box.	Saturday pickup is an extra $9; in outlying areas, it's an additional $45.
Emery Worldwide	Noon, but no money back if it's late.		Minimum charge $40.
Federal Express		Save $2.50 by using a drop-off point.	$10 surcharge for Saturdays.
DHL Worldwide	Noon, but you don't get your money back if it's late.	Save $3 by bringing your parcel to a DHL drop-off point.	No extra charge for Saturday pickup or delivery.
Express Mail (U.S. Postal Service)	Noon, guaranteed.		Express Mail operates 365 days a year. Priority Mail operates Monday through Saturday.
United Parcel Service (UPS)	10:30 AM or your money back.	$8.50 per letter if you go to a customer center or drop-off box.	No service.

Exhibit 3.   Major Air Cargo Competitors and Their Services

Once a competitive advantage and means of differentiation, the speed and reliability of the major air express companies is no longer a differentiating competitive advantage. Instead, it has become an absolute necessity. Furthermore, the intense and cut-throat competition of the latter part of the 1980s has driven the average price per shipment down to approximately half of what high-volume customers paid in 1980. Now, so as not to be priced out of the air express market and maintain profitability, the major players feverishly devise and implement value-added customer services in an attempt to gain a competitive edge and secure market share.

"Computers are now driving the business." This quote from a UPS spokesman, summarizes the importance of technology and information systems to achieving and maintaining a competitive advantage in the air express industry. According to David B. Schoenfeld, Federal Express's vice president of international marketing, delivery reliability and information on the status of the shipment have a primary effect on carrier selections. Price is a distant third in importance for express buyers.

Companies are continuously enhancing the capabilities of their package-tracking computer systems, emphasizing the importance of logistics management and developing computer based systems such as parts banks, and electronic communications for everything from manifests, to invoicing, to on-call pickups. At Federal Express and UPS major efforts in the development of information systems to help manage its operations and provide new services to customers have catapulted the carriers well beyond their smaller competitors. For example, Federal Express' COSMOS tracking enables them to give customers up-to-date information, a service of increasing value as just-in-time inventory systems have become more numerous. Similarly, UPS employs more than 20,000 PCs that support a variety of functions.

Package-Tracking Systems

Essentially a requirement for the air express industry, sophisticated computerized package-tracking systems have evolved into the carriers' electric "eyes," monitoring very closely every stage of the delivery cycle. Notwithstanding the colorful acronyms used to describe the systems and the varying technical specifications, the package-tracking systems of all the major carriers perform basically the same range of functions.

The system typically begins with a customer pickup request or drop-off. Upon receipt of the package, the courier scans the package with some sort of hand held computerized device which "reads" the airbill on each package. Once the package is entered into the system, an optimal routing is computed and the package is classified accordingly. After the package is identified, the scanning device is linked back to the main system which can now provide up-to-date information on the status of the package throughout the course of its delivery.

Electronic Data Interchanges (EDI)

As organizational boundaries begin to blur, the door of opportunity opens for air cargo companies to be accepted as partners. Information between companies can now travel through computer links, permitting quick access to a customer's order and giving them package data they want. As an example, Airborne Express, which caters to large volume business clients typically establishes EDI between customers and itself to offer them better service. In a somewhat similar manner, Federal Express ties its system to that of U.S. Customs, thus improving the transfer of required information and shortening the processing time. The installation of these links poses one of the greatest problems to global expansion for many carriers, because many countries have set their own standards.

SUMMARY

This paper has identified the technological background areas that are needed to understand how to use information technology for competitive advantage. The in-depth analyses of the supermarket and air cargo industries give examples of how these principles are applied in industrial settings.

It is by understanding the technology and understanding the specific operations of various firms and industries that systems for competitive advantage can be developed. This paper has also detailed how technology has opened new opportunities for supermarkets and the air cargo industry. But more importantly, this paper has pointed out that information technology is no longer thought to be a luxury, but rather a necessity for many organizations that want to remain in business.

ACKNOWLEDGMENTS

Information collection, research and first draft preparation for the two case studies in this chapter was performed by three groups of research assistants. For the Supermarket case study assistance was provided by Sergio Vera, Sheng-Yui Wang, Hiroki Izumoto and Stephen Yonaty. For the Air Cargo case study assistance was provided by John Folk, Daniel Gajewski, David Heck and Daniel Elias. Information on EDI was developed by Michael Johnson and Salwa Said.

REFERENCES

Allan, R. 1991. "Database Masters Became Kings of the Marketplace." *Marketing-News* 11.
Brumemback, N. 1988. "Supermarkets Go High-Tech with Electronic Shelf Label." *Electronic Business* 14: 16.
Chain Store Age Executive. 1990. "Price Chopper Quiets Backroom Chaos: Electronic Invoice System Brings Order to Retailer's DSD Process." (January): 76
Childs, W. 1991. "My Oh My, Look at EDI Fly." *Datamation* (May): 120.
Curran, L. 1988. "EDI Makes a Switch." *Electronics* (June): 92-94.
Fox, B. 1991. "Bizarre Idea Gets a Second Chance." *Chain Store Executive* (May): 145.
Garry, M. 1992. "More Joy of DEX." *Progressive Grocer* (January): 65.
Gordon, H. 1986. "Direct Product Profit: Introducing a Comprehensive Measurement of Retail Performance." *Retail Control* (September): 36-43.
Leong, C. C. 1988. "Electronic Data Interchange" *Computer World* (August): 98.

McCarol, T. 1992. "Grocery-Cart Wars." *Time Magazine* (March 30): 49.

Moore, T. 1989. "The Challenge of Change." *Fleet Owner* (September): 63:82.

Nagle, T. 1989. "Automating Paperwork: A Matter of Survival." *Electronics* (February): 126-127.

Personal Interview with former Personnel Representative for Wegman's Food Markets, Inc. April 10, 1992.

Pike, H. 1989. "Check-Out this Supermarket." *Computer World* (November 6): 30.

Pinnock, A. 1989. "Direct Product Profitability." *Management Accounting (UK).* (October): 18-19.

Sherrets, J. 1992. "Space Management." *Discount Merchandiser,* (January): 26.

Shulman, R.E. 1988. "Supermarkets' Competitive Edge Narrows as Other Retailers Adopt Scanning." *Supermarket Business Magazine* (March): 88.

Shulman, R.E. 1987. "How to Coax Greater Productivity from the Front End." *Supermarket Business Magazine* (January): 19.

Shulman, R.E. 1991. "Design your Host DSD System: Why Does It Seem So Difficult?" *Supermarket Business Magazine* (September) 15.

Snopp, C. 1991. "EDI Aims High for Global Reach." *Datamation* (March): 77-80.

Standard & Poors Industry Surveys, Volume 2. January 1992.

Tosh, M. 1992. "Wal-Mart's Big Move." *Supermarket News,* (April 13): 1.

APPENDIX

Technology Transfer: Making Expert Systems Commercially Successful

H. R. Rao

Introduction

Expert systems are steadily moving from the quiet, intellectual AI research community to the bustling field of management applications, from the realm of science and technology to the commercial marketplace. But successful techniques in academic or research settings do not necessarily translate well to a commercial environment, where profit is the prime motivation. The commercial sector prefers problems with high payoffs and few technical risks, and it selects applications that improve productivity and enhance existing products and services. So, the issue for expert systems is no longer one of successful research, but of successful project management. Expert systems must provide a high "return on investment."

However, expert systems have had only limited commercial success so far. Michael Stock, president of Artificial Intelligence Technologies, estimates that only 10 percent of medium to large expert systems have been successful, and many AI practitioners agree (Keyes, 1989). Also, most of the medical expert systems introduced over the past 10 years are not used today (Taylor, 1990). There are two main barriers to the commercial success of expert systems:

1. *Technology issues*—interfacing and integrating with existing systems, picking the correct problem, fulfilling development goals, representing knowledge, acquiring knowledge, and validating and maintaining the system.
2. *Organizational-behavior issues*— deploying and introducing expert systems in an organization, and managing organizational behavior after development is complete.

Overcoming these barriers requires technology-transfer methods that account for an expert system's size and the structure and culture of the organizations involved, among other factors. My discussion here examines such methods based on organizational-behavior issues. (I have discussed other aspects of both sets of issues elsewhere [Rao, 1991].)

Expert Systems for Competitive Advantage

An expert system captures perishable specialized expertise from a human expert and stores it in a problem-solving package of hardware and software.

When called on to solve a problem, the system uses inference to arrive at a specific solution (Rao and Lingaraj, 1988).

When an expert system is designed and used appropriately, the competitive advantage is compelling. Digital Equipment Corporation saves about $25 million a year with Xeon, which configures minicomputer systems and deals with incomplete system orders prepared by sales representatives (Leonard-Barton and Sviokla, 1988). American Express saves about $27 million a year with its Authorizer's Assistant, (Feigenbau, McCorduck, and Nii, 1988) and Campbell Soup has saved about $5 million since installing its Simon system (Ambrosio, 1990).

But until recently, expert systems were characterized by specialized hardware and nonprocedural languages (like Lisp, Prolog, and OPS5) with steep learning curves. Interface management was difficult, and connecting an expert system to a database or spreadsheet was a nightmare. Organizations interested in expert systems had to invest millions of dollars to start up and efficiently run the systems, which still had high risks of failure.

Since those "early days," progress has been made along the learning curve (with a consequent decrease in risk), and expert-system shells have appeared, letting programmers build inexpensive prototypes on standard hardware (PCs and workstations). Still, the transfer of expert-system technology to commercial use must be made carefully. For example, a prototype expert system for centrally distributing cars on the French railway system was technically correct and consistently outperformed human experts in experiments, but the system failed miserably on installation and was finally eliminated (Levine and Pomerol, 1990).

Technology Transfer

Technology transfer involves adapting and appropriating technology—taking concepts and prototypes from the laboratory and making them robust, active, responsive, and supportive for a real problem in a commercial setting. Two easily identifiable groups participate: senders (the research laboratories) and receivers (the target organizations or commercial ventures).

Think of the process as an organ transplant. First of all, from the donor's point of view, an organ contribution would be ill advised if there were no recipient. Assuming there is a recipient, a successful operation requires that the donor and recipient be physiologically alike; without a proper match, the recipient might react violently to the transplant. The process thus requires intermediate agents: the surgeons and the hospital support staff.

A direct technology transfer is practical only when the receiver's desired (stable, high-value) application closely resembles the sender's successful prototype. The application must be valuable to the receiver, so that the receiver's commitment will survive the trauma of adapting and maintaining the system. Without this background, the transfer might not work and might even cause negative reactions, such as operator dissatisfaction and resistance, or a rapid decline in the system's technical quality. Such cases require a technology *transformation*: The application has to be thought through again, from the base level, even after the prototype has been constructed. The system might need to be re-implemented to make it more supportable, evolvable, and efficient. For example, Lisp is a good tool for building prototypes, but building the actual commercial system is usually faster or more cost-effective using C, Pascal, or Fortran.

The Facilitator

Each technology transfer requires multidisciplinary contributions (from planners, psychologists, engineers, and so on) and can involve any number of actors, according to its complexity. The simplest transfer has two actors—the sender and the receiver—and a successful one-to-one duplication of the technology. However, such a straightforward transfer is almost never possible because of technical, social, and economic differences (using the medical analogy, the physiological differences) between the sender and the receiver.

Anything more than a simple transfer requires a third actor: a technology transfer facilitator (or facilitating group). The facilitator—the liaison between the sender and the receiver—must devise an appropriate system for the transfer and coordinate its implementation. Returning to the medical analogy, the facilitator is the surgeon and staff; he conceives and implements the transfer, and is actively involved in preparing the receiver for the transfer. (The construction of a new commercial system requires contributions by engineers, builders, and industrialists. For this discussion, I link the engineers and builders to the facilitator, and the industrialists and members of the financial community to the receiver.)

The facilitator is a catalyst, acting on behalf of the innovator (sender)—whether a laboratory, university, or individual—to exploit research ideas for commercial purposes. He therefore has to work in both the innovator's realm (nature) and the entrepreneur's (society), and bridge the two. For example, the facilitator must closely watch the technology to be transferred and determine the complexity of any adaptations needed for the technology's commercial use. The more complex the required adaptation, the less potential for successful commercial use (Dorf and Worthington, 1990).

By gathering and disseminating technology both passively and actively, the facilitator monitors demand and supply, finds hidden opportunities, and improves the chances for adaptation and innovation. Passive tactics include communicating through research reports, journal articles, videotapes, and other media, while active tactics include personal interactions via teleconferences and on-site demonstrations (Smilor and Gibson, 1991). Active tactics give the facilitator faster and more focused feedback, and consequently spur faster technology transfer. Senders usually pass along technology through diverse channels and mechanisms, so an institutional relationship between a sender and a facilitator provides a purposeful way to generate and distribute technology.

A facilitator can take a receiver's (commercial) problem and work with the sender to assemble a technology that solves it, as opposed to taking a sender's existing "solution" and trying to make it fit a receiver's problem. This process—working back through a facilitator to a research institution— is based on the concept that the commercial company's experience and capabilities should determine a given problem's research needs. Such an approach is the reverse of asking a consulting firm to perform detailed engineering to commercialize a research prototype.

Facilitators have already been used in good advantage in the real world. General Motors and Ford have bought stakes in large software vendors, and several expert-system companies, including Aion, Andersen Consulting, AI Corp, and Carnegie Group, have been instrumental in successful technology transfers (Kupfer, 1987). Campbell's Simon system, for example, was developed using the Aion Development System, and Merced County, California, determines welfare eligibility with the help of Andersen Consulting's Magic system.

The Facilitator in Action. The sender makes his industrial capabilities (documents, organizations, information centers, and trained workers) available for the transfer. He need not worry about adapting these elements for the receiver, but the facilitator does. Informed of the receiver's characteristics through a situation study, the facilitator chooses several executives from both the receiver and the sender to create a "sender-receiver core." This team works toward a consensus on features, performance, and cost; creates a transfer system that accounts for the various transfer steps; and analyzes the jobs to be done within that transfer system (managing men and machines, developing micro- and macrostructures, training, and internal or external recruiting) (Rao, 1980). This team might be only loosely coupled, since senders and receivers can be so different that tight coupling would be a disaster.

Transferring Large-scale Applications

One of the first joint endeavors between a university and private industry—between Carnegie Mellon University and Digital Equipment Corporation—provides some special insights into the transfer of large-scale expert systems and the need for a facilitator (Polit, 1985).

DEC was involved very early with academic and research laboratories to develop and use large-scale AI systems. Even before expert systems were commercialized and DEC entered the AI market, DEC engineers were familiar with AI software projects and techniques. But while its Xcon system was a success, DEC had no central authority to coordinate its various AI research groups, allocate funding, and decide which projects to pursue. Highly trained AI researchers were in short supply, and since several groups were competing for their services, no one group's AI manpower needs were satisfied.

DEC finally established the AI Technology Center (AITC), which includes an engineering applications and advanced-development group, a manufacturing applications group, a marketing group that monitors the AI market and the public's perception of AI, and a coordination committee that makes major decisions and directs DEC's AI activity. AITC also launched a formal program to train qualified AI engineers to develop and maintain complex expert systems using custom tools (Meador and Mahler, 1990).

This approach allows problems to be handled generically at a manageable scale (rather than in a specialized way). But because DEC's structure is decentralized, the approach requires tight integration and alignment of information among departments at the business-process level, strict adherence to data and network standards (to facilitate communication with corporate databases and other applications), and a computer-literate staff (Meador and Mahler, 1990).

The Cluster Approach. One possible architecture for transferring large expert systems is the specialist cluster (see Figure 1). In this approach, the sender is a "nucleus" comprising an R&D organization and a facilitator. The receivers are "satellites" comprising commercial organizations and functional departments within those organizations. The sender and receivers must interact closely at all stages of system development.

Congress gave the cluster concept (or a variant of it) a boost in 1984 when it passed the National Cooperative Research Act. The act legitimized the idea of the R&D consortium, where competing members of the same industry pool their resources to create a legal entity: a nucleus to conduct R&D and to facilitate technology transfer among the members. Such a consortium lets members work at a manageable scale, share the risks of innovation, set standards for new technologies, share complementary knowledge, "cross-fertilize" ideas and processes, reduce excess duplication, and solve the problem of late entrants into the marketplace getting a "free ride."

Boeing used the cluster concept when it created the Advanced Technology Center in 1983 to conduct and oversee AI and allied research, disseminate

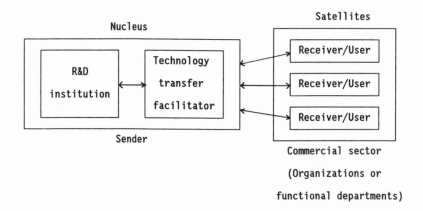

Figure 1. The specialist-cluster approach for large-scale expert systems.

AI's benefits throughout the divisions, and facilitate technology transfer. Also, Microelectronics and Computer Technology Corporation is itself a nucleus, conducting research to be transferred to its 19 satellite members. By the end of 1989, MCC had transferred 84 technologies and dozens of spin-offs and enhancements. One example is Cyc, MCC's project to build a knowledge base of millions of common sense facts, with the goal of engineering the brittleness out of expert systems (Fishetti, 1986). Although Cyc is a long-term project, it has already delivered near-term spin-offs to Bellcore, DEC, NCR, US West, and Apple (Guha and Lenat, 1991). This spin-off technology is the foundation of DEC's Sizer System, which helps sales representatives quickly collect general information about a customer's business and determine its computing requirements.

Transferring Medium-scale Applications

Collaboration allows a project team to develop and share information, resulting in more effective technology transfer. For example, the development of tactical medium-scale expert systems can benefit from the Japanese concept of quality circles (Maletz, 1990). Based on the idea that most employees take pride and interest in their work if they help shape it, a circle is a small group of supervisors and employees who work as a team to solve production problems and enhance product quality. For example, Xerox's Knowledge-Based Systems Circles program creates functional teams (circles) and trains them in knowledge-based techniques (Maletz, 1990). Each team is supported by an umbrella group that provides guidance and system skills, and acts as a catalyst for expert-system development.

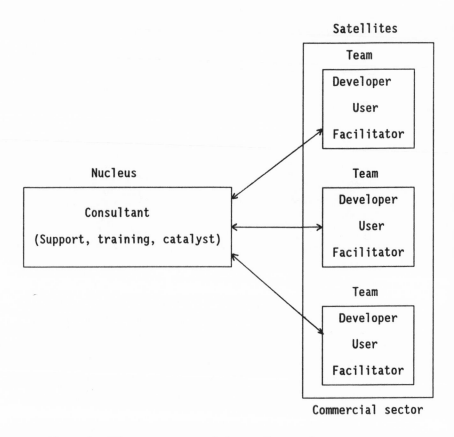

Figure 2.   The team approach for medium-scale expert systems.

In terms of the cluster, the nucleus in this team approach contains only one agent, which acts as a consultant, supporter, and catalyst (see Figure 2). The satellite teams take on the roles of the expert-system developer and the user. Thus, the sender and receiver roles collapse into one (in the satellites). To assimilate the expert system in their own functional areas, the satellites also take on the role of facilitator.

Transferring Small-scale Applications

The generic nature of expert-system shells on standard hardware allows many applications to be developed using the same shell. The "dispersed" technology transfer system that emerges as a result is radically different from the previous two versions. The sender, receiver, and facilitator roles merge in a single organization under the auspices of a nucleus support group, which acts mainly as a catalyst (see Figure 3). The support group's structure is only partly solid, with some permanent members and some members drawn from different functional groups of the organization at different times.

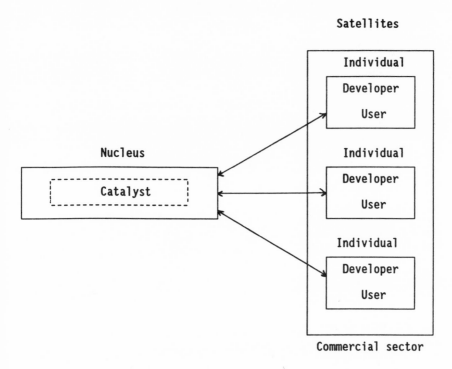

Figure 3. The dispersed approach for small-scale expert systems.

For example, at DuPont, users develop their own PC-based expert systems using standard, low-cost tools. Such systems are usually small, have a short development time, and provide a quick payback. About 1,800 people have been trained to use expert systems under this approach (Meador and Mahler, 1990).

The creation of a sizable expert-system-literate employee base automatically merges the sender, receiver, and facilitator roles into the users. The strength of this grass-roots approach is that smaller expert systems are developed fast—in "programmer days" to "programmer months"—with low costs, broad organizational support, and a high percentage of successful development (95 percent) (Kelleher, 1987). This dispersed approach also demonstrates the increasing significance of the "programmer," a product of the reduced distinction between producers and consumers (Ryan, 1988).

However, since the nucleus support group tends to be overloaded, and lending meaningful support to teams or individuals is a problem itself, this approach is feasible only when:

- The employees are expert-system literate.
- The systems are not highly complex (more like personal support systems).
- The systems are not large (not meant to support departments or organizations, as they are at DEC).

In any case, the DuPont experience is an indicator of things to come as expert system software becomes more powerful, more standardized, and as easy to use as spreadsheets.

Which Approach to Use?

Expert-system applications vary from simple, off-the-shelf packages that run on PCs and cost a few hundred dollars, to huge systems on millon-dollar computers. Thus, when considering a transfer of expert-system technology, the first issue is which approach to use: a large-scale cluster approach, a medium-scale team approach, or a small-scale dispersed approach. Returning to the medical analogy, imagine two kinds of operations: heart transplant, and a surface wound that needs stitches. The transplant requires a specialist-cluster comprising a heart surgeon, an anesthesiologist, an electrocardiogram specialist, a neurophysiologist, a cardiopulmonary physician, and various other specialists. The second operation requires only a general practitioner, or even a nurse practitioner with a broad smattering of dispersed and unspecialized medical knowledge.

A technology transfer approach must match the receiver's culture and structure, especially its knowledge and resource profiles (see Table 1) (Meador and Mahler, 1990; Meyer and Curley, 1991). For example, the cluster approach requires an up-front investment in experienced knowledge engineers. Therefore, a company that prefers high-impact, highly visible projects or whose expert systems must handle voluminous information (and that therefore needs a complex expert system and a cluster approach) must be certain of the benefits before committing to the cost and time needed. At the other end of the spectrum, diversified companies with dispersed knowledge and many problems might prefer the dispersed approach, in which people are trained to develop systems (without the guidance of a knowledge engineer) that might not meet corporate priorities and objectives.

Table 1. Application Characteristics Best Suited to the Three Technology Transfer Approaches.

	Specialist-Cluster	*Team*	*Dispersed*
Orientation	Strategic	Tactical	Operational
Risk	High	Medium	Low
Payoff	High	Medium	Low
Investment	High	Medium	Low
Size	Large-scale	Medium-scale	Small-scale
Problem complexity	High	Medium	Low
Employee literacy	Members of nucleus are expert-system specialists	Some expert-system specialists, some expert-system-literate employees	Many expert-system-literate employees

Planning for Commercial Success. Any successful technology transfer must start with a market study, including needs assessment and target group studies (Harris, 1984). There are three basic segments to the expert-system market: industry, service, and management. Typical industrial and service applications address production planning, quality assurance, worker productivity, and training. But the greatest potential lies in the management segment, where expert systems could aid in decision making, strategic planning, and fusing information from diverse sources.

Once a target group or market segment has been identified, other marketing considerations have to be accounted for, including market size. For example, general-purpose software can be sold to a much broader audience than application-specific software, but it might be more difficult to sell because it is harder to understand exactly how to apply general-purpose software, whereas application-specific software is immediately understood.

A company should examine whether it can leverage the technology, that is, spread its costs by reselling the technology across multiple product and geographic markets. It also should determine market orientation: whether to use a market-driven approach that develops AI technology to meet the market's needs, or a technology-driven approach that brings technology to the market before examining those needs.

A company also needs to consider integration: whether to build a stand-alone system or one that can interact with software from other companies. The system's value would be higher if it worked with existing commercial software. Finally, the company should consider portability, that is, the ability to move the system from one domain to another. Such a move is usually carried out by people without specific AI training, so the designer (the R&D organization and facilitator) must invest heavily in the building process to make such transfers possible.

Generally, an expert system has the greatest chance of success with a market-driven approach and a large market, high integration and portability, and a strong ability to leverage the technology.

Barriers to Commercial Success. Because a successful transfer requires technology that works well and can be managed by the receiver, the sender must clearly understand the receiver's objectives and industrial conditions. But often, a receiver cannot understand, assess, and formulate its own needs, so choosing and implementing a technology will present problems unless the sender knows the receiver well and prepares it for the new technology. The sender's R&D staff can be of extremely high quality, but if the facilitator isn't, or doesn't command attention, then the transfer is destined to be a problem, and the receiver will have trouble understanding and applying the technology. (Returning to the medical analogy, the organ recipient must be prepared mentally as well as physically for the operation.)

Active communication (open meetings, forums, and conferences), articles, newsletters, and personal exchanges help to overcome this barrier. The receiver's engineering staff must be made aware of any design vagaries: simplifications and approximations made in the interest of efficiency, dormant pitfalls, component interactions, and so on. Also, the receiver's management must have a realistic notion of the system's benefits as well as any unavoidable limitations (Enslow, 1989). The receiver must have committed and capable supporters (especially in upper management, perhaps in the form of champions) and support systems to carry the project to commercial deployment. This calls for early on-site involvement by engineering personnel in both the research laboratory and the commercial organization.

Electronic interaction among teams enhances such coordination, helps to build cross-functional skills (Nevens, Summe, and Uttal, 1990), decreases product cycle times, and increases a company's ability to conduct market analyses and quickly react to market changes. Increased interaction also promotes parallel development—where R&D, design, manufacturing, marketing, sales, and service are carried on in parallel—in contrast to the serial model of product delivery.

The slow development of expertise in the commercial sector is another barrier to success. There is a shortage of experienced personnel with an AI background, and those with experience often do not understand real business problems. There is also a shortage of appropriate, reliable, supported tools. Thus, the sender must provide extensive documentation, training, system maintenance, and support. For example, System Development Corporation's successful technology-transfer mechanism moves people who already know the technology into the receiver organization, so they can personally transfer the technology to the uninitiated (Rauch-Hindin, 1988). Another successful approach at DEC uses an extreme form of user involvement, where users are co-developers who actively shape system requirements and direct changes or adaptations during development.

Finally, companies must choose realistic business targets. Expert-system technology can contribute much in many fields, but it does not follow that a company can work in every area with equal success. There must be realistic expectations about the technology's capabilities and its gestation period. For any development effort to have an acceptable payback period and return on investment, its intermediate and long-term goals must be well defined and balanced against its capital requirements and the receiver's available funds. This suggests a two-phase technology-transfer strategy (Harris, 1988) that accounts for a learning curve, which is especially steep for expert systems because they are knowledge intensive. In the first phase, the receiver chooses an almost risk-free application area. The goal here is not return on investment, but to learn about the technology and tools and become well versed in the transfer process. The application in the second phase is not risk free, but has a higher payback and high visibility.

The technology transfer of expert systems calls for imagination and creativity. It does not lend itself to algorithmic implementation. Success requires attention to all aspects of the transfer process, from R&D to marketing. Severe resource constraints and competitive pressures are common problems that call for a focus on those activities that have the greatest impact. For example, initial efforts are usually directed at R&D, but companies that anticipate early commercialization of products should place greater emphasis on marketing activities.

Acknowledgments

Reprinted, with permission, from IEEE Expert, pp. 5-10, April 1992. I thank H.S. Rao and the late Lakshmi Rao for their guidance, the three anonymous referees for critical comments that greatly improved this article, and B. Chandrasekaran for his encouragement.

References

Ambrosio, J. 1990. "Simon Says, Soup is Good Food." Computer World (September 17): 33.
Dorf, R.C. and Worthington, K.F. 1990. "Technology Transfer from Universities and Research Laboratories." *Technological forecasting and Social Change 37.*

Enslow, B. 1989. "The Payoff from Expert Systems." *Across the Board* (January/February): 54-58.

Evan, W.E. and Olk, P. 1990. "R&D Consortia: A New Organizational Form." *Sloan Management Review* 31 (Spring): 37-46.

Feigenbaum, E., McCorduck, P., and Nii, P.H. 1988. *The Rise of the Expert Company.* New York: Times Books.

Fischetti, M.A. 1986. "A Review of Progress at MCC." *IEEE Spectrum* (March).

Guha, R.V. and Lenat, D.B. 1991. "Cyc: A Mid-Term Report." Applied *Artificial Intelligence* 5: 000-000.

Harris, L.R. 1984. "Experience with Intellect: Artificial Intelligence Technology Transfer." *AI Magazine* 5(2): 43-50.

Harris, L.R. 1988. "Bigger AI Isn't Better. *Computerworld* (October 31): 79-83.

Jacobson, H.E. 1986. "R&D Cooperation in AI: Reports on the United States and Japanese Panel, IJCAI, 1985." *AI Magazine* 7 (2): 65-69.

Kelleher, J. 1987. "Interview: Watch the Rabbits." *Computerworld* (November 23): 9-11.

Keyes, J. 1989. "Why Expert Systems Fail." *AI Expert* 4 (11): 50-53.

Kupfer, A. 1987. "Now, Live Experts on a Floppy Disk." *Fortune* (October): 69-79.

Leonard-Barton, D. and Sviokla, J.J. 1988. "Putting Expert Systems to Work." *Harvard Business Review* 66(2): 91-98.

Levine, P. and Pomeral, J.C. 1990. "Railcar Distribution at the French Railways." *IEEE Expert* 5 (5): 61-68.

Maletz, M.C. 1990. "KBS Circles: A Technology Transfer Initiative that Leverages Xerox's 'Leadership through Quality Programs'." *MIS Quarterly* 14(3): 323-329.

Meador, C.L. and Mahler, E.G. 1990. "Choosing an Expert Systems Game Plan." *Datamation* (August 1): 64-69.

Meyer, M.H. and Curley, K.F. 1991. "Putting Expert Systems Technology to Work." *Sloan Management Review* 32(2): 21-31.

Nevens, T.M., Summe, G.L., and Uttal, B. 1990. "Commercializing Technology: What the Best Companies Do." *Harvard Business Review* 68(3): 154-163.

Polit, S. 1985. "AI Technology Transfer at DEC." *AI Magazine* 5 (4): 76-78.

Rao, H.S. 1980. "Diffusion, Absorption, and Adaptation." Proc. Workshop on the Development of Technology, Issues for the '80. Indian Council for Research on International Economic Relations, New Delhi, India.

Rao, H.R. 1991. "Issues in the Management of Expert Systems." *Proc. AI Business Workshop.* National Conference AI (AAAI '91), MIT Press, Cambridge, Massachusetts.

Rao, H.R. and Lingaraj, B. P. 1988. "Expert Systems in Production/Operations Management: Classification and Prospects." *Interfaces* 18 (6): 80-91.

Rauch-Hindin, W.B. 1988. *A Guide to Commercial Artificial Intelligence.* Englewood Cliffs, NJ: Prentice Hall.

Ryan, J.L. 1988 "Expert Systems in the Future: The Redistribution of Power." *Journal of Systems Management* (April): 11-18.

Smilor, R.W. and Gibson, V.D. 1991. "Technology Transfer in Multiorganizational Environments: The Case of R&D Consortia. " *IEEE Trans, Eng. Management* 38 (1): 3-13.

Taylor, T.R. 1990. "The Computer and Clinical Decision Support Systems in Primary Care." *Journal of Family Practice* 30 (2): 137-140.

MANAGEMENT BACKGROUND AREAS

Robert P. Cerveny, C. Carl Pegels, and
G. Lawrence Sanders

INTRODUCTION

The interface of information technology and information systems with management of the various functional areas is pervasive. As a matter of fact it is at this interface where information technology and information systems interact with the functional area management that highest propensity to produce effective strategic information systems exist. The information technology and the information systems areas have the techniques, the tools and the systems, while the functional area management has the expertise and knowledge to prescribe where these systems can be utilized most effectively. The input of functional area management is of utmost import for the development of successful strategic information systems that have high impact on the competitive status of the firm

It is imperative that information technology and information systems managers have a solid background and knowledge of the functional management areas and of how these areas have utilized and are able to utilize information technology.

We shall cover the five major functional areas. They are:

- Management Strategy
- Financial Management and Control
- Marketing Management and Marketing Strategy
- Manufacturing, Technology, and Operations Management
- Human Resources Management

MANAGEMENT STRATEGY

Management strategy is the processes of formulating and implementing business and corporate strategic plans and evaluating managerial strategic performance in complex business environments. This includes issues such as the corporate mission and objectives, industry analysis, competitive analysis, environmental analysis, business strategy, financial strategy, corporate portfolio planning, acquisitions and divestments, organizational implications, international strategy, and entrepreneurship. These topics are very important supplemental material for the SIS manager because they treat strategy formulation from an organizational perspective.

The pervasive forces of technology, which are reshaping industries and deeply affecting the ways to compete, have increased the trend toward globalization. This requires an understanding of not only domestic but also foreign markets. Today's SIS manager needs not only knowledge of technology but also knowledge of management strategy to effectively articulate the vision of the firm into a concrete reality. In general, a SIS manager should have a broad knowledge of topics such as business strategy, corporate strategy, functional strategy, methodology for the development of a strategic plan (industry analysis, environmental analysis, competitive analysis, analysis of acquisitions and divestments), organizational implementation, and evaluating management strategic performance.

Management strategy focusses on several levels, especially for large corporations with operations in many locations serving customers in many countries with a wide range of products and/or services. The four levels of the corporation where strategies are focussed on are:

1. Enterprise level
2. Corporate level
3. Strategic business unit level
4. Functional level

Even for the smallest firms management strategy must focus on at least levels 3 and 4. Larger corporations with focussed products or services should focus on levels 2, 3, and 4. The very large corporations with many divisions, products/services and operating in many markets need to focus their management strategy at all four levels.

An example of an enterprise (level 1) is a large corporation such as General Electric. This company is comprised of many separate corporations involved in such diverse activities as major household appliances, electronic products, aircraft engines, financial operations, television and radio broadcasting, medical apparatus, and others. Each of the diverse activities is usually contained and managed by a separate corporation (level 2).

The strategic business unit (level 3) usually consists of a separate division in a corporation (level 2). The strategic business unit (SBU) is usually able to operate as a separate business with its own functional departments such as marketing, operations, distribution, etc. Because the SBU is a separate unit, it can be evaluated as a profit center independently of other SBU's in the corporation.

Functional level strategy (level 4) is a strategy developed to maximize the efficiency and effectiveness of a functional department such as marketing, operations, finance, distributions, human resources, and so on. These strategies are usually referred to as marketing strategy, operations strategy, finance strategy, distribution strategy, human resources strategy, and so forth.

The direction of overall firm strategy does not entirely evolve from enterprise level strategy down to corporate, strategic business unit and functional department strategies. Strategy evaluation also needs to be upward and interactive. In other words, good and frequent communication between the different levels is an important ingredient in the management strategy process. Management information systems can be particularly effective in aiding this communication process. Such information systems can quite appropriately be called strategic information systems because they aid management in developing successful strategies for the organization.

Strategic Thinking

Strategic thinking is generally defined as a mind set on the part of management, especially upper management, to continuously think about how the organization can utilize and implement strategies to advance their organization. This is not an easy assignment for management to practice. Management, at all levels, is usually focussed on day-to-day operations and problems that need resolution. Time for strategic thinking is usually scarce and a luxury. However, corporations need to think strategically to survive.

There are a variety of methods that upper management can utilize to focus itself and other management levels on strategic thinking. One way is to schedule management meetings, retreats, and other strategic focus activities where management can engage in strategic thinking.

During these special strategic meetings management needs to utilize group activities such as brainstorming to generate ideas and to use affinity diagrams for evaluating constructively the ideas that are generated.

Input to the strategic thinking meetings needs to be extensive and developed by staff members. Specific input can be generated by staff members through industry analysis, competitive analysis, market analysis, benchmarking, economic analysis, demographic analysis, socio-cultural analysis, and other research methods. Information thus generated then needs to be summarized to aid management in generating, considering, and evaluating new strategic ideas.

A management information system which can store the information and provide easy retrieval and summarization of the stored data is an example of a strategic support information system.

Porter's Model for Industry Analysis

Porter's model for industry analysis (Porter, 1980) is a powerful tool for identifying the forces in an industry which control the competitive nature of that industry. The model is depicted on Exhibit 1 and shows the four major forces that determine the competitive nature in an industry. They consist of:

1. Suppliers' bargaining power
2. Customers' bargaining power
3. Threats of new entrants
4. Threats of substitute products/services

The strengths or weaknesses of these four forces determine to a large extent how difficult it is to survive as a competitor in that industry and they also determine the potential profitability of firms in that industry.

Taking the four forces as a given, a firm in an industry must aim to alleviate those forces that reduce its competitiveness. Management information systems have been able to alleviate at least some of the negative forces in many instances. For instance, electronic data interchange (EDI) connecting the firm with its suppliers and its customers has improved the firm's ability to communicate with suppliers and customers. EDI also has enabled firms to supply services to their suppliers and customers which were impossible or difficult to deliver without the EDI link-up.

Developing new services for suppliers/customers using EDI and other information system technology can also increase the barriers to entry for potential new competitors. The threat of substitute products and services

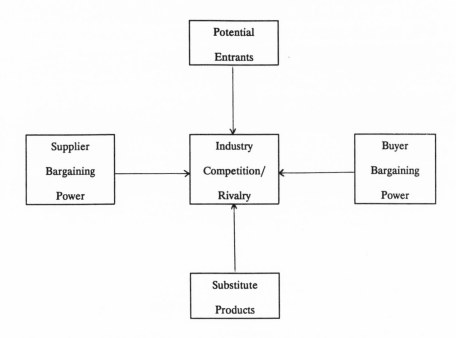

Source: Adapted from Porter (1980).

Exhibit 1.   Porter's Competitive Model

is a continuing threat to any firm. Here continual vigilance is important to ensure that the firm is aware of any new and threatening substitutes so that timely action can be taken to alleviate the impact of the substitutes. Continual vigilance must at least include an ongoing environmental analysis program, including maintenance of an environmental database, which will enable the firm to identify the forces which generate potential substitute products and services.

Strategic Planning Process at Strategic Business Unit-Level

The strategic planning process is an organized activity which usually takes place at the strategic business unit level. It consists of a number of activities which need to be performed over an extended period of time with the full participation of management at all levels. For instance, all of marketing management needs to be involved in the marketing, competitive and external analysis. All managers need to have at least some involvement in all areas.

As management becomes involved in the planning process, it may find that there are numerous other related areas that need exploration, evaluation and analysis in order to develop a complete strategic plan for the organization. The strategic planning process can be described by the following 12 steps:

1. Mission Statement Development
2. Describing the Organization
3. Identifying Strengths, Weaknesses, Opportunities and Threats
4. Developing Goals and Objectives
5. Internal Analysis
6. External (Environmental) Analysis
7. Marketing and Competitive Analysis
8. Industry Evaluation - Porter's Model
9. Resources Evaluation
10. Developing Strategies & Tactics
11. Developing Strategic Plan
12. Identifying Implementation Problems

The above steps do not need to be done in the sequential order indicated. Some of them, however, should be done ahead of others. For instance, steps 2 and 3, describing the organization and identifying strengths, weaknesses, opportunities and threats, should be done ahead of the others. Similarly, before strategies and tactics, and the strategic plan can be developed, the other steps should be completed.

Also, all steps in the strategic planning process need to be done over time while going through several drafts. These drafts need to be refined in response to management comments and suggested changes. In other words, the strategic plan that eventually emerges should have had maximum input from all affected managerial representatives. The eventual strategic plan that will evolve must be viewed as a plan developed by all levels of management and not just a plan which was developed by a staff planning group and supported by top management. Experience has shown that only strategic plans which emerge from, and are supported by, as many levels of management as possible, have the potential for successful implementation. Imposed strategic plans will be treated as NIH (not invented here) plans and will suffer as a result. That is, their implementation will be a failure.

Strategic Planning Process at Corporation Level

The strategic planning process at the corporate level needs to focus on how well the separate strategic plans of the strategic business units (SBU's) can be integrated. The focus at this level tends to be heavily financial performance oriented because this is the common measure which can be applied across a group of diverse strategic business units. Financial measures which can be compared among strategic business units are measures such as absolute volume and annual growth of sales revenues, costs, profits, assets, depreciation, manpower, and so on.

In these comparisons caution must be applied because each strategic business unit is in its own industry and the competitive level between industries varies widely. Additionally, management must decide what businesses (i.e. what industries) it wants to be in. If certain strategic business units do not perform satisfactorily or if they do not fit the portfolio of businesses the corporation wants to be in, then the corporation often divests itself of these undesirable strategic business units. Since these business units are essentially profit centers it is usually not that difficult to find a buyer. The price can, of course, vary widely depending on the expected profitability of the business unit in the future.

Strategic planning at the corporate level also involves decisions as to how much the corporation should invest in a strategic business unit for growth and expansion. Assigning capital for growth to one business unit is usually done at the expense of another unit. Hence, decisions made at the corporate level can have serious positive or negative consequences for each strategic business unit of the corporation.

Enterprise strategic planning is essentially one level higher than corporate strategic planning. At the enterprise level similar comparisons, evaluations and decisions are made for corporations as were made for strategic business units at the corporate level of strategic planning.

Background References

1. Asheghian, P. and R. Ebrahimi. 1990. *International Business*, New York: Harper & Row.
2. Hax, A.C. and N.S. Majluf. 1991. *The Strategy Concept and Processes: A Pragmatic Approach*. Englewood Cliffs, NJ: Prentice Hall.
3. Oster, S.M. 1990. *Modern Competitive Analysis*. New York, NY: Oxford University Press.
4. Porter, M.E. 1980. *Competitive Strategy: Techniques for Analyzing Industries and Competitors*. New York, NY: The Free Press.
5. Porter, M.E. 1985. *Competitive Advantage: Creating and Sustaining Superior Performance*. New York, NY: The Free Press.
6. Porter, M.E. 1990. *The Competitive Advantage of Nations*. New York, NY: The Free Press.

FINANCIAL MANAGEMENT AND CONTROL

The financial management function of the firm encompasses the routine financial processing functions, cash flow management, budgeting, financial control and financing of the organization. For firms engaged in foreign operations there also is the problem of hedging to reduce financial risk of currency fluctuations.

We shall segment our discussion below in terms of:

1.   Financial processing functions
2.   Cash flow management and currency hedging
3.   Budgeting and financial control
4.   Financing the organization

Financial Processing Functions

One of the first areas to be computerized by firms was the financial processing function. Accounts receivable, maintenance and billing were logical areas to computerize because they were quite repetitive and quite laborious. Similarly, maintenance of accounts payable and disbursements were also quickly and routinely computerized. The payroll function followed very quickly. This area also became one of the first outsourcing areas. Firms specializing in payroll operations had economies of scale which allowed them to provide this service for client firms at a lower cost than if the firms did it for themselves.

The early financial processing functions were quickly followed by computer-based inventory systems, inventory tracking systems, client file systems, personnel systems, mailing systems, and others which allowed firms to substantially lower their operating costs for those manual systems.

Cash Flow Management and Currency Hedging

Cash, like inventory, if it is not utilized becomes a cost item. That is, non-earning cash should be kept to a minimum. The management of cash flow is an important and critical activity.

Cash flow management has essentially two dimensions. The first is the utilization dimension. Cash should not be allowed to be a non-earning entity. Cash should be at work as a revenue earner at all times. The financial manager therefore needs to ensure that cash receipts are immediately put to work.

The second dimension is how to allocate the total available cash to various income earning vehicles. Higher cash earnings usually means either more risk or less liquidity. It is the financial manager's task to find that delicate balance. Financial decision support systems have been developed and are available to assist the financial manager in this function.

Currency hedging is a method to protect the firm against losses as a result of currency movements. It is essentially the opposite of speculation. A firm can always protect itself against future currency movements but at a substantial cost. It is up to the financial manager to decide what percentage of exposure (amount held in foreign currency) needs to be protected. Keep in mind that unprotected currencies can behave in three ways: remain unchanged in relation to the home currency; move up; or move down. If the foreign currency becomes more valuable then the firm benefits. Hence, the decision how much to hedge is a very difficult one and requires considerable experience and knowledge of currency markets. However, there are decision support packages available which aid the financial manager in making these decisions.

Budgeting and Financial Control

To ensure that costs are predictable and variations of costs can be controlled a successful firm maintains an extensive budgeting and financial control process. Without adequate control systems, especially financial control systems, not many organizations could survive.

Budgeting involves all levels of management. Each organizational unit, department, section or area makes up a financial budget of its anticipated expenditures for a future planning period, usually a year. These budgets are then accumulated for the organization, evaluated and returned to their originating unit for a repeated cycle of revisions. After one or more budget review and adjustment cycles, the budgets are accepted and each unit is expected to maintain its expenditures within the approved budget. The financial control function thus becomes the policing arm that ensures that each unit remains within budget.

Again, computer-based budgeting and budgets greatly facilitate the budgeting and financial control process. Variations in budgets and budget lines are quickly identified and corrections can be quickly implemented. As a result the computer is an important and critical tool of financial control.

Financing the Organization

Few organizations enjoy the luxury of even inflows and outflows of cash. Cash outflows can especially vary substantially over time. For instance, a firm engaged in a major capital investment project may have substantial cash outflows at certain times during the year. To help smooth these high variations in outflows, the financial manager must make arrangements to have access to cash to help the firm over these situations. The common method is to establish lines of credit with banks. These lines of credit allow the firm to temporarily borrow money from the bank when its cash needs are higher than normal without having to obtain the bank's approval at the time. If the firm has sufficient cash on hand to take care of its own fluctuations, it must ensure that the cash is working in time-based securities such as certificates of deposit while it is being held.

Firms that are expanding or growing rapidly need additional capital for physical expansion, expanded inventory and expanded working capital. In those cases the financial manager needs to arrange for additional capital through long-term borrowing or through issuing more equity in the firm. Either one are steps the firm needs to take cautiously and seriously because timing is important to minimize the costs of acquiring the additional capital.

Although there may be computer software available for the above decisions, the decisions are usually not so simple or straight forward that they can be resolved by a simple computer run. Each one of the above decisions requires careful deliberation and consultation with senior management before the ultimate decision is made.

Background References

1. Anthony, R.N., J. Dearden, and N.M. Bedford. 1989.*Management Control Systems, 6th edition*. Homewood, IL: Irwin.
2. Brigham, E. and L.C. Gapenski. 1985. *Financial Management: Theory and Practice*. New York: Dryden Press.
3. Folks, Jr. W.R. and R. Aggarwal. 1988. *International Dimensions of Financial Management*. Boston: PWS-Kent.
4. Horngren, C.T. and G.L. Sundem. 1988.*Introduction to Financial Accounting, revised 3rd edition*. Englewood Cliffs, NJ: Prentice Hall.
5. Rotch, W., B.R. Allen, and C.R. Smith. 1982. *The Executive Guide to Management Accounting and Control Systems*. Houston, TX: Dame Publications, Inc.
6. Shank, J.K. and V. Govindarajan. 1989. *Strategic Cost Analysis: The Evolution from Managerial to Strategic Accounting*. Homewood, IL: Irwin.

MARKETING MANAGEMENT AND STRATEGY

The marketing management function of the firm encompasses all activities related to the interface between the customer or client and the firm itself. These activities include various marketing and consumer research activities as well as field testing of new products or services. Another set of activities is comprised of environmental analysis, new market screening, potential need evaluation, need satisfaction screening, legal and political screening, and sociocultural screening. A third set of activities is related to channels of distribution, market segmentation, product strategy and marketing mix. Finally, there is the set of activities centered around advertising, publicity and promotion on the one hand and promotion effectiveness measurement on the other hand.

We shall segment the discussion below in four parts. They are:

1. Marketing and consumer research
2. New market and product screening
3. Channels of distribution and market segmentation
4. Advertising, promotion and publicity

Marketing and Consumer Research

Research in consumer/customer/client needs is an ongoing necessary activity for the successful firm. Although the products of a firm may be performing and selling well, this does not preclude the need to do market research. Market research will reveal what features customers like about your products, and what features they do not like. Market research will also reveal what new products, or modifications or extensions of existing products, are required in the market place.

There are a variety of methods to do market research. Information can be collected through questionnaires, interviews, consumer panels, or from field sales forces. Whatever method is used, the data generated needs to be evaluated and analyzed in detail. Statistical models run on computers provide an excellent vehicle to accomplish this.

Firms, therefore, need to make a commitment to do market and consumer research. In other words, market research needs to be done in a methodical manner in order to produce useful results on which important new or modified product decisions can be made.

In the next section we shall discuss an extension of market research, the new market and new product screening process.

New Market and Product Screening

A very important activity of a marketing department is the identification of potential new products based on customer or client needs in the market place. This activity is very critical because of the product life cycle. Existing products eventually disappear, and new products need to take their place. Also, if one firm does not identify new products, another firm will. Being the first on the market with a new product usually provides a strong advantage.

Not all new potential products produce viable and profitable products. For every twenty product ideas only one may become a successful product.

Therefore, product screening is an important activity which helps the marketing department in the evaluation of new potential products. The product screening process takes on several dimensions. Product screening can eliminate potential products at the concept stage, the development stage, the consumer tryout stage, or the test market stage. For a new potential product to become an actual product in the market place requires it to overcome many hurdles.

For the above activities a considerable amount of environmental analysis needs to be done. Databases can be helpful. However, ultimately new products are created through a creative process, and not through data base searches.

Channels of Distribution and Market Segmentation

The choice of a distribution channel is usually dictated by the industry. Most consumer and food products are usually sold through department stores and supermarkets. However, when your products are for industrial markets, there is a choice of distribution channels that needs to be made. Are you going to sell directly to the end user? Will you use manufacturing agents, distributors, or franchised dealers? In other words, in many non-standard situations the choice is not so straight forward.

Market segmentation and product mix are other issues that need to be addressed. Channels of distribution not directly controlled by the firm need a variety of products to motivate their efforts at marketing and selling them. With franchised dealers this is a relatively straight forward issue because dealerships can be organized by geographic area, and overlap only occurs around the interfaces of the dealers' geographic territories.

The most extensive and successful application of information technology has been in the area of electronic communication between the firm and its channels of distribution. Electronic data interchange (EDI) systems are now commonly used to provide quick and rapid communication of information to the firm on sales rates, quality problems, replacement part needs, failures, and so on. Similarly, the channels of distribution can provide rapid information on inventory availability, delivery time schedules, product design changes, problem areas, new product developments and other critical information.

Advertising, Promotion and Publicity

One of the largest discretionary budget items for the firm is the amount it decides to spend on advertising, promotion and publicity. Especially for consumer product firms, the sums spent on advertising and promotion are enormous and necessary to push its products into the consumers' hands.

How effective these product promotion campaigns are is an ever present question. One thing is known, without advertising sales will decline. But what is only vaguely known is how effective each advertising campaign is. Occasionally, claims are made that firms waste vast sums of money on product promotion with little pay off. In other words advertising effectiveness measurement can be a problem.

Information systems which capture buyer behavior at the point of sale and tie the demographics of the buyer directly to the particular product are increasingly being used. These systems have great potential because they identify for the firm exactly who its products purchasers are, what their income levels are, where they live and what other products they buy. The potential to use this kind of information to develop more focussed advertising and promotion is considerable. These systems are of rather recent vintage and the benefits to be derived from these systems are so far limited and only partially explored.

One other example of potential advertising and promotion waste is in new automobile advertising. It is directed at the total audience but only few people, even in a household, make the ultimate product decision and they do so only every five or so years. Using information technology to identify these decision makers and providing them with the critical and important information at the right time is more appropriate. The technology is available to do this and will enable the automobile marketers to save vast amounts of money currently spent advertising their products on national television and other media.

Other examples of how information technology can improve advertising and promotion will be forthcoming. They will show how the productivity of the advertising and promotion dollar can be improved.

Background References

1. Aaker, D.A. 1988. *Strategic Market Management, 2nd edition.* New York, NY: John Wiley & Sons.
2. Boyd, H.W. and O.C. Walker, Jr. 1990. *Marketing Management: A Strategic Approach.* Homewood, IL: Irwin.
3. Committee on Definitions. 1960. *American Marketing Association, Marketing Definitions: A Glossary of Marketing Terms.* American Marketing Association, Chicago, Illinois.
4. Jain, S. C. 1990. *Market Planning and Strategy.* Cincinnati, OH: South-Western.
5. Kotler, P. 1988. *Marketing Management: Analysis, Planning and Control, 6th edition.* Englewood Cliffs, NY: Prentice Hall.
6. Lilien, G.L. and P. Kotler. 1983. *Marketing Decision Making: A Model-Building Approach.* New York, NY: Harper & Row.

MANUFACTURING, TECHNOLOGY AND OPERATIONS MANAGEMENT

The objective of manufacturing, technology and operations management is to focus on operations, production and inventory management problems through the application of information technology, quantitative models, information, decision support, and expert systems. Issues include manufacturing strategy, system design, forecasting, aggregate planning, master scheduling, materials requirements planning (MRP), cellular manufacturing, just-in-time systems, optimized production technology (OPT), and flexible manufacturing systems (FMS). The emphasis is not only in manufacturing operations, but also in the service fields of retail, wholesale, passenger transportation, freight transportation, and elsewhere.

The term computer integrated manufacturing (CIM) has become the catch all term to cover the use of information technology applications in the factory. As such CIM is not very descriptive but its impact on manufacturing operations is significant. In today's economy the non-computer driven factory is no longer competitive in terms of cost control and on-time delivery.

The field of manufacturing, technology and operations management is a broad area. In this brief survey we cannot provide all of the rich detail of this area, but we shall enumerate a number of important sub areas where management information systems are playing an important role.

The management of operations is usually a heavily people-oriented activity. As a result, managing people effectively is an important and critical area. Managing people involves training and development of existing personnel, the hiring and evaluation of new potential employees, development of incentives to maximize efficiency and quality, empowerment of employees, work team formation, developing systems for improvement idea generation, and many other organizational behavior and human resource activities.

Many of the above activities will be more extensively explored in the human resource section of this chapter. There are many technical systems, such as the manufacturing resource planning (MRP) systems, inventory control systems, logistics planning systems, cost control systems, distribution systems, purchasing and vendor relations systems, quality control systems, billing systems and other accounting systems which impact the area.

For longer range planning purposes, there are other activities that require information systems support. They include plant location analysis and design, process analysis and design, technology analysis and design, facilities location systems, project management, forecasting, and so forth.

Information technology systems have been applied to other operations such as services, logistics, distribution, retail, wholesale, and transportation. The transportation sector has become heavily dependent on package delivery and freight tracking systems, and passenger scheduling systems. Tracking systems for package delivery and freight have, in a relatively short period of time, become the norm instead of the special application. Together with the ubiquitous bar code these systems are able to know at any moment where the package or freight is in the system and when it is scheduled for delivery. Although these systems appear to be quite straight forward, the investments required to make them operational have ranged from quite substantial to huge.

Passenger scheduling systems, particularly on airlines, have grown to such enormous size and capacity that they are now housed in separate profitable subsidiaries of the major airlines. Not only do these systems handle passenger reservations but also deal with car rentals, hotel rooms, and other services. Also passenger scheduling is not just done for the owner airline but also for other airlines. These systems are truly strategic information systems because they enable airlines to use variable pricing and other marketing tools to maximize the revenue from each passenger.

At the retail and wholesale level, information technology together with bar coding has enabled retailers to reduce inventories, speed up delivery, more rapidly change prices to move older inventory and forecast demand for most products in a more accurate fashion.

In the toy industry the clout of such large specialized retailers as Toys "R" Us is reshaping the industry. These larger retailers are able to identify, on a daily basis, which toys are selling well and which are not. This information enables them to adjust production levels to match demand resulting in quicker delivery times, lower inventory levels, and less waste because of unwanted inventory. Information technology has provided the means to bring desirable goods to the market quicker with less waste and at lower cost.

The earlier example is only one very visible and focussed example. Other less-known examples abound. When the history of retailing in the last two decades of the twentieth century is written, information technology will receive as much credit for the rapid growth of companies like Walmart as Mr. Walton himself. Without information technology it would be impossible for these large retailers to operate.

Background References

1. Adam, Jr., E.E., and R.J. Ebert. 1992.*Production and Operations Management.* Englewood Cliffs, NJ: Prentice Hall.
2. Dilworth, J.B. 1992. *Operations Management.* New York: McGraw Hill.

88   R. P. CERVENY, C. C. PEGELS, and G. L. SANDERS

3. Evans, J.R., D.R. Anderson, D.J. Sweeney, and T.A. Williams. 1990. *Applied Production & Operations Management*. St. Paul, MN: West Publishing.
4. Gaither, N. 1991. *Production and Operations Management*. Fort Worth, TX: The Dryden Press.
5. Noori, H. 1990. *Managing the Dynamics of New Technology: Issues in Manufacturing Management*. Englewood Cliffs, NJ: Prentice Hall.
6. Stevenson, W.J. 1990. *Production/Operations Management*. Homewood, IL: R.D. Irwin.

HUMAN RESOURCES MANAGEMENT

Human resource management is a comprehensive functional area in the organization. In this brief survey we can only cover certain aspects of it. We shall focus on four areas. The four areas are:

1. New personnel hiring and training
2. Existing personnel development and training
3. Compensation planning, design and control
4. Benefits management and control

New Personnel Hiring and Training

The acquisition of new personnel is a very critical activity for the firm. It is very important that new employees are either properly educated or trained and are able to absorb additional education and training while on the job. The need for teamwork is placing increasing importance on an individual's ability to work effectively and efficiently with others. Other desirable qualities such as commitment and interest in the job, personal discipline, self control, creativity, leadership, and other traits are important qualities for new employees.

To assess a new employee and to determine to what degree he/she has the traits and qualities discussed above is not an easy task. However, most firms are willing to invest time, effort and resources to discover to what degree a potential employee has the above traits and qualities.

Management information systems can be useful tools to help in the potential new employee evaluation system. Profiles of potential new employees can be compared, or benchmarked, against successful employees in the organization. Although this rather objective evaluation is able to assist in the evaluation process, it should by no means be viewed as a singularly decisive approach.

The classic cases of employee evaluation approaches are those used by Japanese firms when they establish assembly operations in the United States.

Before Toyota established its Kentucky automobile assembly operations it interviewed and tested ten applicants for every new hire. Although the cost of this evaluation process appears to be prohibitively high, the long term payoff was substantial.

The training of new employees can also be facilitated if employees with a high propensity to learn and absorb new information are hired. Most of today's jobs, even in the lower-skill job areas, take a lot of training. If the time to train new employees can be reduced, significant savings can be achieved.

Existing Personnel Development and Training

Rapid technological changes force firms to provide ongoing education and training programs. Some firms have their employees spend as much as five percent of their time in classroom or on-the-job training. Whether all employees need this much training is difficult to determine but many firms appear to prefer to err on the high side than on the low side of employee training.

In addition to on-the-job education and training, many firms encourage employees to take up additional training and education in their own time to upgrade their skills and credentials. If there is a match between the employees' educational interests and the firm's needs, non-work time educational activities are or should be of special interest to firms. The problem, of course, is that the match may not always exist.

Information technology has been making increasing contributions to work place training and education. Both the VCR and the PC with appropriate media and software are valuable and relatively low cost contributors to the education and training activities of the firm.

Compensation Planning, Design and Control

Employee compensation planning and design is a critical activity in the human resources management area. If compensation is too high the firm becomes uncompetitive because it will be unable to maintain its costs at the competitive level. If compensation is too low employees are more likely to be dissatisfied and mobile employees are more likely than not to leave for higher paid employment elsewhere.

Another problem in the compensation package development process is to provide an orderly upward progression in employee compensation. More highly motivated and qualified employees may be willing to start at relatively low salaries but will not remain satisfied if their upward progression into higher-paid and more responsible positions is being stifled. A compensation plan must contain a plan for orderly progression based on regular evaluation. Although the evaluation process usually takes place within the affected units and is led by the individual's superiors, the overall plan and process must be planned and controlled by the human resources department.

The degree to which management information systems can be utilized in the above processes, activities and control is fairly extensive. Detailed employee records stored in data bases provide an excellent basis for developing fair compensation and evaluation systems. Also for external evaluation of industry compensation practices, data bases need to be developed or acquired. Without external data it is impossible to compare your compensation policies and practices with those of the competition.

Benefits Management and Control

A very important part of any employee's compensation is the fringe benefit package that accompanies the employee's salary. The two largest components of the fringe benefit package are health insurance and retirement plans. The health insurance component is currently of great concern for the firm because it has been growing very rapidly in recent years, and it is a benefit that is usually available to all employees as they begin employment. The retirement package usually requires several years of employment before it is vested to an employee. As a result, the firm's cost for short-term employees (shorter than vesting time) is low. The two packages combined constitute a substantial cost item and may amount to 25 percent of salary cost for many firms.

Other fringe benefits are the social security (FICA) tax, employee's compensation tax, unemployment taxes, and others. Some firms consider vacation time, personal time and sick time also to be fringe benefits. These, together with the other fringe benefits, constitute a substantial financial burden for the employer.

It is the task of the human resources department to determine how the cost of providing the plethora of fringe benefits can be minimized. This is not easy since most fringe benefits are mandated by state or federal regulation or by collective bargaining contracts. However, certain components, such as health insurance and other insurance, can be controlled to some degree by insurance carrier or health care provider selection and by employee health promotion. To implement any or all of these systems requires extensive data base development to identify cost sources, both internal and external, and then to devise ways to minimize or at least control costs.

Background References

1. Cascio, W.F. 1987. *Applied Psychology in Personnel Management, 3rd edition.* Englewood Cliffs, NJ: Prentice Hall.

2. Larson, P.E. 1989. *Winning Strategies: Organizational Effectiveness Through Better Management of People.* The Conference Board of Canada, Ottawa.
3. Lengnick-Hall, C.A. and M.L. Lengnick-Hall. 1988. "Strategic Human Resource Management: A Review of the Literature and a Proposed Typology." *Academy of Management Review* (13): 454-470.
4. Mintzberg, H. 1979. *The Structuring of Organizations: A Synthesis of Research.* Englewood Cliffs, NJ: Prentice Hall.
5. Snow, C.C. 1989. *Strategic Organization Design and Human Resource Management.* Greenwich, CT: JAI Press.

THE ROLE OF END-USER COMPUTING IN STRATEGIC INFORMATION SYSTEMS

Larry Meile

INTRODUCTION

Starting with the introduction of time-sharing computing environments and accelerated by the introduction of the personal computer and local area networks (LANs), end-user computing (EUC) has become a major means of supplying computing power to decision makers. EUC can promote the strategic information systems (SIS) philosophy by supporting planning, problem solving, and decision making to take advantage of business opportunities. With it, users develop personalized decision support systems (DSS) that help carry out functional tasks such as conducting manufacturing and service operations, assisting marketing management and strategy, facilitating financial management and control, and administering and developing human resources.

For the purposes of this paper, EUC is considered to refer to any application directly manipulated by the user. This definition is broad enough to include applications that are run directly on personal computers, those supported by servers over LANs or other networks, and interactive sessions conducted using a terminal connected to a mainframe computer.

The strategic potential of EUC has arisen from:

- reductions in hardware costs and advancements in end-user software,
- an increased awareness of the productivity gains possible through EUC,
- EUC's ability to effectively deal with time-sensitive and critical business conditions, and
- the existence of roadblocks to using traditional centralized IT resources (slow response time, inappropriate tools, methods, and processes).

As the amount of resources devoted to EUC grows, there will be an increased need to understand the costs associated with the provision of EUC, the determinants of EUC effectiveness, and its strategic value to the enterprise. Because it is so critical, the steps for implementing and maintaining these systems must be understood by the SIS Project Manager.

This broad definition can be further refined by defining end-user types using a modification of Rockart and Flannery's (1983) categorization as shown in Exhibit 1.

This five-level classification implies that end users are a diverse group requiring different levels of education, training, and support as well as access to different hardware platforms, software tools, and sets of data.

The non-programming end user plays a role in SIS only to the extent that the application he or she runs is, itself, part of the organization's SIS. A different strategic role may exist for the other four user types. It is possible that the applications they create possess strategic value, whether or not this value is recognized and incorporated into the organization's SIS. As a result, one critical issue facing the SIS Project Manager is identifying those applications that have strategic value and merging them into the SIS. Further discussion of this topic will comprise the bulk of this paper. Another critical issue is the development of policies for effective and controlled EUC use and growth. A great deal of research and discussion has focused on the effects of management policies toward the level of EUC support and training on end-user effectiveness and productivity. In general, effective use is promoted by management policies that provide training compatible with the skill level of the user and that encourage EUC development and use under guidelines that ensure the uses are congruent with the organization's strategic vision. These policies assume even greater importance for organizations in which EUC is evolving from its tactical beginnings and moving into the strategic realm.

User Type	Definition
Non-programming End User	Runs end-user applications using highly structured interfaces such as menus or spreadsheets designed by others. Does not create applications.
Command-Level End User	Runs end-user applications directly using commands. For instance, creates simple spreadsheets, uses mailmerge, etc.
End-User Programmer	More sophisticated user. Solves problems specific to own job using tools such as Lotus macros, command files, or 4GLs.
Functional Support	Very sophisticated. Writes programs in support of others using tools such as Lotus macros, command files, or 4GLs.
Professional	An information systems specialist hired to design and program software solutions that end-users can employ. Uses procedural or other programming languages.

Exhibit 1.   Definitions of End-User Types

GROWTH OF END-USER COMPUTING

Many corporations have made considerable investment in EUC hardware, software, and accessories. Growth rates through the 1980s ranged from 50 percent to 90 percent per year. Knutsen (1989) estimated that by the end of the decade of the 1980s, personal computers accounted for more than 75 percent of a typical large company's computing capacity. More impressively, it has been estimated that by 1993 EUC expenditures in large corporations will have grown to twice the amount spent for centralized information technology (IT). EUC growth is expected to continue, motivated by the promise of improved productivity obtained by giving end users the ability to automate processes and use IT to support job-related tasks. One of the primary uses of EUC is to provide functionality at the fingertips of the user that can support the corporate mission and related functional strategies.

Since end-user activity can have strategic implications for the enterprise, many of the SIS management issues discussed in the previous chapters relate to the management of EUC as well. To successfully integrate end-user applications into the enterprise-wide SIS the following are required:

- Understanding the organization's mission so that strategic competencies can be defined.
- Establishing who will be responsible for the development and maintenance of SIS within the organization.
- Developing organizational structures and processes which facilitate the identification and migration of EUC applications with strategic value from the end user who developed them to the institution as a whole.

This last issue is particularly important because it provides the means for ensuring that high-quality, effective systems migrate from Personal to Enterprise-wide Systems.

DEALING WITH CHANGING TECHNOLOGY

Information technology and change are synonymous. Sometimes new technology has the potential to transform a business function and the way jobs are done. The strategic implications can be profound: new business products may emerge, new forms of customer interaction may arise, new ways of conducting and assessing operations may evolve.

As EUC technology develops, new hardware and software products enter the organization through two routes: the users themselves identify products they want to use and the technological support staff review products to identify those that may be considered for use. When products are suggested, they must be assessed to see whether or not they offer a significant improvement over existing systems and for compatibility with existing intra-organizational data storage and communication formats. Making new hardware and/or software available can be expensive. Beyond the capital outlay for the technology itself, support staff must be trained and made available to provide assistance, documentation and procedures must be reviewed and updated, and users must spend time to acquaint themselves with the new product.

Changing technology creates an environment in which there will always be something "newer and better" that a department or user may feel is more able to meet specific needs. As a result, "islands of computing" may develop, breaking down effective system integration as a long-term EUC strategy. Consequently, it is important that a unifying policy be established that balances the introduction of innovation (and therefore competitive advantage) with the need to preserve the strategic advantage of a coherent SIS.

END-USER APPLICATIONS AS PART OF THE SIS

One way of classifying EUC applications is by how broad an effect the application has within the organization. Using this approach it is possible to identify three types of computer applications. The first is a personal application which is designed to serve the needs of an individual. Although the data used may come from others, the results generated by the application affect only the individual actually using the system. Most EUC applications start out in this category.

The second type of application is departmental. The output of the application is used by others within a department or other such limited group. Occasionally an EUC application may be designed with the benefit of the group in mind. If this is the case, however, it is necessary to assure an appropriate strategic fit within the SIS and to guarantee system validity and data integrity.

The third type of application is organizational, one which provides data to several groups within the firm. This type, by definition, falls outside the scope of the individual end user. This is not to say that an application originated by an end user cannot provide the foundation for an organization-wide strategic application but it will most likely require extensive refinement before it is rolled out for use by the entire enterprise.

Clearly, if a personal application is used by and affects only the end-user, it does not fall under the purview of the organizational SIS and should not be required to conform to any organizational strategic SIS policies. If, however, the use of the application influences others, it may need to be regulated. Certainly, if the decisions and actions of others depend on the output of an application, it should be required to conform to organizational IT standards (data format and integrity, model reliability, etc.). Furthermore, if the application has influence in areas that the enterprise has deemed to be strategic, it should be folded into the SIS and come under the control of the SIS Project Manager.

Moving an application from the end user's domain to the enterprise's SIS can be viewed as a six-stage process as shown on Exhibit 2. First the candidate applications must be identified. Next an evaluation must be made to determine whether or not the application is truly strategic in nature and, if it is, in what ways can it best be used to further the strategic goals of the organization. If it is selected for inclusion, it must be thoroughly tested to be sure that the model upon which it is based is valid and that it functions correctly. Also, the user interface and the data input and output formats must be assured to conform to the organization's standards. Once ready, the application, along with appropriate training, can be presented to those in the organization who will use it. Of course, as with all IT products, ongoing maintenance is required to maintain the application's viability. These stages will be discussed in more detail in the next section.

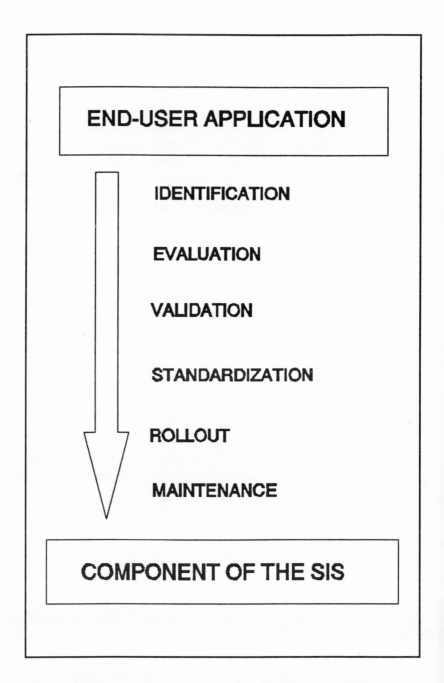

Exhibit 2. Migration of EIC Applications to the SIS

IDENTIFYING END-USER APPLICATIONS
WITH POTENTIAL STRATEGIC IMPACT

Computer-based applications can be considered strategic in nature if they improve the efficiency or effectiveness of the enterprise. Improved efficiency occurs when the application reduces the amount of effort or cost required to accomplish a specific task. Strategic EUC applications that improve efficiency provide improved methods for obtaining or organizing data so that information can be more readily obtained. Examples of applications which improve organizational efficiency include the operational and strategic thrust activities presented in the case studies reporting in succeeding chapters. Strategic EUC applications which improve effectiveness provide the capability of doing things that could not be done before or furnishing new products and/or services (or the distribution thereof) to customers. Examples of applications which improve effectiveness are the customer/client service thrust activities which are also identified in the cases.

The SIS Project Manager should assemble a team which is responsible for assessing the strategic potential of EUC applications. This team should be comprised of IT-literate representatives from each of the functional areas within the organization and one from the SIS office (the SIS Project Manager may be that person). This standing committee will act as an advisory council to the SIS Project Manager helping frame the organization's strategic policies and procedures. It will also will meet whenever an end-user developed application is being considered as becoming part of the SIS.

When a particular application is being considered, the end user who developed the candidate application should be included as an ad hoc member of the team as should representatives from any group directly affected by the potential change (if not already included in the standing committee). The team will be responsible for assessing the perceived strategic value of the application, brainstorming to seek other ways the application may be strategically valuable, and recommending whether or not it is appropriate to assimilate the application into the SIS. If it should be assimilated, the team can assist in this process.

Most end-user developed applications should not be considered of strategic value even though they help the user accomplish his or her job. Since to be considered as strategic, an application must impact the *organization's* efficiency and/or effectiveness, this criterion can be used to segregate strategic from non-strategic end-user applications. Therefore, when an EUC application provides support or information to others or it makes a new product or service possible, it becomes a candidate for inclusion in the enterprise's SIS.

Some end-user oriented applications will be designed from the start as being central to the strategic positioning of the enterprise. As might be expected, however, many will originate with the end user and later be found to have strategic value. It is important, therefore, to have effective procedures for identifying these applications, bringing them to maturity, and incorporating them into the enterprise-wide SIS. A particularly delicate issue to manage here is taking over control of applications that are found to be of strategic value from the original creator, the end user. Specific issues to resolve are listed below. The answers given to these questions suggest general approaches to resolving these issues. However, the specific policies and procedures which should be implemented depend on the particular organization in which they are being installed.

What procedures should be instituted to alert the SIS Project Manager to the fact that an application with strategic potential exists?

Potential strategic EUC applications that are developed by end users can be discovered through two paths: the end-user may suggest that his or her application may have strategic potential or they may be revealed through a periodic organizational IT audit. Therefore, a method should be developed through which end users can suggest applications (either their own or those developed by others) for strategic review. Suggesting an application developed by someone else is valuable since if the application is useful enough for someone else to employ, the application itself (or the function it provides) may have strategic value.

Additionally, periodic organization-wide review should be made of the tasks which are being accomplished using end-user computing. The evaluation should not only seek out new applications but look for previously used application that are no longer employed. New applications can be judged for their strategic potential and those found abandoned can be used as indicators that new ways of accomplishing tasks have been found or that changes have been made in what is being done.

At what point should the application be considered strategic in nature?

An application becomes strategic when its output affects the way an organization conducts its business (affects its efficiency) or when it becomes essential to the production of products or services or their distribution (affects its effectiveness). The boundary between operational and strategic application is not absolute. Nonetheless, when the use of a information technology tool produces an influence beyond the individual user, it starts to fall into the strategic realm and should be considered as a candidate for inclusion into the SIS.

What control should the original creator of the application be given over the use and dissemination of his or her creation?

Once an application is determined to be strategic in nature, it should fall fully under the control of the SIS Project Manager. An application cannot effectively have two "owners". The policies and procedures of the organization's SIS should prevail.

Nonetheless, it makes good sense (and it is ethical) to include the application developer in the absorption process. The user knows the application best, will have his or her own perception of the strategic potential of the application, and can provide valuable commentary on its appropriateness for other purposes that may be suggested. Furthermore, if users feel that their creations are being "stolen," they may resist the process and hide potentially valuable applications from the organization's view. Remember, one of an enterprise's best strategic IS resources is the users themselves.

What reward or recognition is appropriate to acknowledge the originator's efforts?

The primary requirement from a morale standpoint is that the developer be adequately recognized for his or her effort. Certificates, plaques, or gifts given with a proper amount of pomp and circumstance are often appropriate. Rewards in cash or in goods and/or services may be appropriate as well, especially if the strategic value of the application is significant. The amount of reward will depend on the organizational culture and how other achievements of note are recompensed.

Unlike efficiency measures, it is often hard to place an accurate dollar value on the strategic benefits of an application. Consequently, it may be difficult to link in a reward to obtained benefits. Since end-user application developers are often interested in information technology, the provision of hardware and/or software upgrades may make effective rewards. As a side benefit, the organization will be putting advanced IT tools in the hands of those shown to derive advantage from it.

When should formal procedures take over?

It would be inappropriate to have others in the organization use an application that was not fully tested and that did not conform to standards. For other users to adopt new technology, they must trust that it will not cause them to perform their tasks poorly and that it will be reasonably easy to understand and use. To assure that these requirements are met, validation and standardization should be completed before the application is presented as a formal part of the SIS portfolio.

TRANSFERRING APPLICATIONS FROM THE END USER TO THE SIS

When an EUC application has been identified for wider use within the organization, it should be formally included in the organizational SIS. Four steps must be undertaken to complete this transition: application testing, interface standardization, roll-out, and post-implementation review. Additionally, for the life of the application, maintenance will have to be conducted to ensure that the application continues to perform as designed.

Application Testing (Validation)

Although one can argue that any application should correctly model the situation to which it applies, it is imperative that it work right if the results are to be used by others. Therefore the application must be examined for model validity. The relationships expressed in the model must be congruent with reality and the assumptions embodied in the model must be understood. This does not mean that all aspects of the target situation must be faithfully modeled in detail—only those that affect the decisions the application's output supports. This implies that there are limitations inherent in any model. This is acceptable but it means that these limitations be understood and communicated to others using the application (or its outputs).

In addition to determining that the underlying model and its assumptions are valid, it is essential that the end-users faithfully and accurately articulate the code (or logical relationships) used to create the application. Stories have been told about spreadsheet analysis of investment alternatives yielding devastating decisions due to a misplaced decimal point.

Since users, other than the originator, will be employing the application, it must be made resistant to erroneous input and tolerant of incorrect operation. The original developer may be aware of its programmatic limitations but others may not. It must be made as error-proof as possible because other users cannot be expected to know of or be aware of the idiosyncrasies of all applications they use or that affect them.

Interface Standardization

All applications, whether developed by end users or not, should present as uniform an interface as possible to those who will work with them. The terms used (names, data, labels, etc.) should be standardized, the applications should provide a uniform appearance, and inputs should be requested in a familiar sequence. The order in which procedures (data input, analysis, report writing, etc.) are carried out should be as consistent as possible.

Input and output data formats should conform to enterprise standards. It is counterproductive to require a user to reconfigure data in order to use an application or generate output. Not only does it slow the operation down, it provides the opportunity for introducing errors to the input or output.

Rollout

When an application has been tested and standardized, it is ready for inclusion into the organization's SIS. Depending on the situation, it can be made available to a few users or the organization as a whole. A partial deployment will allow for further testing by the users and may result in changes before it is fully implemented. Other situations call for a full scale roll-out to the entire organization, particularly when external customers are affected by the application.

When the application is rolled out, its purpose and expected effect should be explained. Users need to be motivated to change and this is the opportunity to provide them with the required incentive. Also, to make the transition easier, appropriate training and the time to take it should be made available. Resistance to change is not reduced if the training made available is inappropriate (too advanced, too simplistic, none at all) or if the user is under so much pressure to perform his or her present task that the time required to learn the new technique is unavailable or deemed too expensive (causes missed deadlines, incurs superior's disapproval, consumes their own time).

Post-Implementation Review

Once in place it is important to check to see if the system is performing as expected. Are the proposed procedures being followed? If not why not? If so, are the proposed results being obtained? If not, why not? If so, are there any unforeseen opportunities for further strategic advantage?

Organizations are dynamic institutions and the solutions that are appropriate and effective at one point in time may not be best at another. Systems and applications are added when new needs or opportunities arise but may not be decommissioned once they have outlived their usefulness. One way of limiting system proliferation is to institute a periodic review to assess the efficiency and effectiveness of the SIS portfolio of applications. Another way is to have a "sunset" audit performed at some interval after rollout. If the application can prove its value, it can survive. If not, procedures for decommissioning it and giving current users a graceful withdrawal should be automatically carried out.

Application Maintenance

New software and hardware are constantly entering the market place. Will their introduction change the application in any way? What are the effects of any changes in data standards and format? Has new information been made available that the application should include? All IT systems are dynamic entities and any static component is at risk of obsolescence.

FACTORS CRITICAL TO SUCCESSFUL INTEGRATION OF EUC INTO THE SIS

Management and technical support are critical to end-user satisfaction and productivity—and ultimately the strategic value gained from EUC. A positive management attitude toward EUC is a factor most often critical for success. If an end user's superior does not encourage or reward an effort to employ an application in a strategically relevant way, the chances of it being used to its fullest potential are reduced.

User satisfaction with technical training and support is closely related to overall user satisfaction with EUC. The quality of a firm's training plan combined with management's propensity to encourage computer use and data sharing can have a significant effect on the strategic value of EUC applications. To get an idea of how well a firm promotes the inclusion of EUC applications in its formal SIS, the following questions should be asked:

- How willing is the departmental manager to invest company time in an employee's training?
- How much encouragement does an individual receive to learn and be productive using a particular EUC tool?
- How well have previous education and experience prepared users for their current EUC use?
- To what extent does the SIS incorporate and encourage end-user developed applications?

While we are on the topic of training there is an important point to consider: the difference between training and education. Training involves conferring knowledge such as how a software package interface operates. Education is a larger process that teaches a person how to relate ideas and think creatively. End users may become proficient at manipulating information technology yet may become frustrated and disillusioned if they cannot use it to effectively solve their business problems. Therefore it becomes extremely important that users possess strong problem formulation and modelling skills, the foundation of strong business analysis. If these skills are weak, they can be bolstered through formal education classes or other techniques such as one-on-one pairing with those who have these skills. It goes without saying that strong management skills will also improve the potential value of end-user created applications. A skillful manager will not only recognize those tasks that can be enhanced with IT but will be able to effectively communicate these advantages to others.

The specific technical support provided to users depends to a large extent on which SIS development strategy (or combination of strategies) an organization practices. Whatever the specific strategy employed, there are four infrastructures that are key to developing a successful EUC - SIS strategy:

- **Support.** This infrastructure encompasses education, implementation, and leadership strategies, and should preface all acquisitions. It is critical for easing the installation and improving the learning curve.
- **Technology.** This infrastructure focuses on the appropriate hardware, software, and communications equipment. Standards for the hardware and software platforms should be developed in conjunction with the MIS department needs in order to consolidate the support efforts.
- **Data.** This infrastructure is necessary for ensuring data security and integrity as well as for creating a homogeneous, "frustration-free" end user environment. Implementation of user-friendly networks and common operating systems develops an environment that allows the switching of applications from one system to another.
- **Justification and Planning.** This infrastructure views systems as not only an investment, but also as a method for gaining competitive advantage by ensuring that they grow in a measured, meaningful way.

Thus the SIS Project Manager is responsible for seeing that end-users are furnished with appropriate education and support policies, equipped with task-relevant hardware and software, that they are provided with access to a unified data storage and communication system, and are made aware of the potential strategic value of their end-user applications. The primary operational benefits of well-supported end users are: (1) enhanced (more knowledgeable and self-sufficient) users, (2) increased end-user productivity, and (3) better information (both to the individual and the organization). These benefits translate into the strategic benefits of improved organizational efficiency and effectiveness.

End-user developed applications are a vast, often untapped source which can support and/or change a business unit's competitive strategy. It is up to the organization, led by the SIS Project Manager, to mine their full potential. This capability can be obtained by instituting an effective set of policies and procedures to promote and support the migration of these applications from the end user to the organization's SIS. If the issues discussed in this chapter are skillfully managed and resolved, the enterprise will be in better shape to achieve its organizational mission and sustain its competitive posture.

REFERENCES

Knutsen, E. 1989. "Long-Range Diffusion of I/S Poses Challenge to Cost Control" *Chief Information Officer Journal* (Winter): 44-46.
Rockart, J.F. and L.S. Flannery. 1983. "The Management of End User Computing" *Communications of the ACM* (October): 776-784.

OVERVIEW OF INFORMATION TECHNOLOGY APPLICATIONS

Robert P. Cerveny, C. Carl Pegels, and
G. Lawrence Sanders

INTRODUCTION

This and the following papers focus on how, why, and where information technology has penetrated companies in a variety of industries. Also addressed are four specific functional areas where information technology penetration has been particularly visible, necessary and beneficial to the management of those functional areas.

The four functional areas covered are manufacturing and operations management, marketing and sales management, financial management and human resources management. For each of the four broad functional areas case studies have been collected and each case study has been summarized in a standard format for easy review, study, and perusal. In total about 70 case studies are presented.

A wide variety of industries appear in the case studies, including manufacturing, transportation, consulting, banking, insurance, computing and telecommunications, and retailing. Manufacturing firms range from those in the aircraft industry, automobile industry, computers and electronics, to household products. Transportation firms covered are in passenger air transportation, passenger ground transportation, rail freight, truck freight, package delivery, and pipelines. Retailing firms range from the international Toys 'R' Us chain, the corner store cookie retailer chain, Mrs. Field's Cookies, and Dillards, a department store chain. The insurance industry is represented by firms such as John Hancock and the New England Insurance Company. Consulting firms include Coopers and Lybrand and KPMG Peat Marwick. Several firms from the computer and telecommunications industry were analyzed including AT&T, IBM, Unisys, and GE Information Services.

This paper will present an overview of how information technology and specifically strategic information systems are being applied in these sectors. Additionally, it describes the major trends that are emerging in the application of information technology to business operations. The following chapters will review the functional areas of manufacturing and operations management, marketing and sales management, financial management and human resources management. Each of these chapters is preceded by an overview of how information technology is being applied in each respective area. The case studies, and their respective information technology applications, are presented following the overview for each paper. In this overview we focus on several information technology developments which in one form or other have been utilized in the case studies presented in each chapter.

STRATEGIC ISSUES IN INFORMATION TECHNOLOGY DEVELOPMENTS

The term strategic information systems (SIS) was coined a number of years ago. To many the term meant the development of a specific information technology application congruent with a specific company strategy. As detailed in the earlier chapters many definitions have been proposed for strategic information systems. What emerged is that SIS is a complex concept which organizations should not dismiss. SISs are not merely systems, but embody a philosophy which emphasizes planning, managing and utilizing information technology to solve problems and to take advantage of business opportunities.

Strategic Information Systems have become a primary focal point for developing and implementing corporate strategy. Additionlly, SIS is taking on a new role to shape corporate strategy and to determine the way companies will be doing business in the future.For instance, American Hospital Supply's (AHS) approach to connect their regular customers with an electronic data interchange (EDI) system was a specific strategy. The result was that AHS customers could order by way of EDI, could be given current prices by way of EDI, and could be invoiced by way of EDI. In addition, the AHS system provided inventory planning and control tools to those customers who wanted to use them. The AHS approach worked very well. They already had a large market share and through the AHS system provided services other suppliers could not immediately provide. In other words the AHS strategic information system gave AHS a competitive advantage.

Another example of a strategic information system is the Federal Express (FEDEX) package tracking system, whereby FEDEX can track all packages in the system on a real time basis. A customer calling about the status of a package or a shipment can be provided with the exact location of the shipment as well as its scheduled delivery. Again, this is an example of a service feature which gave FEDEX a competitive advantage over its competitors. As can be observed in the United Parcel Service (UPS) case study, discussed in the next paper, UPS had to react to the FEDEX service feature and literally spend hundreds of millions of dollars on information technology to be able to give the same service as that provided by FEDEX.

In several instances strategic information systems have also been used to assist senior management in the actual planning process. One of the case studies for Rockwell International describes an executive information system (EIS) which provides information to executives and allows executives to search databases for information for decisions affecting current and future operations. The common usage of the term strategic information systems, however, focusses on the use of information technology to improve operational efficiency and productivity to gain competitive advantage.

Two profound trends are beginning to have an impact both on organizational efficiency and on the way that organizations will do business in the future. They are:

- The role of Electronic Data Interchange (EDI) in Inter-Organizational Systems (IOS).
- The role of systems integration in restructuring organizational systems.

These important issues which involve both technological and managerial knowledge are discussed below.

INTERORGANIZATIONAL INFORMATION SYSTEMS

With the proliferation of telecommunication technologies, the traditional internal focus of information systems (IS) has shifted to entities beyond the organization's boundaries, such as customers, suppliers, and even competitors. This type of IS is described as an inter-organizational system

(IOS). The IOS plays a vital role in changing industry structure and potentially providing competitive advantages to the adopting firm. Electronic Data Interchange (EDI) systems are a special class of IOS.

EDI has been defined in numerous but similar ways. Almost all the definitions of EDI contain a few common key words such as intercompany, standard or structured format, and computer-to-computer communication. These key words will be explained further in order to clarify the concept and to differentiate EDI from other electronic communication applications.

First, intercompany communication indicates that data transfer occurs between two separate companies. Cooperation between the two is required to make the system work properly. A company that initiates the development of the EDI system and prompts its trading partner firms to adopt the system is called a "hub company."

Second, standard format communication implies that information to be transmitted must be formatted according to a predefined layout so that a computer can process the information without human assistance. Four types of EDI standards exist: proprietary, industry-specific, cross-industry, and international. A proprietary standard is set by one company which has enough leverage to ensure that all trading partner firms use its standard. An industry-specific standard is set by an industry trade group and promotes industry-wide electronic communication. Due to the industry specific growth of EDI, multiple industry-specific standards exist. Examples are the Uniform Communication Standard (UCS) in the grocery industry, the Transportation Data Coordinating Committee (TDCC) standard in transportation, and the Warehouse Information Network Standard (WINS) in warehousing, to name a few. These separate standards issues are now beginning to be resolved by a cross-industry standard, called X.12, which was developed by American National Standards Institute. At the international level, a standard, called EDIFACT (EDI For Administration, Commerce and Trade), was developed by the United Nations. Typically, a company chooses an EDI standard that will facilitate communication with the maximum number of trading partners.

Finally, computer-to-computer communication refers to the fact that information flows directly from a hub company's application system to the trading partner's application system or vice versa without human intervention. For computer-to-computer transmission to be possible, a communication network must be established to interconnect both companies' computer systems. There are basically two ways to develop an EDI network: (1) establish one's own network, or (2) use a third-party value-added network. Large EDI users are more likely to set up their own communications networks because of the sheer number of communication links involved. Advantages of private EDI networks include additional security, and the possibility of using proprietary EDI standards to exert more control over trading partner firms. However, except for the very large corporations, a third-party network is a more feasible solution. Popular third-party EDI network providers are General Electric Information Services (EDI*Express), McDonnell Douglas Integrated Business Systems Division (EDI*Net), Control Data Corp. (REDINET), Sterling Software, Inc. (ORDERNET), and IBM Corp. (IBM Information Network).

Many authors have documented the expected benefits from the use of EDI and then classified them into direct and indirect benefits. Direct benefits come from reducing the cost associated with handling paper transactions. They include elimination of keyboard data entry, improved order entry procedures, eliminated manual sorting, matching, filing, reconciling, mailing, decreased paper materials, reduced need for overnight couriers, reduced telephone costs, reduced need for paper storage space, and elimination of data entry facilities. Indirect benefits include effective use of data received electronically for better inventory management, streamlined manufacturing operations, and enhanced customer-supplier relationships.

According to recent estimates about 25,000 U.S. companies currently use EDI. With regards to industry, some are well established in EDI utilization, such as the automotive, grocery, transportation, and chemical industries. They have established their industry-specific standards and are actively using EDI. Others, such as healthcare, insurance, telecommunications, and electronics, are just beginning to use EDI.

SYSTEMS INTEGRATION

Organizations are facing complex internal and external forces which are having a profound impact on the way they compete. Product life cycles are shorter, market encroachment is the norm, and sophisticated technologies are being introduced at a breath-taking rate. End-users in functional areas (financial management, human resources, marketing and operations) often complain that they cannot retrieve data from organizational databases, that reports are delivered too late and that they are inaccurate. A particularly troublesome problem identified by end-users is that their localized processing needs and decision making needs are not being met by the centralized information systems department.

Several solutions have been proposed to deal with the uncertainty and turbulence that characterize the current competitive environment. The development of *strategic information systems planning* and *systems integration* are two popular solutions that require the commitment of senior level managers. The strategic information systems planning process was reviewed in the earlier chapters. From our review of the case studies and an analysis of several industries, *systems integration* appears to be gaining momentum. The concept is so popular that many major consulting firms and hardware vendors are specializing in systems integration.

Systems integration is generally defined as the merging of diverse hardware, software, and communications systems into a new operating unit serving the enterprise.

Most system integrators concentrate on supplying hardware and telecommunications solutions to interconnecting equipment from various vendors. This somewhat myopic view of systems integration does not always address the central issues of providing access to organizational data and providing end-users with localized processing capabilities. But the major problem with most systems integrators is that they do not provide adequate assistance to the organization in identifying information needs.

The primary objectives of systems integration are to:

- Standardize, centralize and integrate organizational data
- Provide users, departments, and functional areas with localized processing and decision making ability.

Systems integration, as a solution to dealing with environmental complexity, is not an easy assignment. The objectives of systems integration form a doubled-edged sword because they are both competing and complementary.

An enterprise-wide systems integration project requires a multifaceted strategy. It requires top-down managerial involvement, enterprise-wide participation of functional area personnel, and attention to technical details. The Strategic Enterprise-Wide Integration (SEWI) process and similar approaches have been found to be effective in guiding the integration process. SEWI consists of the following activities:

- Strategic data planning and enterprise-wide data modeling.
- Identifying the appropriate hardware architecture.
- Implementing the integrated database using a relational database engine and provide access with a fourth generation language.

The relationship of information systems planning with corporate planning has been extensively discussed in earlier chapters. The important consideration here is that corporate goals and objectives provide a pivotal reference for guiding the SEWI process. The other two points will be discussed next.

STRATEGIC DATA PLANNING

Strategic data planning and enterprise-wide data modeling form the foundation for integrating organizational databases (Sanders 1990). The strategic data planning process dictates assembling a project team comprised of senior level managers and functional area representatives. An important outcome of strategic data planning (sometimes referred to as information engineering) is that it encourages the development of standards throughout the organization. A more important outcome, however, is that it promotes internal assessment and organizational communication.

As part of the SEWI process it propels senior level managers to look towards operations for strategic opportunities. But it also cultivates a strategic perspective in functional level managers because it forces them to look at the data relationships throughout the firm and understand systems interdependence. Finally, the SEWI approach often leads to uncovering areas in which an organization needs to capture and maintain data, and assists in identifying irrelevant or outdated systems.

IDENTIFYING THE APPROPRIATE HARDWARE ARCHITECTURE

Identifying the appropriate hardware architecture involves two competing philosophies. The first philosophy is based on the situation where terminals are connected to a centralized mainframe and all applications are run on the mainframe. The second philosophy involves the development of local area networks (LANs) and wide-area networks (WANs) and all applications are run on microcomputers or at times on minicomputers. When an organization abandons the mainframe solution in favor of the microcomputer based LAN this is referred to as *downsizing*.

DOWNSIZING

The terms *downsizing* or *rightsizing* have received extensive press coverage lately. Downsizing has been promoted as a way to reduce costs, speed applications development, and put computing power in the hands of the end-users. Downsizing usually involves scaling back the hardware platform. In a typical scenario the organization migrates from a centralized mainframe to a microcomputer-based LAN architecture. The resultant microcomputer configuration is often referred to as a client/server architecture. However, this is somewhat misleading because in practice any size computer can be designated as the file server and any size computer can be designated as a client. For many businesses the client/server approach involves a variety of personal computers and mainframes with integrated connectivity.

Cost effective Electronic mail (E-mail) and relational database applications are pushing the demand for the microcomputer-based client/server architecture. E-mail systems have given organizations a powerful tool and they are less expensive and more flexible on a PC based network. Although mainframe-based relational databases have a longer history than the personal computer-based client/server architecture, many companies have developed or are in the process of developing reliable implementations of the relational database language SQL. Personal computer hardware is indeed cost effective from the performance perspective. For instance, consider that currently the cost of a personal computer MIPS (millions of instructions per second) is $1,000 while a mainframe MIPS costs $100,000.

But not all of the news about the personal computer-base client/server architecture is good news. First, all large mainframe computers and their accompanying centralized databases have been around for several years and as such from a technical standpoint they are comparatively stable. Second, they have the ability to handle far more transactions on a central data repository than any microcomputer-based database engine. As a third related issue, many so-called common systems related to financial data, employee records, and customer databases require centralized maintenance and are relatively standard. Finally, so-called mission critical applications which are the foundation of day-to-day operations demand a stabile, reliable platform. But as noted by LaPlante the personal computer-based client/server architecture poses significant technical and managerial problems (LaPlante, 1992). These problems are:

- There are not enough off-the-shelf applications for a distributed environment.
- Information systems development and operations need to be redesigned for the distributed environment.
- Distributed applications require a significant investment up-front in resources for hardware, software, and systems development.
- There are compatibility problems with the client/server mix involving the development language, the network architecture, the operating systems, and the hardware.
- System crashes are an inevitable part of many distributed environments.

Personal computer-based LANs are also more vulnerable to security risks than their larger mainframe counterparts. As noted in the section on human resource information systems, there is no way to prevent someone with the technical know-how and motivation from breaking into a network using the DOS operating system and Novell's NetWare. It has been estimated that there are 25,000 people with knowledge about the backdoor entry into this network software.

Whether a firm utilizes the personal computing-based client/server architecture or some other hybrid architecture, downsizing has significant managerial implications. Downsizing involves cutting staff, restructuring jobs, changing the physical layout of the organization, and in essence redesigning the organization. Before taking the downsizing route an organization should address the following (Glass, 1992):

- Will additional staff cuts seriously undermine the ability of the organization to satisfy customers and meet operational needs?
- What are the true costs of downsizing? Will the newly installed technology require more or less expenditures on maintenance and training? Will the technology be able to handle future transaction workloads? Will the technology be reliable and stable?
- Should the organization consider outsourcing? Organizations can enter into contracts with other companies to assist in facilities management, managerial and technical support, and to meet temporary staffing needs.

There is some sentiment that LANs require more administration and maintenance than multi-user systems because there are many issues related to network configuration and equipment selection.

IMPLEMENTING THE ENTERPRISE-WIDE DATA MODEL

Enterprise-wide data modeling provides structure and stability in the development of an integrated data architecture. However, integration can also be viewed as being rigid and confining. Flexibility can be imparted to this rigidity through relational database engines with an accompanying fourth generation language. Data modelling provides an overlay of structure and discipline so that the data retrieved through the relational database engine is well-behaved. Relational database engines are currently the most popular way to integrate and distribute organizational data. They are available on the personal computer-based LANS as well as on large mainframes. The relational database language SQL is the current industry standard. Relational databases when *coupled* with data modeling and a fourth generation development language provide the following benefits:

- They provide data independence. That is the physical characteristics of data storage devices are insulated from applications.
- Multiple views of data can be maintained and users can concentrate on their data requirements.
- Data redundancy is minimized, resulting in reduced storage requirements and greater levels of data consistency after updates.

- Improved security and integrity is realized by controlling access to the database and by having backup and recovery mechanisms.
- Concurrency control is maintained so that simultaneous updates are handled in a consistent manner.
- Flexible retrieval and updates of records and data in the database.
- Fast report generation, customized electronic input and output forms, and graphic support facilities are available.

The primary benefits of enterprise-wide data modeling and relational database systems with a fourth generation language accrue to end-users and data administrators because they can focus on data requirements. The goal, after all, of the systems support infrastructure is to provide information which supports the organizational mission.

CONCLUSION

Information technology is playing an increasingly critical role in how organizations will compete. Virtually, every organizational activity can be made more efficient and effective with information technology because it provides a platform for organizational communication. Communication can lead to more efficient production processes and reduce the redundancy inherent in many organizational activities. Better communication with suppliers can improve throughput and delivery delays. Better communication with customers can lead to increased understanding of their needs and ultimately result in more sales. In the next four chapters we shall review how information technology is being utilized in the four areas of manufacturing and operations management, marketing, and sales management, financial management and human resources management. Information technology applications and expecially strategic information systems enable firms to function more effectively and also provide a competitive advantage.

REFERENCES

LaPlante, A. 1992. "Chipping Away at the Corporate Mainframe." *InfoWorld* 14: 40-42.
Sanders, G.L. 1990. "Strategic Database Planning." *Database Programming and Design* 3(11): 52-56.

STRATEGIC INFORMATION SYSTEMS FOR MANUFACTURING AND OPERATIONS MANAGEMENT

Robert P. Cerveny, C. Carl Pegels, and

G. Lawrence Sanders

INTRODUCTION

Several information technology developments over the past two decades have been influential in the emergence of strategic information systems in the manufacturing and operations management (MOM) area. Although these developments by no means comprise every information technology development in the MOM area, they do comprise the vast majority of information technology developments.

The information technology developments consist of: (1) airline passenger booking systems; (2) manufacturing requirements planning or manufacturing resource planning (MRP) systems; (3) item (package, part, product, component) tracking systems; and (4) logistic information systems which link manufacturer to supplier and manufacturer to customer by electronic data interchange (EDI) links.

The four information technology developments mentioned have been developed over a considerable time period and are still developing today, and will most certainly expand and become more capable in the future. Underlying the development of these systems has been the growth in sophistication and speed of hardware which allowed the development and implementation of these systems. Also the developments in relational database technology, the appearance of the work station, the developments in fault-tolerant computing, the development of both local area networks (LANS) and wide area networks (WANS) have contributed to the developments listed above. Next we shall look at each of the four main information technology developments separately.

AIRLINE PASSENGER BOOKING SYSTEMS

Airline passenger booking systems have been around for a while. As a result of both hardware and software developments, these systems have become very sophisticated and enable the users of these systems to utilize the systems for a variety of strategic and tactical applications.

Strategic applications include studies of traffic patterns, traffic loads, passenger demand forecasting, passenger load forecasting, and in general capacity planning. Tactical applications include variable pricing, block pricing, modifying seat inventory block pricing as the departure date approaches when seats are still unsold plus a variety of other tactical uses which enhance revenue and maximize profitability of each flight.

The airline passenger booking systems also allow the airline which owns the booking system to promote its service (product) ahead of the competition. Although there are limitations on what is legally allowed, the owner of the booking system is able to direct travel agents to its product (service). In addition, the owner airline is able to provide a variety of incentives, as well as varying incentives depending on demand, to its travel agents. Hence, the airline passenger booking system has become a very valuable and important marketing tool for the airline industry.

The results of the above success has led to the airlines forming separate corporations for the airline passenger booking systems. These separate corporations have become valuable assets which frequently are more profitable than the basic function of the airlines, transporting passengers and freight.

In recent years with the globalization of the airline industry, the separate airline passenger booking systems corporations are forming a basis for international cooperation. UAL (United AirLines), AMR (American AirLines), and Continental Airlines now share and co-own their airline passenger booking systems corporations with their foreign competitors and frequently partners.

MANUFACTURING RESOURCE MANAGEMENT SYSTEMS

Manufacturing resource management systems started out as manufacturing requirements planning (MRP) systems. These systems have evolved from an information system designed to handle ordering and scheduling raw materials, parts and subassemblies in a product manufacturing operation to a complex manufacturing resource information system. When first developed the system was quite revolutionary because it tied several operations, which formerly had been viewed as quite separate, together. It starts out with the finished assembly (product) production plan over a defined time period tied to product delivery dates. It then works backward and based on lead times and requirements determines by date when all raw materials, parts and subassemblies must be ordered or placed in production. The entire system can be viewed as a series of product structure trees for each batch of products that is to be delivered on a given date. Needless to say this information system, even from its very beginning, needed to be rather complex. It was therefore considered to be a great advance in computer software technology development when the systems first became available in sophisticated form in the sixties.

The original MRP systems were very expensive to develop and required extensive computing facilities (large mainframes) to operate. As a result the original MRP systems were only affordable and accessible to large-scale manufacturing firms. The resultant implementation of a large-scale, expensive and very complex computer-based information system in a manufacturing environment met with very disappointing results. The rather chaotic conditions in a large-scale manufacturing plant were just not conducive to implementation of a computer system which requires data input from a very well organized and stable environment. Also the data input had to come from a work force not familiar with information systems and with the discipline required to utilize information systems. Needless to say the initial success of MRP systems in the complex and chaotic manufacturing environment was poor to non-existent. Management, which had approved large expenditures for these costly computer-based systems was obviously disappointed but could do very little about it initially. To be sure quite a few systems were installed but their effectiveness was rated from barely acceptable to poor.

What went wrong with the initial MRP systems? The technical nature of the MRP systems, even the early ones, was fine. What had not been fully considered was the nature of the manufacturing system with all of its behavioral, human, organization, technical, and other complexities. It was just not ready to be transferred into the highly disciplined format required for MRP implementation. As a result management had to first reorganize its manufacturing system, impose a discipline on it, before it could even consider implementation of the MRP system.

Today, MRP systems are widely used and most manufacturing systems could not function without them. In the interim, MRP systems have become available first for mini-computer applications, and more recently for the expanded and networked PC computer systems. Cost of software for the small systems had decreased substantially to the point where even a manufacturer employing twenty people can afford, and needs, a MRP system. What was also initially overlooked, the implementation of a MRP system in a small-scale environment, a factory employing 20 people, is much easier than trying to do the same in a factory employing 2000 people.

Today's MRP system has evolved from manufacturing requirements planning to manufacturing resource planning. The systems have evolved to include both the work force scheduling function as well as the marketing, sales, and billing functions. In addition, the present-day systems are able, in simulation mode, to be used for capacity planning in the short as well as long run. Hence, the MRP system, now called MRP II in its expanded format, has become a truly strategic information system for the manufacturing environment.

ITEM (PACKAGE) TRACKING SYSTEMS

The item tracking systems have become very successful in the transportation industry. Led by Federal Express, which developed a highly sophisticated package tracking system, other package and freight transportation firms have invested vast amounts of money to develop systems to suit their own needs.

These tracking systems have been an indirect outgrowth of bar-code applications. Although bar-code was largely originated and utilized by the retailing industry especially the food retailers, it has now become an important feature of item tracking systems.

Item tracking systems also have wider applications in other areas. Wherever a single item needs to be followed over a period of time, the focus on that item drives the system, and the future will see many more developments based on item tracking.

LOGISTICS INFORMATION SYSTEMS

Whereas item tracking systems were driven by the bar-code development and the need to provide superior customer service, logistics information systems were driven by information technology developments especially those in electronic data interchange, or developments in data communication.

Electronic data interchange (EDI) allows corporations, or units in a corporation, to communicate extensive and detailed blocks of information in digital format and without operator intervention. It is thus therefore a substantial improvement in communication but also a substantial improvement in the efficiency of communication.

EDI systems are now used extensively by manufacturers to communicate with their component and parts suppliers on issues related to technical details, orders, modification to orders, and so forth. The supplier in turn can query the manufacturer on any problems. In addition it can use the EDI system for invoicing purposes.

Manufacturers also use EDI systems to communicate in a forward vertical dimension with their customers, retailers, wholesalers, or dealers. Again the customer can utilize the EDI system to place orders, modify orders, and otherwise communicate with the manufacturer. As a result EDI systems have become pervasive and by the end of 1992 over 25,000 EDI systems were installed and in use in the United States.

The above reviews the various applications of information systems in the manufacturing and operations management area. Not reviewed are information systems used for pure technical operations such as computer numerical control (CNC) systems, and other such systems which direct and control the functions of complex machines, transfer lines and robots.

CASE STUDIES

This chapter evaluates and analyzes manufacturing and operations management information technology developments in recent years in 25 firms. The studies of the information technology development in the 25 firms are called case studies. The 25 case studies are based on prior reports published in such journals as *Datamation, Computerworld,* and so forth.

The 25 firms on which the case studies are reported represent a fairly wide variety of industries in the manufacturing, transportation, and other service sectors. The activities the firms are engaged in can also be simplified to manufacturing and service. Specifically, there are 17 manufacturing firms, 6 transportation firms, one automobile rental firm, and one retailing firm.

The focus of the 25 firms is on operations related activities. Financial related activities were not covered in this group of case studies unless they were explicitly reported and if they interfaced with operations-related activities.

Analysis of the 25 completed case study summaries revealed that there were ten specific strategic thrust oriented activities on which information technology developments were focussed. The ten specific strategic thrust oriented activities were found to be clustered into three groups consisting of an operations and strategic thrust group, an organizational thrust group and a customer/client oriented thrust group.

INFORMATION TECHNOLOGY
DEVELOPMENTS IN MANUFACTURING AND OPERATIONS MANAGEMENT

Based on the 25 case studies of firms in various manufacturing, transportation and service industries we have been able to identify three strategic thrusts which the 25 firms represented by the case studies are trying to implement utilizing information technology developments. The three strategic thrusts are:

1. *Operational and Strategic Oriented Activities. Information technology developments focussed on operational and strategic improvements consisting of:*

    ... Improving the pricing of services and products and segmenting services in various categories or classes.
    ... Forecasting demand for products and services and also potential shortages so that steps can be taken early to avoid the shortages.
    ... Improving efficiency and effectiveness in order to position the firm in a more competitive position.
    ... Improving the flow of finished products and supplies to speed up response times and reduce customer/own firm inventories.

2. *Organizational Activities. Information technology developments focussed on organizational improvements consisting of:*

    ... The integration of databases and organizational activities.
    ... Speeding up and improve quality of communication internally and externally to the firm.
    ... Centralizing the firm's activities, including a flattening of the organization chart.

3. *Customer/Client Service Oriented Activities. Information technology developments focussed on customer/client service oriented activities consisting of:*

    ... Improving the user-friendliness and simplification of use by computer systems users.
    ... Providing tracking of such items as packages, passengers, automobiles, freight cars, projects, etc. for better management.
    ... Improving informational and functional services to customers thus assisting them in their operations.

Included in each of the strategic thrusts are the activities described above, consisting of four operational and strategic oriented activities, three organizational activities, and three customer/client service oriented activities.

Exhibit 1 provides a matrix showing the relationship of the 25 case studies with the ten strategic thrust activities. Exhibit 2 lists the 25 firms and the industries in which they operate.

CASE ANALYSES

Activity 1a, improving the pricing of services and products and segmenting services in various categories or classes, was practiced by a mixture of product manufacturing and service-oriented firms. Nine of the 25 firms utilized this strategic activity. The firms included Cummins Engine, Hewlett Packard, Helene Curtis, American President Lines, American AirLines, CSX Transportation, Dylex, Avis International, and Harley Davidson. Note that three firms were in manufacturing, three firms were in transportation, and one was in the retail sector.

Activity 1b, forecasting demand of products and services and identifying potential shortages, was utilized by five of the 25 firms. It is interesting that the firms are engaged in a variety of activities consisting of manufacturing, retailing and transportation. The firms include Andreas Stihl, Helene Curtis, Dylex, American AirLines, and Rockwell International.

Activity 1c, improve efficiency and effectiveness in order to improve competitiveness, was utilized by nearly all firms, to be exact by 24 out of 25 firms. This near-total utilization of this strategic thrust is not surprising. Maintaining competitiveness requires continuous focus on efficiency and effectiveness.

Activity 1d, improve the flow of products to improve customer service and lower inventory, was practiced by 19 of the 25 firms. Fourteen of the firms are in manufacturing one is a retailer and four are engaged in various forms of transportation. The firms include Corning Asahi, A.T. and T. Technologies, Schering, Cummins, Helene Curtis, B.M. Products, Raymond Industrial, Texas Instruments, American Cyanimid, American President Lines, CSX Transportation, Ethyl Corporation, Bi-State Transit, Dylex, Control Data, Nissan, BRK Electronics, and Harley Davidson.

Activity 2a, integration of databases and organizational activities, was practiced by 15 out of 25 firms. The firms not included did not mention this important and critical activity explicitly but, based on the description of their information technology activities, appear to be engaged in the integration activity also.

Activity 2b, speeding up and improving communication, was practiced by 19 out of 25 firms. Firms which did not identify this activity were more

Strategic Thrusts/ Activities	Firm Identifiers for Case Studies													
	MOM1	MOM2	MOM3	MOM4	MOM5	MOM6	MOM7	MOM8	MOM9	MOM10	MOM11	MOM12	MOM13	MOM14
1a						x	x	x						
b		x		x				x						
c	x	x	x	x	x	x	x	x	x	x	x	x	x	
d	x		x		x	x	x	x	x	x	x		x	
2a		x	x	x				x	x	x				
b		x	x	x				x	x	x	x	x	x	x
c				x			x	x	x	x	x	x	x	x
3a				x	x								x	
b					x					x		x	x	
c						x	x	x		x				x
Number	2	4	4	6	4	4	5	8	5	7	4	4	6	3

Exhibit 1. Mapping of Case Studies on Strategic Thrusts/Activities

Strategic Thrusts/ Activities	Firm Identifiers for Case Studies											
	MOM15	MOM16	MOM17	MOM18	MOM19	MOM20	MOM21	MOM22	MOM23	MOM24	MOM25	Total
1a	x	x	x			x	x				x	9
b		x										5
c	x	x	x	x	x	x	x	x	x	x	x	24
d	x		x	x	x		x	x	x	x	x	19
2a	x	x	x			x	x	x	x	x	x	15
b	x	x	x	x	x			x	x	x	x	19
c		x	x	x	x	x	x	x	x	x	x	19
3a		x				x	x	x			x	7
b	x		x	x	x	x	x	x	x	x	x	14
c	x	x	x	x	x	x					x	12
Number	7	8	8	6	6	7	7	7	6	6	9	

Strategic Thrusts/Activities

1. Operational and Strategic Thrust Activities

   a. Improve pricing;
   b. forecast demand;
   c. improve efficiency/effectiveness; and
   d. improve just in time.

2. Organizational Thrust Activities

   a. Integration of databases;
   b. improve communication; and
   c. centralization.

3. Customer/Client Service Oriented Thrust Activities

   a. Improve user friendliness;
   b. provide item tracking; and
   c. improve customer services.

Note See Exhibit 2 for list of firms.

Exhibit 1. (Continued)

125

Identifier	Industry Area	Firm
MOM1	Manufacturing	A.T.&T. Technologies
MOM2	Logistics in Manufacturing	Andreas Stihl Chain Saws
MOM3	Manufacturing	Corning Asahi Video Prod.
MOM4	Manufacturing	Rockwell Int'l
MOM5	Manufacturing	Schering AG
MOM6	Manufacturing	Cummins Engine
MOM7	Manufacturing	Hewlett Packard
MOM8	Sales/Manufacturing	Helene Curtis
MOM9	Manufacturing	B.M. Products
MOM10	Manufacturing	Raymond Ind. Prod.
MOM11	Manufacturing	Texas Instruments
MOM12	Manufacturing	Gen'l Motors
MOM13	Manufacturing	Am. Cyanimid
MOM14	Transportation	UPS
MOM15	Transportation	Am. Pres. Lines
MOM16	Air Transportation	Am. Air Lines
MOM17	Railroad	CSX
MOM18	Shipping	Ethyl Corp.
MOM19	Metrop. Transit	Bi-State Transit
MOM20	Auto Rental	Avis Corp.
MOM21	Retailing	Dylex
MOM22	Manufacturing	Control Data
MOM23	Manufacturing	Nissan
MOM24	Manufacturing	BRK Electronics
MOM25	Manufacturing	Harley Davidson

Exhibit 2.   Listing of Industry Areas and Firms for Case Studies

focussed on other activities. The non-reporters consisted of A.T. and T. Technologies, Avis Corporation, Dylex, Schering, Cummins, and Hewlett Packard.

Activity 2c, centralize the firm's activities and flatten the organization chart, was practiced by 19 out of 25 firms. Firms utilizing this activity included United Parcel Service, American AirLines, CSX Transportation, Avis Corporation, Rockwell International, Hewlett Packard, Helene Curtis, B.M. Products, Raymond Industrial, Texas Instruments, General Motors, American Cyanimid, Ethyl Corporation, Bi-State Transit, Dylex, Control Data, Nissan, BRK Electronics, and Harley Davidson.

Activity 3a, improving user-friendliness and simplification of use, was practiced by seven out of 25 firms. The number is low because firms which utilize computer systems with many internal and especially external users consider this a very important activity. However, not many firms fall in this category. The firms include Schering, American AirLines, Avis Corporation, Rockwell International, American Cyanimid, Control Data, and Harley Davidson.

Activity 3b, providing tracking of items critical to a firm's operations, was practiced by 14 out of 25 firms. The firms consist of Schering, Raymond Industrial, General Motors, United Parcel Service, American President Lines, CSX Transportation, Avis Corporation, Ethyl Corporation, Bi-State Transit, Dylex, Control Data, Nissan, BRK Electronics, and Harley Davidson.

Activity 3c, improving informational and functional services to customers, was practiced by 12 out of 25 firms. This activity was generally driven by trying to be more competitive or responding to competitors. Firms utilizing it include Cummins, Hewlett Packard, Helene Curtis, Raymond Industrial, United Parcel Service, American President Lines, American AirLines, CSX Transportation, Avis Corporation, Ethyl Corporation, Bi-State Transit, Control Data, and Harley Davidson.

DIFFERENCES BETWEEN MANUFACTURING AND SERVICE ORIENTED FIRMS

Utilization of information technologies had a distinctly different focus for manufacturing and service firms. Based on the 25 case studies summarized in Exhibit 1, service firms, especially those in the transportation sectors, appear to be achieving more benefits from intensive use of information technologies than do manufacturing firms. This difference could be explained by the perceived or actual larger benefits service firms can obtain from more extensive information technology developments in comparison with manufacturing firms. Extensive computerization in manufacturing is usually accompanied by extensive investment in manufacturing machinery and equipment. As a result, to achieve substantial benefits from computerization in manufacturing requires a considerable investment. This is a relatively larger investment on average than for service sector firms.

Evidence for the above can be observed from Exhibit 1. Note that seven of the 17 manufacturing firms only utilized two to four of the ten strategic thrust activities. Specifically, Corning Asahi, Schering, Cummins, Texas Instruments, General Motors, and Andreas Stihl utilized four strategic thrust activities and A.T. and T. Technologies utilized only two. Three manufacturing firms, Hewlett Packard, B.M. Products, and American Cyanimid utilized 5 of the ten strategic thrust activities. Of the remaining manufacturing firms, three utilized six strategic thrust activities, two utilized seven strategic thrust activities, one utilized eight strategic thrust activities, and another utilized nine strategic thrust activities. On the other hand the eight service-oriented firms utilized from four to eight of the ten strategic thrust activities. Only United Parcel Service utilized four strategic thrust activities. Two firms, Ethyl Corporation and Bi-State Transit utilized six strategic thrust activities. American President Lines, Dylex, and Avis Corporation utilized seven strategic thrust activities and American AirLines and CSX Transportation each utilized eight of the ten strategic thrust activities.

Based on the above we can observe that service-oriented firms appear to be gaining significantly more from intensive information technology developments than do manufacturing firms. Specifically, we find that the 17 manufacturing firms used on average 5.29 strategic thrust activities while the eight service firms utilized on average 6.63 strategic thrust activities.

The individual case studies for the 25 firms included in this section of the report are shown below:

Number:	MOM1
Industry:	Integrated Circuits
Area:	Manufacturing
Firm:	A.T. and T. Technologies Kansas City Works (Integrated Circuit Mfr.)
Location:	Lee's Summit, Missouri
Manager:	Jeffrey M. Neve
Size:	Revenue: $36 Billion (company-wide)
Summary:	Computer simulation was used to study various aspects of Integrated Circuit manufacturing including installation of just-in-time (JIT) manufacturing, allocating equipment to process steps, and increasing the output of critical (bottleneck) operations. As a result of the computer simulations operations were modified with the following results. Cycle time was reduced about 40 percent while wafer starts per week increased by 10 percent. Product shipments and yields increased also. Cycle time in testing operations increased by a factor of two.
Source:	Neve and Crossland (1988/1989).

Number:	MOM2
Industry:	Chain Saws
Area:	Logistics in Manufacturing
Firm:	Andreas Stihl Chain Saws
Location:	Stuttgart, Germany
Managers:	Hans Peter Stihl and Eva Mayer-Stihl
Size:	Largest producer of chain saws (27% market share) Revenue: DM 1 Billion

Summary:	Stihl has developed a market oriented logistics system whereby the customer market and supplier organizations have been integrated. Stihl views itself as a communication link between its customers (and their orders) and its supplier (and their shipments). The purchasing function is no longer handled by just the purchasing department, but engineers and technicians form an integral part of the purchasing process. All of the above have been accomplished by use of computer integrated management systems.
Source:	Busch (1990).

Number:	MOM3
Industry:	Industrial Glass
Area:	Manufacturing
Firm:	Corning Asahi Video Products (39% owned by Asahi)
Location:	State College, Pennsylvania
Plant Manager:	Mark Mitchell
Size:	Revenue: $2.94 Billion (company-wide)
Product:	Glass for TV tubes
Summary:	Installed computer integrated manufacturing (CIM) in 1985, as well as total quality control (TQC) and JIT principles. By 1990 manufacturing costs were 22 percent lower than in 1985. In 1989 gross margin had tripled in comparison with 1985. CIM integrates all accounting, ordering and billing procedures. The glass-making process had 215 steps and 6500 variables which must be monitored continuously. CIM is helpful in doing so.
Source:	Betts (1990).

Number:	MOM4
Industry:	Aircraft
Area:	Manufacturing
Firm:	North American Aircraft Division (NAAD) of Rockwell International
Location:	El Segundo, California
Manager:	John Pierro, Division President
Size:	Revenue: $13.38 Billion (company-wide)
Products:	Military Aircraft

Summary: This firm is making a serious attempt to develop
                executive information systems (EIS). It is a formidable
                task both from a technical and implementation point
                of view. The primary requirements are a user-friendly
                system which provides useful services. The system used
                was one developed by Command Center from Boston-
                based Pilot Executive Software. An implementation
                package with the Company's Advantage/G Applica-
                tion Generator was used. The system was strongly
                supported by Mr. Pierro, the Division President who
                insisted that his senior executives use it. At the
                development end a senior executive served as a
                "champion" of the system. Data providers and data
                keepers are important people that keep the system
                useful for the users. The EIS developers must have
                technical skills, business understanding, toleration for
                ambiguity and interpersonal skills. They must also
                play the roles of teacher, salesperson, detective and
                diplomat. Acceptance of the system has ranged from
                enthusiasm to resistance. It requires changing the
                executive culture. The system is not fully operational
                yet but promises to improve the lines of communica-
                tion at NAAD, especially at the senior executive level.

Source: Armstrong (1990).

Number: MOM5
Industry: Pharmaceuticals
Area: Manufacturing
Firm: Schering AG
Location: Berlin, Germany
Manager: Not Available
Size: Revenue: $3.2 Billion (company-wide)

Summary: The company built a decision support system for
                planning chemical production of active ingredients.
                A traditional manufacturing resource planning
                system (MRP) type production planning system was
                insufficient due to the cyclical structure of the
                production process. A number of co- and by-products
                are recycled which traditional MRP systems cannot
                handle. The decision support system (DSS) aids in
                determining the time phased production quantities of
                all active ingredients and intermediates for the whole

planning horizon. The key elements of the DSS are: Relational database containing production data, Model base that models the system as mixed integer programming problem and a Dialogue system to interface with the users.

Source: Jager, Peemoller, and Rohde (1989).

Number:	MOM6
Industry:	Diesel Engines
Area:	Manufacturing
Firm:	Cummins Engine Company
Location:	Columbus, Indiana
Manager:	Not Available
Size:	Revenue: $3.46 Billion (company-wide)

Summary: In 1986, Cummins implemented Computer Numerical Control (CNC) machining in its manufacturing system. The CNC machines were designed as stand-alone systems to increase flexibility. Since its adoption, the cost to customers have decreased by 30 percent and the time to market a new design has decreased by 2 years.

Source: Venkatesan (1990).

Number:	MOM7
Industry:	Computer
Area:	Manufacturing
Firm:	Hewlett-Packard
Location:	West Coast
Manager:	Not Available
Size:	Revenue: $9.8 Billion (company-wide)

Summary: Hewlett-Packard implemented a computerized system to track and interpret the quality-control data in the production of hard-disk packs. Hewlett-Packard reduced both the failure rate and the time required to correct the defects by more than 90 percent. In addition, materials and labor costs were halved, and the time needed to serve customers was reduced by two-thirds.

Source: Haas (1987).

Number: MOM8
Industry: Consumer Products
Area: Sales/Manufacturing
Firm: Helene Curtis Industries
Location: Chicago, Illinois
Manager: Tom Gildea
Size: Revenue: $629 Million

Summary: The IS department at the company plays a crucial role in business planning throughout the company—from coordinating a new fully automated warehouse to arming sales representatives with laptop computers loaded with information from the corporate database. The company uses a centralized, relational database that links a variety of customized applications, enabling all company divisions to share key information about manufacturing, distribution and sales.

Source: Johnson (1989).

Number: MOM9
Industry: Moulding
Area: Manufacturing
Firm: BM Products
Location: St. Louis, MO
Manager: Not Available
Size: Not Available

Summary: The company developed a decision support system (DSS) for production scheduling in its blow moulding operations. A DSS, instead of a more traditional MIS system was required because a DSS allows the moulding department personnel the opportunity easily to control changes in the data and perform sensitivity analysis to improve the solution. The DSS allowed the moulding department management to occasionally experiment with alternative production methods to identify the impacts of possible changes in production times and set-up times. The system also allowed the management to productively use their machines by scheduling routine maintenance during slack times which the system explicitly identified. The DSS appears to be an efficient and effective computer-based decision aid.

Source: Kwak, Freeman, and Schniederjans (1989).

Number: MOM10
Industry: Forklift Trucks
Area: Manufacturing
Firm: Raymond Industrial Equipment Inc.
Location: Brantford, Ontario, Canada
Manager: Not Available
Size: Revenue: $147 Million

Summary: In 1979, the company adopted MAPICS (Manufacturing Accounting Production Information Control System). MAPICS covers all of the applications that a manufacturer needs, including tracking production, feeding information into the ordering system, general ledger uses and more. Since its first installation, the system has been upgraded several times and it has now evolved into "a company wide piece of software that is totally integrated." Presently, the materials area uses it for inventory planning, the production area uses it for planning goods and the accounting area uses it to pay their vendors.

Source: Wintrob (1990).

Number: MOM11
Industry: Electronics/Computers
Area: CIM
Firm: Texas Instruments, Inc.
Location: Lubbock, Texas
Manager: William Rolland, Executive Director of the Automation Forum; Ken Barnes, Equipment Engineering Manager at the Lubbock facility
Size: Revenue: $6.57 Billion (company-wide)

Summary: The Lubbock plant of Texas Instruments, Inc. (TI) uses a highly automated, continous-flow production system that turns raw plastic pellets into a finished calculator (ready to ship) in 20 minutes. This CIM system not only lowers the production system cost but also provides real-time monitoring of the assembly line, giving immediate feedback on throughput, scrap and yield from start to finish. An Ethernet network links the shop floor to TI's accounting and inventory systems. In addition, TI's suppliers can call into the factory's minicomputer to find out if any parts were defective.

Source: Betts (1990).

Number: MOM12
Industry: Automobile
Area: Manufacturing
Firm: General Motors Corp.'s Fort Wayne Assembly Plant
Location: Fort Wayne, Indiana
Manager: Monty Hansen, EDS Account Manager
Size: Revenue: $124 Billion
                   Employees: 761,000 (company-wide)

Summary: GM's Fort Wayne Truck and Bus Group Assembly Plant, one of the most technologically advanced plants in GM, has recently implemented several monitoring systems to track down the manufacturing process and troubleshoot it at approximately 5,000 points in the plant. The project is designed to improve specific plant functions; a problem-tracking system was installed for the paint shop, another for maintenance and an upgrade was installed for the inspection feedback system, a crucial part of GM's quality assurance system. These plantwide monitoring systems are developed and installed by Electronic Data Systems Corporation (EDS), a GM subsidiary. In addition to performing the traditional IS functions, EDS's staff also do the surveys for Occupational Safety and Health Administration (OSHA) and create the computerized instruction manuals that meet the requirements by the OS and H Administration.

Source: Fitzgerald (1990).

Number: MOM13
Industry: Chemical
Area: Manufacturing/R&D
Firm: American Cynamid
Location: Wayne, NJ
Manager: Robert Fay, Engineer
Size: Revenue: $4.82 Billion
                   Employees: 35,000 (company-wide)

Summary: American Cynamid, a chemical company operates many plants of various sizes. The company has aggressively implemented computer technology in the area of process control. Cynamid has concentrated on developing systems which have flexibility and can be programmed by an engineer. By not having to hire a programmer, the company can save money. Also, an engineer is the one who understands a process well. To achieve this objective Cynamid has ensured that the process control engineer can talk directly with the vendors. It also created a committee to make each group aware of what is being done throughout the company and coordinate efforts where appropriate. The use of computers at Cynamid has resulted in the improvement of product quality, lowering of energy costs, increase of plant capacity, conservation of raw materials and, compliance to environmental and safety standards.

Source: Heller (1989).

Number: MOM14
Industry: Package Delivery
Area: Transportation
Firm: United Parcel Service (UPS)
Location: World-wide
Managers: Kent Nelson (Chairman)
        Frank Erbrick (Sr. V.P. of IS)
        James Flynn (EDI Services Manager)
Size: Revenue: $13.6 Billion (1991) (company-wide)

Summary: UPS has vastly expanded its IS operations from a low investment in the early eighties to an approximate $1.5 billion investment today. Its annual IS operating budget is $300 million covers 1400 IS employees. Most of its IS budget is focussed on package tracking from pickup to delivery. Barcoding and hand-held data collectors are extensively used. The latter are scheduled to be put on-line through radio communication in the future. Once installed, UPS will know instantly the status of any package it is handling. UPS has 2000 package sorting centers and operates in 118 countries.

Source: Crockett (1991).

Number: MOM15
Industry: Container Transportation
Area: Transportation
Firm: American President Lines
Location: Oakland, California
Manager: Michael E. Cromar, Director of Information Services
Size: Revenue: $1.8 Billion (1989)
Service: Ground and Sea Transportation by Computers

Summary: American President Lines (APC) transports contain-
                 erized goods between land locations in the United
                 States and trans-Pacific destinations. APC used a
                 computer-based interpretation system made by
                 Metaphor Computer Systems of Mountain View,
                 California which provides reports from databases in
                 30 minutes. Before the reports took up to two weeks
                 to prepare. It uses a Terdata relational data base
                 machine. APC also uses computer-aided logistics
                 systems to load and unload cargo ships (i.e., ships stop
                 at many ports for delivery and containers need to be
                 loaded in a certain order). APC's customers in the
                 United States can keep track of cargo location through
                 a voice response system triggered by touch-tone
                 telephone service. Also United States importers are
                 able to track their imports from the time a purchase
                 order is issued to final delivery. Computer is also used
                 for freight rate-setting purposes.

Source: McCusker (1988)

Number: MOM16
Industry: Passenger Transportation
Area: Air Transportation
Firm: American AirLines (AMR)
Location: Dallas, Texas
Manager: Not Available
Size: One of the World's Two Largest Airlines
Service: Provide Passenger Air Line and Freight Service

Summary: American Airlines has moved in three directions to
                 accommodate to market pressures. They developed: (1)
                 Travel reservation systems; (2) Independent MIS
                 subsidiaries; and (3) Competitive in-house operations
                 for customer service. American's Sabre system handles

as many as 1.5 million fare changes overnight when a price war kicks off. American receives $1.70 for every transaction on its reservation system and gets about 20 percent more business from agencies that use Sabre than from those that do not. Airlines seek to gain and keep travel agencies (who write 70 percent of all airline tickets) by enhancing their reservation systems to be more reliable and easy-to-use. The major competitors now provide travel agents with PS/2 workstations which enhance the agent's ability to do many other routine tasks. American provides word processing, database and spreadsheet capabilities as well as user-friendly ticket writing abilities. The PS/2s have also off-loaded many small tasks from the Airlines main frame computers. American's MIS subsidiary now sells packages to hotels to provide similar reservation and pricing services similar to those it developed for its own Sabre system.

Source:	Horwitt (1988).
Number:	MOM17
Industry:	Freight Transportation
Area:	Railroad
Firm:	CSX Transportation
Location:	Richmond, Virginia
Manager:	Jack Cooper, President of CSX Technologies
Size:	$10 Billion transportation firm - rail, ocean, barge, trucking, warehousing and distribution
Service:	Freight Transportation

Summary: CSX has over 800 databases which are accessed over 200 million times per day. They are used to keep track of 1.4 million railroad cars (10% owned by CSX) and 22,000 miles of track. Sales people access databases to sell the use of specific cars. Service people handle customer inquiries and billing people need access to data. Currently, PS/2 workstations allow users to access four mainframes at the same time thus providing access to many databases. Internal operations helped by this new system include billing services, freight collection, strategic pricing, interline accounting and rating and pricing. Errors are reduced significantly because of fewer required key entries.

Source: Robinson (1990).

Number: MOM18
Industry: Natural Gas Transportation
Area: Ship Scheduling
Firm: Ethyl Corporation
Location: Richmond, Virginia
Manager: Not Available
Size: Revenue: $2 Billion

Summary: The Ethyl Corporation utilizes a fleet of bulk ocean-
                       going tankers to deliver gasoline antiknock com-
                       pounds to distribution and customer terminals all over
                       the world. Managing this fleet involves strategic
                       planning decisions, as well as many day-to-day
                       operational decisions. However, the central issue
                       around which most of these management decisions
                       evolve is that of how to schedule each ship in the fleet
                       so that inventory needs at all terminals are satisfied in
                       the least-costly manner. The Ethyl Corporation
                       developed a decision support system to address the
                       problem. The system has proven to be very effective
                       in addressing "what-if" questions to modifications in
                       the operating plans. Following the implementation of
                       the system, the variable scheduling costs at the
                       corporation have decreased by 5 percent-15 percent.

Source: Miller (1987).

Number: MOM19
Industry: Passenger Transportation
Area: Metropoliton Transit
Firm: Bi-State Transit Agency
Location: St. Louis, MO
Manager: Not Available
Size: A fleet of 750 buses

Summary: A computerized system was developed to facilitate
                       assignment, parking and dispatching of buses for the
                       metropolitan transit system. The major objectives of
                       the system were: (1) increase the ease with which the
                       system is restored after an interruption in service
                       through bus breakdown, (2) increase bus operator
                       satisfaction, and (3) improvements in bus mainte-

nance. The system relies on mathematical heuristics and decision rules developed from intensive observation, computer simulation, and on-site experimentation. Significant gains were achieved following the implementation of the system. The most important was the 13 percent reduction in the total mechanic-hours in maintenance.

Source: Smith, Nauss, and Bird (1990).

Number: MOM20
Industry: Rental Industry
Area: Automobile Rental
Firm: Avis Corporation
Location: Garden City, NY
Manager: Peter Fittler, V.P. of Wizcom, Avis Subsidiary
Size: Second Largest automobile rental firm
Service: Automobile Rental

Summary: Avis developed Wizard as a management tool which impacts on virtually every area of the company and enhances operations. It is on-line in 20 countries. All transactions are fed back to the host computer at head office. A fleet system tracks Avis vehicles from time of purchase to time of sale. Previously several separate systems covered these areas. Avis roving rapid return system uses a hand-held computer to print out customer invoices as they return their cars while they are unloading their luggage. Wizcom sells many of its services to the hotel industry, an industry with DP needs frequently similar to the car rental industry.

Source: Robinson (1990).

Number: MOM21
Industry: Retailing
Area: Inventory Management
Firm: Dylex
Location: Toronto, Canada
Manager: Not Available
Size: Sales: $1 Billion

Summary: Dylex operates over 1500 stores in Canada and about 150 in the United States, selling men's and women's fashion clothing. In 1990, Dylex incorporated a computerized system to integrate 900 of its retail stores.

The system is mainly used for inventory management. Information is tracked from the time that a purchase order is raised with a supplier through the time that it reaches Dylex's distribution center in Toronto. The goods are also tracked from the shipment to the stores until they leave the stores in a customer's arms.

Source: Wintrob (1990).

Number: MOM22
Industry: Computers
Area: Manufacturing
Firm: Control Data Corporation (CDC), Peripherals Division
Location: Minneapolis
Manager: Randy Gottwaldt, Divisional Materials Control Manager
Size: Over $1 Billion in Sales (company-wide)

Summary: Control Data's Peripheral Division had been using an in-house MRP system on a CYBER 175. The system was too slow because of the software developed in the sixties. It would take 48 hours to do a full run. Management decided to change to an MRP II system that can run on personal computers. The system was developed by Fourth Shift, Inc. of Minneapolis and comprises 15 AT-compatible 10 MHz PCs on a Novell network using a Compaq 386 as the file server. The Compaq's disks, which house the database are CDC's own 70 MB Wren II. The system supports eight users at a time and 10,000 transactions per week, more than adequate for their needs. One of the limitations of PC-based MRP II systems, including Fourth Shift's system, is that financial modules are not fully integrated with the inventory software. CDC, however, decided to consolidate financial data with other corporate financial software hosted on large systems. The integration of the new system took two months and the system was fully operational in 5-1/2 months. The low cost and high flexibility of the micro-based system appears to have been the right decision for Control Data's Peripheral Division.

Source: Brady (1988).

Number:	MOM23
Industry:	Automobile
Area:	Manufacturing
Firm:	Nissan Motor Manufacturing, USA
Location:	Smyrna, Tennessee
Manager:	Robert Frinier, VP/Director of Production Control
Size:	Second Largest Japan Automobile Producer

Summary: Nissan's MRP II system runs under MVS/XA on an IBM 3081K mainframe configured with 32MB of main memory and 24 channels. Also used is IBM's IMS database. Nissan decided to write their own MRP II system because the cost of acquiring and modifying existing packages was considered to be as huge as writing their own system. The MRP II system was designed with Arthur Andersen assistance and written by the information systems department in IBM's COBOL which calls on the IMS database system. The planning system goes five months out giving a supplier exact delivery times and volumes three months into the future. The system is JIT oriented and safety stock from overseas supplier has been reduced to five days. Local suppliers, especially those with bulky items, are expected to supply as often as twice per shift. The system has been so successful that Nissan was considering adoption of it at other overseas locations.

Source: Brady (1988).

Number:	MOM24
Industry:	Smoke Detectors and Timing and Sensing Devices
Area:	Manufacturing
Firm:	BRK Electronics, a division of Pitway, Inc.
Location:	Aurora, Illinois
Manager:	Dale Berman, Director of MIS
Size:	$130 Million in Sales/1000 employees

Summary: BRK switched from a Service Bureau to the Xerox MRP II software designed as a turnkey system and runs on IBM 370 systems. BRK uses an IBM 9370 with 16MB of memory and 3.2 GB of disk. The system supports between 75 and 80 terminals on the system. BRK's two plants operate under a work order system instead of repetitive manufacturing. The Xerox software is fully capable of handling direct input from factory floor devices.

Source: Brady (1988).

Number: MOM25
Industry: Motor Cycles
Area: Manufacturing
Firm: Harley-Davidson Motor Company
Location: York, Pennsylvania
Manager: Robert Miller, VP/General Manager
Size: $300 Million in 1986

Summary: Just-in-Time and computer-based planning has helped the company become the primary producer of large motorcycles. Harley Davidson's main survival tool has been MAN - Materials as Needed, a JIT tool. The system is a combination of computerized planning system and Kanban system. On floor scheduling is handled by the manually-driven Kanban system while the formal scheduling is done by computer using capacity planning, inventory, bill of material, master production scheduling and purchasing. The software modules run under VM/CMS on the factory's host computer, a 16MB National Advanced Systems AS/6630 IBM-compatible mainframe with 28 CDC 33301 DASD units. The host computer supports 51 plant floor and factory office terminals. Each customer order is assigned a bar code which is attached to the bike's chassis. Harley Davidson's 240 suppliers are given a firm one year order with a rolling forecast for deliveries frozen one month in advance. The combination of Kanban and MRP has positioned Harley Davidson in a very competitive manufacturing position.

Source: Brady (1988).

REFERENCES

Armstrong, D. (1990). "The People Factor in EIS Success." *Datamation* (April 1): 73-79.
Betts, M. (1990). "TI Factory Cited for Automation." *ComputerWorld* (November 5):
Betts, M. (1990). "Corning TV Stays Alive with CIM." *Computerworld* (September 3): 47.

Brady, S. (1988). "School of Hard Knocks" *Software Magazine* (April): 37-44.

Busch, H.F. (1990). "Integrated Materials Management." *International Journal of Purchasing and Materials Management* 18 (7): 27-39.

Crockett, B. (1991). "Major 5-Year IS Initiative Positions UPS for the '90s." *Network World* 8 (27): 63.

Fitzgerald, M. (1990). "Troubleshooting for Success." *ComputerWorld* (November 5).

Haas, E.A. (1987). "Breakthrough Manufacturing." *Harvard Business Review* 65(2): 75-81.

Heller, S.R. (1989). "Technology Moves Forward in the Chemical Industry." *Chemicalweek* (March): 30-47.

Horwitt, E. (1988). "Carriers Land Profits by Empowering DP Units." *ComputerWorld* (March 7): 73-80.

Jager, K., W. Peemoller, and M. Rohde. (1989). "A Decision Support System for Planning Chemical Production of Active Ingredients in a Pharmaceutical Company" *Engineering Costs and Production Economics* 377-387.

Johnson. M. (1988). "Helene Curtis' IS Makes Waves" *ComputerWorld* (December 4): 71, 76.

Kwak, N.K., J.S, Freeman, and M.J. Schniederjans. (1989). "Minimising Moulding Production and Material Storage Costs." *The International Journal of Physical Distribution & Materials Management* 18-26.

McCusker, T. (1988). "Ocean Freighters Turn to High Tech on the High-Seas." *Datamation* (March 1): 25-26.

Miller. D.M. (1987). "An Interactive, Computer-aided Ship Scheduling System" *European Journal of Operational Research* 367-379.

Neve, J.M., and P.P. Crossland. (1988/1989). "From Push to Pull: Improving the Productivity of an Integrated Circuit Manufacturing Line" *National Productivity Review* 8, (1): 35-43.

Robinson, M. (1990). "In the Transportation Industry, IS Offers New Advantages" *Transportation Industry Systems*, IBM Corporation.

Smith, L.D., R.M. Nauss, and D.A. Bird. (1990). "Decision Support for Bus Operations in Mass Transit System." *Decision Sciences*, 21(1) 183-203.

Venkatesan, R. (1990). "Cummins Engine Flexes Its Factory." *Harvard Business Review* 68(2): 120-127.

Wintrob, S. (1990a). "MAPICS Carrying the Load for This Forklift Truck Firm." *Computing Canada*, (November): 8.

Wintrob, S. (1990b). "Dylex Stays with Vendor, Plunges into S/390 Waters." *Computing Canada*, (November): 8.

Appendix follows

APPENDIX

Recent Advances in Crew-Pairing Optimization at American Airlines

Ranga Anbil, Eric Gelman, Bruce Patty, Rajan Tanga

Abstract

Crew-pairing optimization, the most important and computationally intensive part of crew assignment, contends with union and FAA work rules and pay guarantees to arrive at a low cost solution for assigning crews to fly a monthly schedule. The trip re-evaluation and improvement program (TRIP) generates annual savings in excess of $20 million. Considered the pre-eminent solution mechanism for problems of this type, TRIP has been sold to 10 major airlines and one railroad.

Introduction

American Airlines (AA) employs more than 8,300 pilots and 16,200 flight attendants to fly one of the largest fleets in the United States with over 510 aircraft. Total crew cost, which includes salaries, benefits, and expenses, exceeds $1.3 billion every year and is second only to fuel cost. But unlike fuel costs, a large part of crew costs are controllable. Therefore, a priority of the crew resources department at AA is to develop crew assignment plans that achieve high levels of crew utilization. To meet this goal, crew resources has come to rely heavily on optimization systems, spending about 500 hours of processing time each month on an IBM 3090 mainframe computer.

AA schedules its flights once every month. Each flight in the month must be assigned a crew (pilots and flight attendants). Crews reside in 12 different cities called crew bases; therefore, the assignment of a crew to flights must be such that the crew works a sequence of flights that starts and ends at the same crew base. This sequence of flights is called a *pairing* and typically lasts three days. A crew works four to five pairings each month. These four to five pairings together form what is called a *bidline* (Jones, 1989). Since crew costs are affected much more by the quality of the pairings than by bidlines, we focussed on optimizing pairings.

Crew pairing optimization is an enormously complex combinatorial problem because the set of possible pairings is innumerable. All large airlines find it impossible to solve this problem globally. It has been a subject of intense research since the 1950s for two reasons: small improvements leverage into large dollar savings, and all known approaches have produced suboptimal solutions. In fact, a one percent increase in AA's crew utilization translates into $13 million savings each year. Recently, researchers became more interested in crew-pairing optimization because of emerging parallel and vector architectures and because of the development of interior point methods for solving very large optimization problems.

AA's crew pairing optimization system is known as the trip re-evaluation and improvement program (TRIP). TRIP is based on an approach in which the pairings are iteratively improved by generating and solving a series of subproblems; the greater the number and size of subproblem trials, the better the solution quality. In practice, the number of subproblems tried is limited only by the available computer time.

Over the past three years, American Airlines Decision Technologies (AADT) has spent about 15 man-years improving TRIP. The major objectives of this effort have been to increase TRIP iteration speed, to solve larger subproblems, to improve pairing generation, to improve TRIP's ability to minimize the impact of local minima problems, and to reduce the cost of matching available crews at different crew bases to the demand. All of these objectives have been met. The enhancements to TRIP have resulted in annual savings of about $20 million.

Work Rules. Figure 1 shows an example of a typical pairing that starts and ends in Dallas/Fort Worth (DFW), an AA crew base. The construction of crew pairings is complicated by a complex array of union and Federal Aviation Authority (FAA) work rules. These rules vary by crew type (pilot or flight attendant), crew size, aircraft type, and type of operation (domestic or international).

Work rules concern duty periods and rests. A stringent union rule specifies maximum duty length, which varies between 14 and 16 hours. We impose a shorter duty length in the planning stage in anticipation of delays during actual operations. This duty length permitted by work rules is shortened further when the duty involves night flying. Other, less constraining duty rules govern the maximum flying time allowed and the maximum number of flights permitted.

The FAA imposes rules to minimize crew fatigue and ensure passenger safety. Minimum rest requirements are tied to the flying time scheduled in a moving 24-hour window. Without going into detail, satisfaction of the rest requirements can be verified only after the entire pairing has been constructed. TRIP ensures that the final set of pairings satisfies all the FAA and union rules.

Costs. AA uses a complicated set of rules to determine the cost of a pairing. The principal cost component is called *pay and credit*: it is the guaranteed hours of pay minus the hours actually flown. These hours are also called *synthetic* or *nonproductive* hours.

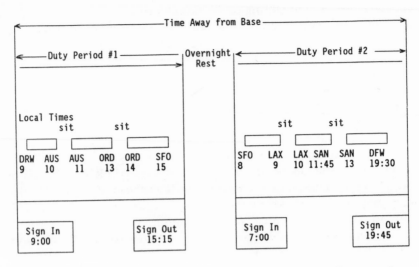

Figure 1. A typical pairing displaying such pairing attributes as duty periods, sits within duty periods, overnight rests, and sign-in and sign-out times.

The guaranteed pay for the whole pairing is computed as the maximum of several individual guarantees and is never less than the scheduled flying time. Individual guarantees are based on pairing attributes, such as duty length, number of duty periods, the total time spanned by the pairing, and the number of *deadhead* hours (when crews are transported as passengers). Apart from deadheads, the two main causes for pay and credit are long or frequent *sits* within duty periods and long overnight rests between duty periods.

Hotel, per-diem, and ground-transportation costs make up the rest of the pairing cost. While these costs are close to $100 million every year, there are not many opportunities to reduce them. These costs are closely tied to the overnighting aircraft in the schedule and thus are not greatly affected by crew assignments.

Other Factors. In addition to the airline schedule size, work rules, and costs, five important factors make crew assignments difficult. First, solutions that keep the crew with the aircraft as long as possible are preferred, since this improves the dependability of operations. This issue is addressed in TRIP by penalizing pairings in which crews change aircraft.

Second, crew assignments must utilize the number of crews available at different crew bases.

Third, crew assignment optimization must consider changes to the airline schedule made to respond to seasonal demand, competition, new business opportunities, aircraft deliveries, and the acquisition of new routes. Such changes are fairly frequent and destroy the regularity of the schedule, complicating the crew assignment process.

Fourth, the schedule is based on a hub-and-spoke network that greatly increases the problem size. This network is similar to a bicycle wheel, where the flight segments serve as spokes connecting outlying cities on the rim to a hub city in the center. AA has two major hubs (Dallas/Fort Worth and Chicago O'Hare) and five other, smaller hubs (Nashville, Raleigh/Durham, San Juan, San Jose, and Miami). These hubs provide many connecting opportunities which lead to an explosion of possible crew pairings.

Finally, the maximum number of days that a pairing is allowed to operate limits the total number of possible pairings. It is company policy to keep the value of this parameter as small as possible, in part, because it is difficult to reassign crews scheduled to work long pairings in the event of weather and maintenance delays during actual operations. More important, long pairings rarely save pay and credit, and enormous resources can be wasted looking at the possibilities. Crew resources sets this TRIP parameter at three to six days, depending on whether it is planning crews for domestic or international operations.

The Crew-Assignment Process. At the heart of crew assignment is the airline schedule. Forty days prior to the targeted month, the scheduling/ capacity planning department provides crew resources with a monthly flight schedule. Crew resources has three weeks to assign crews to the schedule.

Crews are assigned on a fleet-by-fleet basis because pilots are qualified to fly only one particular fleet. AA has two very large domestic fleets (McDonnel Douglas 80 and Boeing 727) and six other smaller fleets (Douglas Corporation 10, Airbus 300, Boeing 737, Boeing 747, Boeing 757/767 and British Aerospace 146). The approach AA uses to assign crews originated in the 1950s. This approach attacks a targeted month's schedule by solving three consecutive problems known as the *daily* problem, the *weekly* problem, and the *changeover* problem. Each of these three problems is optimized independently. The daily problem consists of pairings that contain flights that operate every day of the month; the weekly problem consists of pairings that contain flights that operate only during weekends; and the changeover problem consists of pairings that contain flights that operate once a month (Figure 2). It has been essential to employ this scheme of decomposition given the enormous size of the monthly problem and the limited technologies to date.

TRIP History. Until the early 1970s, crew analysts constructed pairings for the daily, weekly, and changeover problems manually. They punched

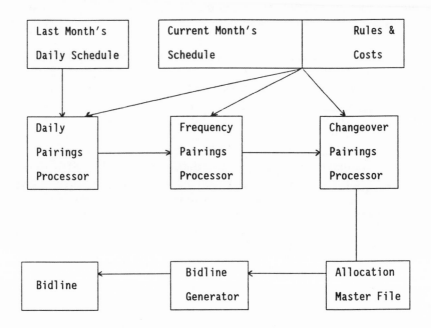

Figure 2.   An overview of the crew assignment system.

flight segments on cards with flight number, departure station and time, arrival station and time, aircraft type, and the aircraft's next flight number and sorted these cards manually into legal pairings. Legality checking was tedious and time consuming. Overall, delivering the monthly assignment on time left little time for pairing optimization.

The first major improvement came in 1971; TRIP was developed at AA to solve the daily problem. It was based on the methodology developed by Rubin (1973), (Figure 3). To start the procedure, the analysts manually constructed an initial set of pairings on cards. These pairings did not have to be legal or of high quality. The TRIP program iteratively improved this solution while removing all illegal pairings in the process, thus saving a great deal of time.

Each TRIP iteration has three basic steps: subproblem selection, pairing generation, and pairing optimization. In subproblem selection, TRIP selects two to five parings from the total solution, either randomly or systematically from a list of all possible subproblem combinations. All other pairings are locked out of the iteration. A miniature daily problem is obtained from the subproblem segments, which is then solved globally by exhaustively generating all possible combinations of pairings in the second step and solving for the best pairings in the third step. If the best pairings

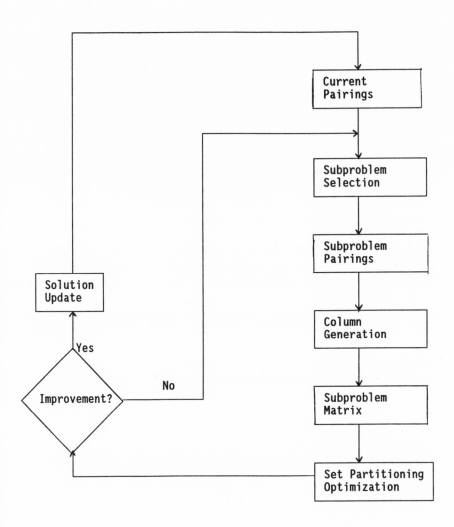

Figure 3. The TRIP subproblem methodology.

are different from the incumbent subproblem pairings, it implies an improvement, and the best pairings replace the incumbents. This iterative scheme is continued for the computer time specified.

Each subproblem is formulated as a set-partitioning problem (Garfinkel and Nemhauser, 1972). This well-researched problem uses a zero-one matrix where the rows represent the generated combinations of pairings. A matrix entry of one implies that the corresponding pairing covered the particular segment, and a matrix entry of zero implies otherwise. The objective is to find the set of minimum-cost columns that cover all the rows exactly once.

To solve this problem, TRIP used an implicit enumeration method that handled matrices with at most 50 rows and 300 columns. The TRIP subproblem size was therefore kept to at most five pairings. Typically five pairings in a subproblem would result in 50 flight segments (rows) and generate 300 different combinations of pairings (columns). The appendix describes this problem in mathematical terms.

Although the TRIP methodology has not changed since 1971, operations researchers at AA have periodically improved both its scope and its technology. They have improved its scope by extending it to process weekly and changeover pairings, adjusting the pairings to satisfy the number of crews available at different crew bases, and accommodating new work rules as well as the rules of other airlines. They have made technological improvements in all three areas of TRIP: subproblem selection, pairing generation, and subproblem optimization. Gershkoff (1987, 1989) describes the enhancements made to TRIP until 1986. We will discuss AADT's improvements to TRIP over the last three years.

Recent TRIP Enhancements. In recent years, AADT has made an effort to enhance TRIP for two reasons: small improvements leverage into large dollar savings, and TRIP produces suboptimal solutions. In fact, a one percent increase in crew utilization translates to savings of $13 million every year. This effort has focussed on the daily problem because of the potential savings involved and had the following objectives:

- To increase TRIP iteration speed,
- To solve larger subproblems,
- To improve pairing generation,
- To improve TRIP's ability to minimize the impact of local minima problems, and
- To reduce the cost of achieving the desired crew levels at different crew bases.

TRIP Iteration Speed. AADT performed a study in mid-1986 that clearly showed that TRIP produced significantly better results as it performed more subproblem trials. Table 1 summarizes the results of this study. Clearly additional savings could be realized if the crew resources department had a faster TRIP system.

In the three-year period from 1986 to 1989, AADT significantly increased TRIP iteration speed by improving both hardware and software. AADT

Table 1.

Monthly Schedule	Solution Used	Solution after 300 CPU Minutes	Missed Savings
Jan 727, 1986	$2,025,390/mo	$1,801,890/mo	$222,000/mo
Feb 727, 1986	$2,073,930/mo	$1,942,980/mo	$129,450/mo
Mar 727, 1986	$2,003,190/mo	$1,857,030/mo	$144,660/mo
Apr 727, 1986	$2,120,610/mo	$1,966,800/mo	$153,810/mo

Note: The first column shows the monthly schedules used for this study; the Boeing 727 was chosen because it was the largest fleet at that time. The second column contains the costs of the crew assignment plans obtained by the crew resources department in the three-week time frame available. The third column shows the costs of the solutions produced by TRIP using the crew resources solutions as inputs. Each of the runs were made for 300 CPU minutes on an IBM 3090 computer and had about 900 TRIP subproblem trials. The last column shows the missed savings after subtracting the CPU cost at $5 per minute.

investigated new hardware systems from work stations to supercomputers, as well as parallel and vector architectures and recommended that TRIP be run on powerful work stations during business hours when mainframe turnaround time is prohibitive.

In the software area, AADT has increased TRIP speed tenfold. TRIP spends 99 percent of its time in two areas: column (pairing) generation and optimization. AADT achieved tenfold speedup in TRIP by improving both pairing generation and optimization. The latest TRIP version performs 30 iterations per minute compared to three iterations per minute in the 1986 version on the same IBM 3090 computer.

TRIP's speed in generating pairings has been increased tenfold by reducing the data processing necessary. The 1986 TRIP version had a design flaw in that it assumed only 640K of mainframe memory. Consequently, it relied on constant regeneration of data. In the last three years, we have developed customized techniques to preprocess data and to maintain interim data that have greatly reduced data processing. To support these techniques, we created new data structures using pointers and linked lists. The TRIP pairing generation today produces 5,000 pairings a second compared to 500 pairings a second in 1986 on the same IBM 3090 computer.

To solve set-partitioning problems, TRIP used an LP-based optimizer developed by Marsten (1974). It took a lot of time to solve problems with more than 100 rows. Recently, AADT, in a joint effort with Thomas Chan of Southern Methodist University, developed a novel hybrid algorithm involving both Lagrangian relaxation and linear programming. The basic idea is to quickly determine a good set of Lagrangian multipliers (Chan, Bean, and Yano, 1987) and to initiate the LP at an advanced starting point. This hybrid algorithm is about 10 times faster than the 1986 optimizer. The largest TRIP subproblem that the 1986 TRIP optimizer could solve contained 100 rows and 5,000 columns, and it would take the 1986 TRIP optimizer about 10 seconds to solve this problem on an IBM 3090 computer. The hybrid algorithm solves this problem in one second on the same computer.

Larger Subproblems. Solution quality is affected by both subproblem size and the number of subproblem trials performed. At the start of the execution, a small subproblem size of five to 10 pairings is used and thousands of subproblem trials are performed. But as cost reductions taper off, a larger subproblem size is necessary. Table 2 illustrates how the search space (all possible combinations of pairings) exponentially increases with the number of pairings in a subproblem. The 1986 TRIP version could handle subproblems with at most 5,000 generated pairings; as a result, the subproblem size was limited to about 10 pairings. Now, subproblems with up to 100,000 generated pairings can be solved using column screening techniques developed by AADT. The basic idea in column screening is to reject a pairing if its reduced cost exceeds a threshold value. Reduced costs are computed efficiently using heuristics based on Lagrangian relaxation (Geoffrion, 1974; Fisher and Kedia, 1986). Using these techniques, we can now achieve global solutions for AA's small fleets and use much larger subproblems for the large fleets.

Table 2.   The number of pairings generated for differet subproblem sizes.

Subproblem Size (Pairings)	Number of Pairings Generated
2	20
5	200
10	1,000
15	10,000
20	25,000
25	100,000

Pairing Generation. Since 1986, AADT has implemented new techniques to generate pairings selectively. These techniques reduce the number of pairings generated per subproblem and increase the TRIP iteration speed. One effective technique limits the search at the hubs to crew connections during the same day. Another technique focuses on overnight crew connections at outlying (non-hub) cities using heuristics based on crew planning experience. A third technique maintains a history of "good" crew connections in low, reduced-cost pairings as the pairings are generated over many subproblem trials and imposes them during subsequent pairing generation.

Local Minima.   A major concern in using any subproblem approach is that different sequences of subproblems can lead to different solutions because of the presence of local minima. There is no way of knowing a priori which sequence will provide the best solution. In recent years, AADT has developed three techniques to minimize the impact of local minima.

Often, for each subproblem, alternative optimal pairings may exist. Selecting one alternative over another may trap the procedure in a local minima. The first technique simultaneously considers alternative optimal pairings and the solution paths they generate, allowing TRIP to minimize the impact of local minima. This is a very innovative enhancement.

The second technique to reduce the impact of local minima is to solve larger subproblems. Local minima for the larger subproblems are then closer to the global minima for the entire problems.

The third technique used to avoid local minima is to allow the model to make moves that initially may not reduce the total cost. After several subproblem trials, however, the procedure may find new directions that result in lower cost (Glover, 1986). This technique has been customized to AA's hub-and-spoke flight network.

Crew Manpower.   Pairings in a crew assignment can originate from different crew bases. However, the distribution of pairings over the originating crew bases must be such that the flying time in those pairings matches the number of crews available at those bases. In recent years, because the number of crew bases has grown, manpower balancing has been both difficult and expensive. To solve this problem, AADT has developed innovative goal programming devices within the context of subproblems that have been particularly effective at achieving the desired manpower levels.

Impact.   The relative impact of each of the recent enhancements to TRIP is given in Table 3. These enhancements have results in tremendous cost savings for AA. These savings have been estimated to exceed $20 million annually compared to 1986 (Figure 4). The performance is measured in terms of the pay-and-credit percentage, the ratio of nonproductive time over productive flying time in the schedule. This parameter has shown a steady downward trend with a few seasonal fluctuations for both the pilots and flight attendants.

In 1986, the average pay-and-credit percentage was 6.275 for pilots and 3.858 for flight attendants whereas in 1989, the average pay-and-credit percentage was 3.858 for pilots and 2.790 for flight attendants (Figure 4). The pilots account for 75 percent of the total crew cost and the flight

Table 3. The relative impact of each of the recent enhancements on the cost savings since 1986.

Enhancements	Impact percentage
TRIP Iteration Speed	20
Larger Subproblems	25
Pairing Generation	15
Local Minima Strategies	15
Manpower Balancing	20
Schedule Changes	5
Totals	100

attendants for the remaining 25 percent. Taking a weighted average (75% for pilots and 25 percent for flight attendants), the pay-and-credit percentage was 5.670 in 1986 and 3.591 in 1989.

Pilot and Flight Attendant Pay and Credit

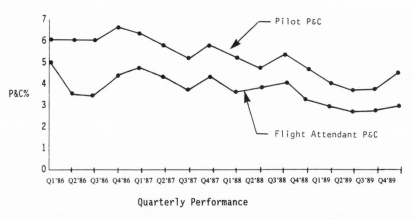

Quarterly Performance

Figure 4. The quarterly performance of TRIP from 1986 to 1989.

The difference in the pay-and-credit percentage between 1986 and 1989 translates into a savings of $27.027 million annually (2.079 percent of total annual crew cost of $1.3 billion). AA used the same amount of computer resources for crew-pairing optimization (about 6,000 IBM 3090 CPU hours) in 1986 and 1989.

In 1987, changes in the FAA and union work rules helped reduce pay and credit. We performed a TRIP study to evaluate the economic impact of these changes in the work rules. We found that these changes caused about 25 percent of the reduction in pay-and-credit. Therefore, 75 percent of the $27.027 million annual savings ($20.27 million) can be attributed to the recent enhancements in TRIP. In practice, these savings imply an increase in crew utilization, allowing AA to operate with a proportionally smaller crew work force in the future.

We have achieved a tenfold speedup of TRIP since 1986, creating better interaction between the crew resources and capacity planning/scheduling departments. Capacity planning provides crew resources with a monthly schedule about 40 days in advance of its operation. At that time, capacity planning is still refining the schedule and can make slight modifications in the schedule that do not affect marketing. Crew resources has about a week to request changes to the schedule. It is not uncommon for minute changes in a schedule to generate significant crew cost savings.

For example, postponing the departure of a flight by a few minutes might make a pairing legal and reduce the cost of the crew assignment plan. As another example, an aircraft's routing may be changed so that the crew does not have to change aircraft at a city. Keeping the crew with the same aircraft reduces nonproductive time involved in changing aircraft. Such opportunities are now being seized with the faster TRIP system that allows sensitivity analyses of the schedule in the first week.

In addition to saving costs internally, TRIP has generated revenue externally. A rewrite of TRIP, completed in 1987, made it more portable and flexible with many inputs being specified as parameters. If these parameters are changed, TRIP can be used for other schedules operating under different sets of work rules. As a result, AADT has sold TRIP to 11 major airlines and to one railroad company.

In addition to its use for optimizing crew pairings, the current version of TRIP is used for certain what-if studies. It produces results that are closer to the global optimal than the 1986 TRIP and therefore more accurate results. This allows for better decision making. We have not included savings from the what-if studies in the savings claimed for the recent TRIP enhancements.

TRIP is used regularly to study the economic impact of adding or closing crew bases. For example, a study was done for Miami in conjunction with AA's acquisition of Eastern' South American routes. The study showed that by adding a new Boeing 727 crew base at Miami, AA could save several million dollars. This base was opened in June 1990.

TRIP is also used to help decide whether a crew base should be closed. For example, the Los Angeles Boeing 727 crew base was closed because crews could be moved to other bases more economically.

TRIP is used to find the manpower required to operate each crew base. Sometimes, when major airline schedule changes occur, crew must be relocated from one crew base to another.

TRIP is used to evaluate the economic impact of changes in pilot and flight attendant rules during contract negotiations. For example, the Allied

Pilot Association proposed changing the pilot union rule that guarantees three hours of flying in every duty day to 3.5 hours. AA used TRIP to assess the cost of changing this union rule.

TRIP is also used to evaluate the economic impact of changes in operational rules. For example, the minimum time required to change aircraft at hubs is set at 35 minutes. It was proposed that this requirement be increased to 50 minutes to improve the dependability of operations. However, increasing the connection time for crews from 35 minutes to 50 minutes increased the operating costs by more than $35 million.

Future Directions. AADT continues to invest heavily in TRIP research for three important reasons: First, because TRIP uses a subproblem approach, there is scope for improvement. The solution space investigated by TRIP is very small compared to the total problem space. Second, small savings leverage into large dollars savings. Each percentage drop in pay and credit (nonproductive time) is equivalent to $13 million. Third, AA is expected to grow 50 percent by 1995, and this will further increase the size and complexity of the problem. It will, therefore, be impossible to hold the cost savings at the present pay-and-credit levels without enhancing today's technology.

Consequently, AADT is spending a great deal of effort to develop the next generation crew-scheduling system that will be able to handle the larger problems expected. This system will solve problems that consider all the flight segments at once instead of solving a series of subproblems that consider subsets of the flight schedule. Although it is impossible to generate the complete problem for the big fleets, much less to solve it, the challenge for the next generation crew-scheduling system is to identify, generate, and solve those parts of the problem that yield significant savings.

We have achieved a breakthrough in this research. In this approach 12 million pairings were selected from 10,000 subproblems. We obtained an LP solution using a new optimizer developed by IBM called Optimization Subroutine Library (OSL). We developed a novel integer programming technique in a joint effort with Ellis Johnson of IBM (1989) to obtain the integer solution. The estimated annual savings from this improvement are $5 million per year.

AA is moving the crew-assignment system, which includes TRIP, from the mainframe to powerful work stations. There are several reasons for this move. The first is to provide a more responsive and user-friendly environment that will make it easier for schedulers to learn and use the system. The second is to provide dedicated machines so that crew resources analysts (TRIP users) do not have to wait for batch processing jobs to execute on the mainframe, especially during business hours. The mainframe CPUs work at about 99 percent of their capacity at AA and consequently jobs queue up to be executed. Work stations are much cheaper than mainframe computers, while the processing speeds of the two are rapidly converging. These factors justify the costs of moving the crew-assignment system to high-speed work stations.

AA is also looking at more powerful optimizers based on both the more traditional exterior-point algorithms and the newer interior-point algorithms (Forrest and Tomlin, 1988; Marsten et al., 1988). These optimizers would be used in conjunction with integer programming techniques (Falkner and Ryan, 1987, 1988). AA is also evaluating the benefits of emerging technologies such as vector and parallel processing.

Preliminary results have been very encouraging. TRIP spends about 30 percent of its time costing pairings. This process has been vectorized with a resulting 15 percent improvement in time spent performing this function. An improvement of 800 percent in total TRIP time has been achieved during an experiment using 10 parallel processors on a Sequent computer.

Conclusions

The recent enhancements to TRIP save over $20 million annually. These enhancements include algorithmic improvements and more efficient data processing. The next generation crew-scheduling system currently under development at AADT promises to continue this trend of improvement through both software and hardware advances.

Appendix

The crew-pairing optimization problem can be expressed as the following set-partitioning problem:

$$
\begin{aligned}
\text{minimize} \quad & c'x \\
\text{s.t.} \quad & Ax = 1 \\
& x = (0,1),
\end{aligned}
$$

where the rows of the matrix A are related to flight segments in the schedule, while the columns are related to pairings, and

$$
a_{ij} = \begin{cases} 1 \text{ if segment i is part of pairing j,} \\ 0 \text{ otherwise;} \end{cases}
$$

$$
x_j = \begin{cases} 1 \text{ if pairing j is part of a solution,} \\ 0 \text{ otherwise;} \end{cases}
$$

$$
c_j = \text{the cost of pairing j.}
$$

Acknowledgments

Copyright 1991. The Institute of Management Sciences, reprinted with permission from Interfaces, Vol. 21, No. 1, pp. 62-74, January-February 1991.

References

Chan, T.J. J.C. Bean, and C.A. Yano. 1987. "A Multiplier-Adjustment-Based Branch-and-Bound Algorithm for the Set Partitioning Problem." Department of Operations Research and Engineering Management, Southern Methodist University.

Falkner, J.C. and D.M. Ryan. 1987. "A Bus Crew Scheduling System Using a Set Partitioning Model." *Asia Pacific Journal of Operational Research* (4): 39-56.

Falkner, J.C. and D.M. Ryan. 1988. "On the Integer Properties of Scheduling Set Partitioning Models." *European Journal of Operational Research*. 35 (3): 442-456.

Fisher, M.L. and P. Kedia. 1986. "A Dual Algorithm for Large Scale Set Partitioning." Department of Decision Sciences, The Wharton School, University of Pennsylvania.

Forrest, J. and J. Tomlin. 1988. "Vector Processing in Simplex and Interior Methods for Linear Programming." *IBM Research Report*, RJ 6390. New York: Yorktown Heights.

Garfinkel, R.S. and G.L. Nemhauser. 1972. *Integer Programming* New York: John Wiley and Sons.

Geoffrion, A.M. 1974. "Lagrangian Relaxation for Integer Programming." Pp. 82-114 in *Mathematical Programming Study 2: Approaches to Integer Programming.* edited by M.L. Balinski. Amsterdam: The Netherlands.

Gershkoff, I. 1987. "American's System for Building Crew Pairings." *Airline Executive* 11 (9): 20-22.

Gershkoff, I. 1989. "Optimizing Flight Crew Schedules." *Interfaces*. 19 (4) 29-43.

Glover, F. 1986. "Future Paths for Integer Programming and Links to Artificial Intelligence." *Computer and Operations Research*, (5): 533-549.

Johnson, E.L. 1989. "Modeling and Strong Linear Programs for Mixed Integer Programming." Pp 1-44 in *Algorithms and Model Formulation in Mathematical Programming*, edited by S.W. Wallace. Berlin: Springer Verlag.

Jones, R.D. 1989. "Development of an Automated Airline Crew Bid Generation System." *Interfaces* 19 (4): 44-51.

Marsten, R.E. 1974. "An Algorithm for Large Set Partitioning Problems." *Management Science* 20 (5): 774-787.

Marsten, R.E., M.J. Saltzman, D.R. Shanno, G.S. Pierce, and J.F. Ballintijn. 1988. "Implementation of a Dual Affine Interior Point Algorithm for Linear Programming." CMI-WPS-88-06, Department of Management Information Systems, University of Arizona.

Rubin, J. 1973. "A Technique for the Solution of Massive Set-Covering Problems with Application to Airline Crew Scheduling." *Transportation Science* 7 (1): 34-48.

Spitzer, M. 1987. "Crew Scheduling with Personal Computer." *Airline Executive* 11 (10): 24-27.

STRATEGIC INFORMATION SYSTEMS FOR MARKETING AND SALES MANAGEMENT

Robert P. Cerveny, C. Carl Pegels, and

G. Lawrence Sanders

INTRODUCTION

Marketing and Sales Management Information Systems (MKIS) are aimed at assisting the marketing and sales functions within organizations. Staff members from the clerical to the senior management level utilize these systems.

One way to view a MKIS (Mayros, 1990) is as an organized set of data that encompasses multiple origination points, entries, and outputs. These information systems assist in improving revenue, market opportunities, market positioning and customer support. They may also be used to answer routine questions about the company's product, customer, sales force and markets. Additionally, marketing managers and executives use the information which sales and marketing systems provide. The next generation of these systems will integrate external information and intelligence with internal data on financial, production, sales and customer trends. The result will be an electronic executive briefing system that details trends and projections in markets, customer segments, competitors, industries, and technologies. The evolution of use of these systems forces companies to restructure existing data files and link those files to tools on end user workstations. Managerial and executive needs will continue to be met by developing special purpose programs to extract the information needed.

Close (1991) suggests that automating marketing and sales information is useful for improving related productivity. Marketing and sales activities cost an average of 15 to 35 percent of total corporate costs. It is estimated that the cost of marketing and sales activities can be decreased by 10 percent to 30 percent through automation. In order to implement these automated information systems, companies must evaluate their current sales and marketing information systems, define clear and specific objectives and goals, designate a task force to carry out the project, and obtain an open-ended system, preferably using a fourth generation language with a relational database. The information system must be capable of corporate-wide use by field sales, telemarketing, customer service, marketing, and sales-support management. The system should have unlimited, user-defined screens allowing it to be tailored to the firm's specific business information needs. Other desirable features should include unlimited dated note-field areas, continuous scroll windows, scripting, unlimited query fields, multiple contacts per organization, mirroring, word processing for mailing lists, letter generation, direct mailings, reporting and tracking capabilities and a security system with several levels. Look-up lists, pop-up windows, and help menus are important for the learning phase and continued use by marketing people.

According to Douglass (1990):

... highly integrated systems—those that link direct selling, distributor relationships, telemarketing and direct mail operations—allow organizations to:

1.   generate, qualify, rank-order, distribute, and track sales leads;
2.   fill prospect's requests for product and price information;
3.   update customer and prospect files;
4.   provide sales and technical product support by telephone;
5.   and automate order entry and sales reporting.

Past studies indicate that business to business sales calls cost about $250 per call. Any assistance that these systems can provide in finding customers has the potential to have a high payoff.

COMPUTERIZED SALES SUPPORT SYSTEMS

According to Taylor (1991), management of the sales force (including control and feedback) is the single most important benefit from computerized sales support (CSS) systems, followed closely by productivity improvements, better access to data, and faster response to customers. Companies are now rushing to computerize and gain benefits in four major areas: productivity, information, customer support and communications. Pinpointing benefits from CSS systems can be difficult, however, and many companies report few realized gains in these areas. Computerization can provide higher quality, longer-lasting customer relationships which translate into a competitive advantage. However, companies must watch for increases in the amount of time salespeople spend on administrative work as support personnel are eliminated. It has been found that administrative work often takes more time than before the system was implemented. CSS systems are making salespeople a conduit for information for both the customer and the supplier. Customer specific information is being created to meet needs because feedback from salespeople is being better recorded and utilized. CSS systems provide hard and soft paybacks. Hard paybacks are cost savings and soft paybacks are such things as better sales personnel morale and customer satisfaction which leads to more sales at lower cost.

TEST MARKETING SUPPORT SYSTEMS

Yet another area of opportunity in MKIS lies in computer-support of test marketing a product (Little, 1990). Changes in the marketplace and distribution chain have brought a greater emphasis on speed and efficiency in product testing. Life cycles are shortening because competitors are increasingly adept at copying successful ideas. Running a year-long market test is no longer an option. However, technology now plays a part in predicting market results. **Behaviorscan**, by Information Resources, Inc. runs tests in markets where it has profiled customers and given them identification cards which are scanned each time they shop. This system can monitor cable television viewership and direct different advertisements at individual homes and then determine the effectiveness of the ads. In another approach developed by Nielsen, Inc., the TV market share people, personal scanners are provided to 15,000 households for use at home after shopping. The Nielsen information is downloaded every few weeks via telephone. It is more geographically dispersed than the **Behaviorscan** data and also provides information on the effectiveness of advertising and promotional campaigns. Mall interviews are now being supplemented with computers and interactive PC graphics will soon allow respondents to review new product features.

ELECTRONIC MARKETING SYSTEMS

Still another use of MKIS lies in their use in creating and managing electronic markets for buyers and sellers (Malone, 1989). By using computers to help customers order supplies or provide services, such as the making of airline reservations, these companies are creating electronic markets. Innovative companies using this technology have boosted their profits and net worth and permanently altered the competitive dynamics of their industries. This evolution of computer-aided buying and selling has the potential to disrupt conventional marketing and distribution patterns. Some companies, especially those that make or wisely use electronic markets, will emerge as winners and others, those who are unwittingly eliminated from the distribution chain or who try to lock in customers through obsolete arrangements will lose. By reducing the costs of negotiating and consummating deals and by helping buyers find the best supplier, electronic markets will make it more attractive to buy certain goods and services. Vertical integration will become less appealing to many companies. Electronic networks for companies that perform different steps in the value-added chain may become a major industry.

Successful electronic sales channels give customers real value in the form of convenient on-site terminals, elimination of paperwork for purchasing and reduction of inventories through just-in-time delivery. Sellers create a captive audience and competitors find cannibalizing sales difficult. But all companies usually want several suppliers, so electronic markets fill that need. Electronic markets are ideal for companies which sell standardized products where customers can make purchasing decisions based on database information. Electronic markets are ideal for complex products which the seller has differentiated so that customers can narrow their search according to attributes. Electronic markets help companies and consumers find the most efficient providers of goods and services in as short a time period as possible.

RETAILING AND MAIL ORDER SUPPORT SYSTEMS

In the area of supermarket retailing (Shulman, 1990), supermarkets are using frequent shopper programs to learn about their customers and ultimately to increase the purchases and profitability of each class of customer. They use electronic scanning to generate information on purchases, often linked with the customer's background data. Shoppers are asked to fill out information forms and are then issued cards with codes. Clerks then scan the card each time the customer shops so purchases are automatically recorded in the data base. The scanners also acknowledge electronic coupons automatically. Supermarkets use the data to determine sales, units to be purchased and profits for the departments to help in merchandising and buying. Customers are segmented and target markets determined.

Another major user of MKIS are mail order firms (Kay, 1991). With increased competition for the limited shopping time of today's consumers, mail-order companies are relying more heavily on information systems to create innovative marketing and inventory applications. These systems analyze, massage and manipulate demographics and other assorted customer information that has been collected by their own and other firms.

Banks are using MKIS for bank customer information files (McAllister, 1989) (CIF) which are often used for storing simple transaction and balance data, but could also be used for much more. CIFs allow a view of the full customer relationship. CIF functions can consist of: multiple cross-referencing to define and track relationships, insider identification to track various "sensitive" groups, special codes to identify members of bank affinity groups, marketing codes to identify customer group characteristics, and profitability by customer. The files can detect accounts which produce losses, help in strategic planning, identify relationships between customers and accounts for which they are not the primary owner, and analyze specific groups for marketing purposes. Past customers' needs can be pinpointed for further consideration.

In the retail banking industry, banks must provide first class service to their most lucrative market—individual customers. Because the services are not likely to change any time soon, the way banks service these customers is becoming very important. This is being accomplished by using a data base which is accessible by desktop (called platform automation) and has all of a customer's records and personal information included in it. Customers can be serviced faster and more efficiently and every encounter is a potential sale and because a customer's complete history is available, there is often no waiting time for credit approval. ATMs are becoming easier for the customer to use and include more features such as multilingual access and the ability to order checks or look at mortgage rates. Computers are also increasing service in the areas of balance inquiries (a computer answers the phone and the customer dials through the system to get the information). Off-hours access is provided via electronic scanners and records are kept of phone messages for service representatives.

GEOGRAPHIC INFORMATION SYSTEMS

Finally, the use of Geographic Information Systems (GIS) for marketing (Goodchild, 1991) needs to be discussed. GIS provide geographic access to records. This requires substantial technology including specialized hardware and software for input and output, and special techniques for storing coordinates. But with these enhancements, a conventional database can answer simple geographic questions such as the demographic characteristics of an area or the location of regular customers. Marketing use includes spatial organization of information, exploratory spatial analysis, site modeling, and spatial-decision-support systems. The ability to examine data in its spatial context is enormously important because you can "eyeball" geographic proximity (distance becomes an explanatory factor). Exploring geographic options (patterns and structures) with GIS aids real estate analysis and enhances the products that can be obtained from traditional analysis. Site modeling with statistical analysis allows regression analysis on variables associated with the site's particular characteristics, such as parking volume when sales are in progress, and so forth. Location allocation provides the optimal site selection for a group of stores within a given area. Many of these features suffer from the same informational problems encountered in market research. Regions may change, software capabilities may have limits and certain types of analysis are not applicable.

CASE STUDIES

Twenty case studies were identified which discuss recent developments in Marketing Information Systems. The firms involved range from manufacturing to service providers showing a wide range of applications of these systems in American industry. These firms range in size from relatively small to quite large, again showing the flexibility of these systems. These systems are used for internal control purposes and external competitive advantage purposes. There are three strategic thrusts along which these systems may be examined. These consist of:

1. *Operational and Strategic Oriented Activities. Information technology developments focussed on operational and strategic improvements consisting of:*

    a. Improving the pricing of services and products and segmenting services in various categories or classes.
    b. Forecasting demand for products and services and also potential shortages so that steps can be taken early to avoid the shortages.
    c. Improving efficiency and effectiveness in order to position the firm in a more competitive position.
    d. Improving the flow of finished products and supplies to speed up response times and reduce customer/own firm inventories.
    e. Improving the planning process for products or services.

   f.   Providing information to allow product development, product
        quality or product enhancements.

The most common strategic thrust activity utilized was strategic thrust
activity 1c, improving efficiency and effectiveness in order to position a firm
in a more competitive position. Of the 20 case studies reviewed, 18 firms
utilized this strategic thrust activity. The second most important activity was
activity 1e, improving the planning process for products or services. The
other four strategic thrust activities appeared less often.

2.   *Organizational Activities. Information technology developments
     focussed on organizational improvements consisting of:*

   a.   The integration of databases and organizational activities.
   b.   Speeding and improving the quality of communication
        internally and externally to the firm.

Both of these two organizational strategic thrust activities were commonly
utilized by many of the 20 firms studied. Activity 2a, integration of data bases
and organizational activities, was utilized by 15 of 20 firms. The other
activity, 2b, speeding and improving the quality of communication
internally and externally to the firm, was utilized by 12 out of 20 firms. Based
on the above, it is clear that organizational thrust activities are important
in the development of marketing management information systems.

3.   *Customer/Client Service Oriented Activities. Information technology
     developments focussed on customer/client service oriented activities
     consisting of:*

   a.   Improving the user-friendliness and simplification of use by
        computer systems users.
   b.   Providing tracking of such items as packages, passengers,
        automobiles, freight cars, projects, and so on, for better
        management.
   c.   Improving informational and functional services to customers
        thus assisting them in their operations.
   d.   Insuring that customer accounts are properly managed.
   e.   Management of the qualification process for new customers
        (prospecting).
   f.   Using systems to gain competitive advantage.

The most common strategic thrust activity utilized was strategic thrust
activity 3c, improving informational and functional services to customers,

assisting them in their operations. A total of 12 out of 20 firms utilized this activity. The next most common strategic thrust activity was activity 3e, management of the new customer qualification process. A total of 10 out of 20 firms utilized this activity. The other four strategic thrust activities were less commonly utilized.

CASE ANALYSIS

Activity 1a, the use of information technology in pricing of services and products and segmenting services in various categories or classes allowed firms to be more competitive along a number of dimensions. These systems ranged from tracking price history of customers (Yellow Pages Publishers), to managing pricing of related products during promotions, to being able to charge a premium price for a product due to the customization allowed by the use of information technology (National Bicycle Industrial Co.), to systems which allow managers to understand competitors' pricing so they may position themselves appropriately (GE Information Services). Firms using information systems in this manner included a Yellow page publisher, a PC systems integrator, a bicycle manufacturer and a provider of information services.

Activity 1b, forecasting product demand and understanding potential shortage areas is used by firms in a wide variety of industries to understand what is happening to them in time to manage their inventories. Banking firms and others are using the technology to customize products and services to a market segment of one and to understand what the demand for such products will be. A retailer (Dillard's) is using very close monitoring of product movement to decide how much product to stock and when to order more. By watching very closely trends in product sales, Dillard's has not only been able to reduce inventory, but they can also detect trends very early and order more of "hot" moving items from their suppliers in time to capitalize on the trend. This makes them much more efficient and competitive than before.

Activity 1c, using information technology to improve efficiency and effectiveness, was practiced in one form or another by almost all firms in the study. This ranged from building custom bicycles (National Bicycle Industrial Co.) for individual buyers to being responsive as to exact locations of shipments (Sea-Land Service, Inc.) to letting store managers know what toys are selling so proper stocks of inventory can be acquired (Toys 'R' Us).

Activity 1d, improving the flow of finished goods to allow better inventory control, was practiced by a number of firms. Food companies, with their stocks of perishable goods, are a good example of this type of activity. Companies are using information technology to understand demand for their products, allowing them to tailor production and supply for their retail outlets with the proper amounts of needed goods. A clothing retailer (Dillard's), faced with the ever-changing tastes of customers is using information technology to allow them to keep abreast of the changes and reduce the amount of non-performing inventory while maximizing quantities of moving items.

Activity 1e, improving the planning process for products or services, is used by firms ranging from manufacturing, to financial services, to telecommunications to insurance. Uses range from improving proposal preparation (Metropolitan Life Insurance Company), to strategic planning (Cincinnati Bell Telephone), to planning the number of campaign operators to have available (AT&T American Transtech).

Activity 1f, using information technology to improve product development, quality or enhancements, is used by a wide variety of firms. This activity consists of credit unions using information technology to target appropriate services to individualized customers (State Employees Federal Credit Union), food suppliers developing new products for consumers (Frito-Lay, Mrs. Fields Cookies), and AT&T providing the closest towing service for its customers (AT&T American Transtech).

Activity 2a, integration of databases and organizational activities, was practiced by the majority of the firms. Uses ranged from creation of a database which tracks points awarded to retail customers for purchases which then are redeemable for prizes (Zellers, Inc.), to databases of customer referrals (BellSouth Enterprises, Melton Truck Lines), to providing databases which customers can scan (Prodigy).

Activity 2b, improving communications, was used by a large number of firms. Uses ranged from communications with customers (State Employees Federal Credit Union), to internal communications among executives (Cincinnati Bell Telephone), to communications among different parts of the company so sales leads were not lost (BellSouth Enterprises).

Activity 3a, improving user-friendliness, was used by firms to insure that representatives who were contacting customers were dealing with people who had potential interest in the firm's products (Melton Truck Lines), or directing customer calls to the proper parties within the firm (AT&T American Transtech), or to insure that the services provided were accessible to the customer (Prodigy).

Activity 3b, tracking items, was used by firms to track actual location of products in shipment (Sea Land), where product is within the company (Dillard's) or what items or services are being sold to customers by whom (Baxter Credit Union).

Activity 3c, information technology applications which assist customers in their operations, are used by firms to monitor company representatives in their dealings with customers (Cincinnati Bell Telephone), distribution of food products (various), and a variety of other applications which monitor the interface between the customer and the company to improve the service the customer receives and to insure that it is satisfactory.

Activity 3d, information technology applications that insure proper management of customers, includes management of telemarketing campaigns (Unisys), lead follow-up (Melton Truck Lines), tracking order status (Microsolutions) and insuring proper customer hand off (BellSouth Enterprises).

Activity 3e, information technology applications for prospecting for new customers, include promotional activities (State Employees Federal Credit Union) and insuring that a proper sales representative is contacting prospect (BellSouth Enterprises, Melton Truck Lines, AT&T American Transtech).

Activity 3f, information technology applications which are attempts to give the company competitive advantage include using information systems for points award systems which lock customers who want to acquire points for prizes to their stores (Zellers, Inc., Sears, S&H Green Stamps, Walden Books), direct products customers are currently demanding to the store while the demand is "hot" (Dillard's), and keep overhead staff to a minimum so prices can be kept low (Mrs. Fields Cookies).

Exhibit 1 provides a matrix showing the relationship of the 20 case studies with the 14 strategic thrust activities. Exhibit 2 lists the 20 firms and the industries in which they operate.

The 20 case studies of marketing and sales management information systems follow:

Number:	SMM1
Area:	Marketing Customer Information Files (MCIF)
Firm:	State Employees Federal Credit Union
Location:	Albany, NY
Manager:	John Lawler, VP/marketing
Size:	Not Available

Summary: In addition to market segmentation, marketing customer information files (MCIF) can be used for strategic planning, product development, member survey development and performance evaluation. Direct mail shows the most benefits by matching customers to variables so they will be included or excluded from the mailing. The system also has a word processing function which allows personalization. The MCIF is valuable in identifying prospects for loan campaigns and other promotions. It can create response groups which help in test mailings. This has

Strategic Thrusts/Activities

		Firm Identifiers for Case Studies									
Activities	SMM1	SMM2	SMM3	SMM4	SMM5	SMM6	SMM7	SMM8	SMM9	SMM10	SMM11
1a						x					
b		x						x			
c	x	x	x	x	x	x	x	x	x	x	x
d				x							
e	x		x		x	x				x	
f	x			x						x	
2a	x	x	x		x		x	x	x	x	x
b		x		x		x	x		x	x	x
3a									x	x	x
b		x									
c			x	x	x	x	x			x	x
d	x						x	x	x		
e	x						x		x	x	x
f					x						
Number	6	5	4	5	5	5	6	4	6	8	6

Exhibit 1. Mapping of Case Studies on Strategic Thrusts/Activities

Strategic Thrusts/ Activities	Firm Identifiers for Case Studies									
	SMM12	SMM13	SMM14	SMM15	SMM16	SMM17	SMM18	SMM19	SMM20	TOT
1a		x			x	x		x		4
b	x			x	x	x	x	x		6
c		x	x	x					x	18
d				x						2
e		x		x	x	x	x	x		10
f	x	x					x			6
2a	x	x	x	x	x	x	x		x	15
b				x	x	x				12
3a										3
b				x		x				3
c	x	x		x	x	x		x		12
d			x							6
e	x		x		x	x	x	x		10
f				x		x				3
Number	5	5	4	9	7	8	5	5	2	110

Strategic Thrusts/Activities

1. Operational and Strategic Thrust Activities

   a. Improve pricing;
   b. forecast demand;
   c. improve efficiency/effectiveness;
   d. improve just in time;
   e. improve planning; and
   f. improve product development, quality, improvement.

Note See Exhibit 9-2 for list of firms.

2. Organizational Thrust Activities

   a. Integration of databases; and
   b. improve communication.

3. Customer/Client Service Oriented Thrust Activities

   a. Improve user friendliness;
   b. provide item tracking;
   c. improve customer services;
   d. improve customer account management;
   e. prospecting; and
   f. competitive advantage.

Exhibit 1. (Continued)

Identifier	Industry Area	Firm
SMM1	Credit Union	State Employees Federal Credit Union
SMM2	Credit Union	Baxter Credit Union
SMM3	Telecommunications	Cincinnati Bell Telephone
SMM4	Food Production	Various
SMM5	Mass Merchandising	Zellers, Inc.
SMM6	Manufacturing	Anonymous
SMM7	Telecommunications	BellSouth Enterprises, Inc.
SMM8	PC Systems Integrator	Microsolutions, Inc.
SMM9	Transportation	Melton Truck Lines
SMM10	Telecommunications	AT&T American Transtech, Inc.
SMM11	Telecommunications	IBM, Inc. and Sears, Roebuck & Co.
SMM12	Various	Various
SMM13	Transportation	National Bicycle Industrial Co.
SMM14	Telecommunications	Unisys, Inc.
SMM15	Retailing	Dillard's
SMM16	Network Services	GE Information Services, Inc.
SMM17	Transportation	Sea-Land Service, Inc.
SMM18	Retailing	Mrs. Fields Cookies
SMM19	Insurance	Metropolitan Life Insurance Co.
SMM20	Retailing	Toys "R" Us

Exhibit 2. Listing of Industry Areas and Firms for Case Studies

revealed errors in segmentation strategies and mail pieces. Mailing procedures are streamlined by identifying households versus individuals. The system also generates a series of reports that are used to track sales efficiency and accounts/services per household or individual. The statistics are now used in performance review. The system can identify accounts with incomplete social security numbers, generate correspondence to members affected by changes and auditors use it to check accounts.

Source: Lawler. (1990).

Number: SMM2
Area: Credit Unions Using Computers to Help Sales Function
Firm: Baxter Credit Union, division of Baxter International, Inc.
Location: Deerfield, IL
Manager: Not Applicable
Size: Not Available

Summary: Baxter Credit Union (BCU) uses customized Lotus spreadsheets to track sales representatives' efforts. Representatives record weekly sales, then fax tally sheets to managers who add up the numbers and generate reports and graphs. Trend analysis and profitability studies are also done. BCU also has an Electronic Data Systems, Inc. system which aids in tracking sales results as well. Twin City Co-Op Credit Union (TCCCU) uses a Data General mainframe to run Symitar Systems software to track sales and get report-writing help. Branch-by-branch tracking is also possible. The next step will probably be individual sales tracking and providing individual incentives. North Island Federal Credit Union (NIFCU) operates a phone information center which provides all the services of a branch office. The TelPlus system hooks up to a personal computer and shows managers what's happening in the department at any one time, number of people on the phone, number of transactions, etc. The system also tabulates and stores this information for later recall and analysis. It can tell the response to specific promotion or marketing materials.

Source: Minderman. (1990).

Number: SMM3
Area: Executive Information System (EIS) by Comshare Inc.
Firm: Cincinnati Bell Telephone (CBT)
Location: Cincinnati, OH
Manager: Not Applicable
Size: Sales: $900 Million
Assets: $1.4 Million

Summary: CBT's goal is to increase the quality of customer service. To do that, Commander EIS (executive information system) was purchased to more efficiently communicate internally and monitor service to customers as well as centralize data collection and reports. Commander EIS is made for top level executives, emphasizing strategic information reporting organized into "Briefing Book," "Newswire," and "Execu-View." Features include color coded reports identifying problem areas and the ability to browse through multidimensional information models of ad hoc investigation and analysis. Executives can tell how many customers are out of service by geographical location and for how long. This allows better prioritizing of action. The system also monitors all services the company provides, such as operator-assisted calls and dial tone completion speeds. Commander EIS includes financial reports, historical performance overview and Peer Group (PG) Comparison reports. All budgets are on line. The PG Comparison reports track performance against the competition. Executives use AT&T's 6386 WGS personal computers with EGA color monitors, 1.2 Mbps floppy disks, 68 Mbps hard drive and 2 Mbps of RAM. Courier modems transfer data to the mainframe. CBT plans to add marketing applications enabling the telephone company to monitor point of sale terminals at Phone Center Stores. There are also plans to track call volumes and average wait time for directory assistance and the talking Yellow Pages. Commander EIS will help CBT serve and monitor customer service, plus plan future marketing strategy.

Source: Shanks, and Forsythe (1989).

Number: SMM4
Area: Computers in Food Production, Marketing & Distribution
Firm: Various
Location: Not Applicable
Manager: Not Applicable
Size: Not Applicable

Summary: Between the consumer and food there is now computer-crunched demographic analyses, electronic data interchange (EDI) links, computer-integrated food factories, automated warehouses, truck mounted data terminals, computerized shelf-management systems, direct product profitability calculations, barcode scanners, and debit-card networks. Food companies must please increasingly picky and diverse customers by using systems to streamline the supply chain, add flexibility and efficiency to productions systems, and help marketers read consumer desires.

Shaw's Supermarkets (East Bridgewater, Mass) uses scanner data in conjunction with EDI to streamline direct store deliveries. Ralphs Grocer Co. (Compton, CA) uses scanner data for merchandising analysis and space management and has an automated warehouse for just-in-time (JIT) deliveries. The Vons Companies (California) excels in electronic funds transfer using bank cash cards. Frito-Lay uses hand-held terminals to track inventory and sales. Campbell Soup Co. has used scanner data to become a data consultant to many stores, offering demographic analyses and evidence that promotions increase sales, as well as using artificial intelligence in its factories. RJR Nabisco is noted for its computer-integrated manufacturing. It is heading the DSD EDI movement (direct supply delivery). Sara Lee successfully manages systems in a decentralized corporation and has individual divisions known for managing shelf space and participating in DSD EDI efforts. McDonald's is committed to Integrated Services Digital Network (ISDN). It now has a high-tech restaurant with modem and fax jacks in dining booths. Mrs. Fields has a legendary flat structure due to its use of PCs that run expert systems which have valuable knowledge from its founders to use in daily business operations. Hardee's has superlative financial reporting systems.

Source: Steinberg (1989).

Number: SMM5
Area: Marketing MIS for Competitive Advantage
Firm: Zellers, Inc., Mass Merchandiser, division of the Hudson Bay Co.
Location: Canada
Manager: Not Applicable
Size: $2.1 Billion sales, 200 outlets, 25,000 employees

Summary: Zellers is a mass merchandiser aimed at middle to lower income buyers. It created a mass merchandising campaign modeled after the airline frequent flyer program in 1986 called Club Z. It also has more than 50 percent of Canadian households as members of the program. Basically each member gets 100 points for each $1 of purchase and can redeem the points for gifts.

Gifts start at 30,000 points and go up. Gifts are things that are not carried by the store. When customers make a purchase, they give the clerk a membership card to identify themselves. The points generated by the purchase are automatically added to the customer's data record and the sales receipt shows the points to date. Customer does not have to keep up with stamps or points or anything. Central computer does this. Customer can ask for point status at any time in the store. Some promotions involve offering additional points if you buy a certain product. Zellers can also track purchasing activity of members through sales information generated. System has created customer loyalty and given competitive advantage. Sears, S&H Green Stamps and Walden Bookstores, Inc. have developed similar systems.

Source:	Wightman (1990).
Number:	SMM6
Area:	Marketing Decision Support Systems
Firm:	Yellow Pages Publisher and a Consumer Manufacturer (both anonymous)
Location:	Not Available
Manager:	Not Available
Size:	Not Available

Summary: Yellow Pages created a data base with the advertiser's account number, the heading under which the ad appeared, the size and features of the ad, and what the charge for the ad was. Follows year-to-year changes so it can follow performance by area headings, sales area and sales representative. System has four modules, (1) external variables, external demographic information to allow sales forecasting and analysis, (2) salesforce allocation, (3) pricing, and (4) advertising.

Another system by a consumer goods manufacturer ties retailers and the manufacturer together so they can plan sales promotions. If the manufacturer is planning a promotion on window cleaner the retailer may wish to promote paper towels to boost the sales. The system allows both parties to plan together so enough supplies can be on hand. Paper towel promotion may increase effectiveness of window

cleaner promotion more than manufacturer anticipated, and system allows them to prepare.

Finally, article concludes with lessons learned from
these systems: "Integrate all the marketing phases into
an overall system. Cross organizational bounds,
especially target customer service applications.
Provide access to a variety of information sources.
Establish areas of responsibility. Watch for hidden
costs."

Source: Douglass (1990).

Number: SMM7
Area: Providing Customer Telephone Related Services
Firm: BellSouth Enterprises, holding company for **unregu-
                   lated businesses** of BellSouth Corp., one of regional
                   Bell companies.
Location: Los Angeles, CA
Manager: Not Applicable
Size: Sales: $395 Million
                   Assets: $176 Million

Summary: Twenty-four businesses are covered in this segment,
                   including cellular telephone service and equipment,
                   advertising in Yellow Pages, data communications
                   equipment, and so on.

The author describes the system as "... internal
voice response system to help the sales representatives
in different businesses refer customers to each other.
The network, which uses a patchwork of voice
processing, electronic mail, fax, live operators and a
customer database, is an example of a relatively simple
but clever use of technology to support the organizations's marketing efforts. The system is used to pass
customer queries about different products to the right
sales representative. The Yellow Pages representative,
for example, knows little about cellular phones. The
representative had difficulty knowing who to pass
customer to if customer wanted information about this
area. Now representative either faxes or calls a routing
center with an internal 800 number where a voice mail
system prompts representative for necessary information. Voice message is then rekeyed into the electronic
mail system and, using the product and geographic

location of the customer, sent to the proper sales representative. Database keeps track of leads, representative must act within 2 days or data base will alert a supervisor. Data base generates monthly reports about lead, if sale made, for how much, if lost, why, and so on. System works well because, (1) easy to use so original sales representative does not waste time trying to figure out who to refer lead to, (2) several ways to get data into system so people can use what makes sense for them and (3) used existing technology so start up costs were low.

Source: Douglass (1990).

Number: SMM8
Area: Providing Customer Service
Firm: Microsolutions, personal computer systems integrator
Location: Dallas, TX
Manager: Not Available
Size: Not Available

Summary: Microsolutions is creating a system that takes an integrated customer data base and makes it available to all employees who have a personal computer. Anyone with a personal computer can answer questions about an order, such as what the price quote was based on, and so forth, or, after a customer has placed an order, the status of the order. Order status tracking is done by bar coding the order when it starts the production process and scanning it as it moves from station to station. The data base keeps current with the order status.

Source: Douglass (1990).

Number: SMM9
Area: Truck-load Transportation
Firm: Melton Truck Lines
Location: Not Available
Manager: Not Applicable
Size: 400 trucks, 700 trailers,
Revenue: $45 Million/year

Summary: Melton Truck Lines transports truck load quantities of building supplies, steel and machinery. They use an automated system to (1) assign ownership of accounts, (2) insure necessary actions happen on time and (3) evaluate sales lead sources. They use the Marketing and Sales Management system from Marketing Information Systems, 906 University Place, Evanston, IL 60201. The system creates a database of sales leads: ones who have responded to ads or called for information or taken from rented lists of potential customers and have telemarketers call them to determine if they are interested in Melton's services by following scripts on a series of screens. If a lead is qualified, it is automatically assigned to a sales representative according to geographic territory. Sales representative then contacts lead and assigns an activity code. Some of these automatically generate a customized letter and a brochure to be mailed to the lead. Six days later a tickler file reminds the representative to call the lead. Requests for price quotes work in a similar manner. Closing is still done face-to-face. System creates a customer history that gives information about best closers, best sources of leads, and so on. System also used to query customers as to quality of service, and so forth.

Source: Douglass (1990).

Number: SMM10
Area: Direct Marketing Service Bureau
Firm: AT&T American Transtech, Sub of AT&T, founded 1983
Location: New York, NY
Manager: Not Applicable
Size: $37 Billion of Revenue (for AT&T)

Summary: Combines information systems with telecommunications technology for (1) incoming call management, (2) operator productivity enhancement and (3) caller information collection. For various kinds of promotions, incoming calls arrive at different times and with differing frequency. To balance work loads the system keeps track of which toll-free number the caller is responding to and brings up a screen with the promotion name and a script for the agent to work from. This way one agent can handle more than one promotion. It keeps the agent busy. The company contracts with others and agrees to respond within certain parameters. System "stacks" calls according to conditions set by client company. Managers can determine how long a call will wait before being put in a queue, how long it will be in a queue before an agent is free to respond, when the caller will be asked to call back, and so on. Lots of data is available on the calls, such as number of idle agents available for a call; the number of calls handled; the average speed of answer and length of call; the number of callers that have hung up while waiting in queue; the number of callers in the queue, and so on. System also notifies a manager if response rate is somehow falling below the contracted rate, allowing managers to take corrective action. Also allows historical comparison of agents.

Operator productivity is enhanced via the use of Integrated Services Digital Network (ISDN) technology. The system allows Automatic Number Identification (ANI) which can identify a caller's telephone number. An example of productivity improvement came from an automobile dealer locator service. Originally, when a call came in to locate the nearest dealer, the agent would ask the caller for his zip code, enter the zip code into a data base and retrieve the dealers near that zip code. Now, the system uses the caller's telephone number to automatically search the data base and when the agent picks up on the call, a list of the nearest several dealers is automatically displayed on his screen. This saves an average of 12 seconds per call (valued at 3.6 cents per call) or a 10 to 12 percent improvement in productivity. Another example is a client offers roadside service for customers whose autos break down.

When the customer calls a toll-free number, the data base is automatically searched on the basis of ANI and the nearest several towing companies used by the auto dealer are identified. The information is given to the customer by a recorded voice. This has led to a 30 to 40 percent reduction in costs.

Customer information becomes available as soon as the phone number is known. Data bases exist with demographic and psychographic profiles organized for small groups of people. Area codes and exchange information group people close together. A company can run a television promotion and give a number to call. American Transtech can provide information on the location of callers, the median income by area of callers, and so forth. This provides a good analysis of who responded to the advertisement. They can show areas which over- or under-responded for the nation, region or locally. These systems were originally developed for micro-computers but now also run in mainframe environments. System may be used for lead generation.

Source: Douglass (1990).

Number: SMM11
Area: Videotex (Prodigy)
Firm: IBM and Sears, Roebuck and Co.
Location: Not Applicable
Manager: Not Applicable
Size: Not Applicable

Summary: Prodigy is an on-line information source for use with home personal computers (PC)s. Prodigy offers access to EAASY SABRE (the airlines and hotel reservation system), financial services, shopping, information, education and classified ads. The cost is $9.95 per month. Advertisers pay $40 per month for each 1,000 subscribers who call up their electronic ads on PCs. Prodigy takes 10 percent or more for every item subscribers order. Industry experts are still lukewarm about it because it is slow and the screens do not contain enough information. And the products are expensive (no discounts). Advertisers and service providers say that Prodigy delivers on its promise of an upscale audience. Prodigy executives are making the system more useful with additional features and increased distribution.

Source: Rothfeder (1990).

Number: SMM12
Area: Database Marketing
Firm: Bank of America, Arby's Inc., Pinpoint Information

	Corp., "Time," "Fortune," Cabela's, Inc., General Foods USA.
Location:	Not Applicable
Manager:	Not Applicable
Size:	Not Applicable

Summary: The theme for the 1990s is marketing to a "segment of one." That means creating a corporate database full of details about the buying habits of individual customers and prospects — called database marketing. This requires the firm to extract key data from its own databases and add layers of demographic, financial and lifestyle data from outside sources. The database may be on a mainframe with data base management software, a dedicated database machine, or on compact disks for use in desktop computers. The marketing applications include producing highly targeted direct-mail and telemarketing programs, customized catalogs and newsletters, and special coupons and promotions. The idea is to keep the relationship with each customer going from diapers to death.

Source: Betts (1990).

Number:	SMM13
Area:	Custom Bicycle Production
Firm:	National Bicycle Industrial Co., subs. of Matsushita
Location:	Kokubu, Japan
Manager:	Koji Nishikawa, head of sales
Size:	20 Employees

Summary: This company has a computer capable of design work which allows the firm to create bikes based on the customer's body, weight and size. This all happens within two weeks (there is a wait because the company feels the customer should wait for something this special — production capability is several days). Customers go to bike shops, are measured on a special frame and the specifications are faxed to the factory. They are then punched into a Digital Equipment Corporation minicomputer which automatically creates a blueprint and produces a bar code attached to a shapeless mass of tubes and gears. This becomes the customer's bike through hand crafting. The code serves as a kind of DNA double helix, determining the size, color, and design. At every point in production, a computer reading the code knows that each part belong to the specific customer's bike and tells a robot where to weld or a painter which pattern to follow. A computer-aided-design (CAD) (the basis for all of this) creates blueprints in 3 minutes versus 3 hours for a draftsman.

Source: Moffat (1990).

Number: SMM14
Area: Telestar and Business Television Programs
Firm: Unisys
Location: Not Available
Manager: Not Applicable
Size: $8.6 billions of revenues (Unisys)

Summary: By partnering with Unisys in the promotional efforts, value-added marketers (VAM) can now acquire a broad range of proven marketing methods at a minimal cost. Essentially, Unisys has made available two of their most effective marketing systems to its network of distributors and resellers. Telestar services include obtaining databases, mailing lists, making direct calls and executing mail drops. Unisys also provides a comprehensive step-by-step manual for developing successful telemarketing and direct mail campaigns. The program is very cost-effective for firms to subscribe to because Unisys offers the services well below market average costs. Telemarketing allows value-added marketers to concentrate sales resources on those prospects who have expressed interest in a system solution and are qualified to purchase products. Unisys Business Television enables companies to reach qualified prospects, existing customers and their own sales personnel using Unisys' television broadcasting facilities. VAMs can deliver sales and training presentations to 90 sites simultaneously.

Source: Anonymous (1991).

Number: SMM15
Area: Clothing Retailer

Firm:	Dillard's
Location:	Little Rock, Arkansas based - many Western stores
Manager:	William Dillard, Sr. - Founder and Chairman
Size:	$2.7 Billion per year, 167 stores

Summary: An important factor in Dillard's phenomenal success in an industry characterized by takeovers and bankruptcies is the company's near-fanatical focus on computer technology. Their system can break down sales by store, departments within the store, and items within the departments - daily. Its most important feature is the ability to get goods onto the floor at twice the normal rate for department stores. The program, called Quick Response (QR), reorders basic items from the vendor every week (based on the previous week's sales) without human intervention. Goods that normally take a month to reorder only take 12 days with QR. Sales on these items increased 50 percent in 1988 and suppliers like to work with the system because inventories are reduced as production becomes lot sized.

Source: Caminiti (1989).

Number:	SMM16
Area:	Sales Support Software
Firm:	GE Information Services (GEIS)
Location:	Fairfield, CT
Manager:	Not Applicable
Size:	293,000 Employees

Summary: GEIS introduced a new system designed to automate standard sales support activities and integrate them with value-added network services. It combines an integrated software package with GEIS network services and is intended to help users in lead tracking, order entry, scheduling, sales forecast, and price and product information. The system is based on GEIS' BusinessTalk System, communication software that combines the functions of a key word search textual data base, electronic mail, electronic bulletin board and news clipping services. Each workstation manages its own relational data base of sales files that can be exchanged through the BusinessTalk system.

Salespeople can access information from other corporate departments. Data can be extended to trading partners and customers creating closer vendor/customer relationships. GEIS also allows access to informational public data bases for lead qualification, market research and competitive information, for example. Other divisions can also use the data. Haggar Apparel Co. used the precursor to the system which allowed them to eliminate the data entry function and streamline the entire process. Employees now sell more intelligently through more comprehensive data analysis which lets sales and marketing personnel know their customers better and target sales opportunities accordingly.

Source: Molloy (1991).

Number: SMM17
Area: Transportation and Logistics
Firm: Sea-Land Service Inc.
Location: Elizabeth, NJ based with worldwide operations
Manger: John Parker, Senior VP of Information Resources
Size: $3 Billion provider of services worldwide

Summary: Sea-Land acquired computer capabilities which provide fast, easy and effective access to information in its Pacific Division based in Seattle. This has resulted in a market-driven and customer-focused company. The company's sales and marketing operations have a wealth of useful information in SMART (the Strategic Mapping and Revenue Tracking system). SMART pulls information from a variety of sources including federal import declarations, field representatives and internal records. Revenue tracking allows marketing managers to easily break out revenue by region, country, market segment, salesperson and customer. Overall performance and that of individual sales representatives and managers is tracked, as well as competitor comparisons. Sales and marketing representatives have quick access to transit times and schedules of the vessels and to market share for the top 15 carriers, plus marketing objectives and sales performance for 24 westbound and 26 eastbound market segments. SMART can be used to sort prospects according to potential financial return, helping to pinpoint high-margin customers. The information also yields forecast growth, competitive performance and strengths and weaknesses in each segment.

Source: Bertrand (1991).

Number: SMM18
Area: Retailing of Cookies
Firm: Mrs. Field's Cookies
Location: Park City, Utah (headquarters)
Manager: Not Applicable
Size: Operates 600 stores in 37 states
Revenue: $1 Billion

Summary: The company built a flat management system supported by a sophisticated information system. A single corporate database is maintained on IBM AS/ 400 and S/38 computers. The single database enables the firm to update all functions nearly simultaneously. Also a very lean headquarters staff is required (115 people) to provide all headquarters operations. Each store has or will have an IBM compatible PC with a 20 MB hard disk tied into the cash register. On a daily basis headquarter staff receives performance reports on each of the stores. Store employee interviewing and training is also done through the central computer system. In addition store managers are trained to do employee scheduling using the central computer system. Other functions the computer provides is an equipment failure diagnostic system and a raw material utilization control system. At any one time, the responsible headquarters staff person knows how his/her stores are performing.

Source: Hartman (1990).

Number: SMM19
Area: Insurance
Firm: Metropolitan Life Insurance Company
Location: United States
Manager: Senior Vice President Dan Cavanagh
Size: Not Available

Summary: Customer records for Metropolitan Sales Support
                              Systems were originally centralized on an IBM
                              mainframe. They have subsequently developed a
                              network of desktop PCs, laptops, and LANs connected
                              to 11 central IBM mainframes. The system called
                              SONIC—Sales Office Network of Intelligent Compu-
                              ters—has reduced the amount of time necessary to
                              prepare sales proposals, improved customer service,
                              and reduced the training time for the 15,000 sales
                              people in 1,000 offices. The system has over 100
                              functions, including E-Mail, and is believed to be an
                              essential element in redesigning business procedures
                              throughout the company.

Source: Santosus (1992).

Number: SMM20
Area: Retailing of Toys
Firm: Toys 'R' Us
Location: World-wide
Manager: Dennis Healey, VP - MIS
Size: Operates 451 domestic stores and 97 foreign stores
                              (1991). Also operates 164 Kids 'R' Us stores

Summary: The system currently has Digital clusters in automated
                              warehouses, a Digital VAX in each toy store and one
                              Digital VAX in each Kids store. There are 18
                              distribution centers connected via local leased lines.
                              High speed lines connect each distribution center to the
                              Central Office. Each store can communicate with its
                              distribution center and with other stores. DOS-based
                              IBM-compatible PCs are used throughout the chain.
                              In addition to sales and item-tracking the system is used
                              for employee scheduling, payroll, accounting, and
                              forecasting. Each item is tracked closely on a day-to-
                              day level to determine if its sales are rising, flat or
                              declining. Especially trend markets such as California's
                              are closely watched to discern trends. Early trends help
                              the firm to avoid future shortages or surpluses of its
                              shelf items. Due to communication limitations the IS
                              in foreign operations is not always as far advanced as
                              in the United States.

Source: Robins (1991).

REFERENCES

Anonymous. 1991. "Value Added Marketers Provide New Services." *Unisys World* (December): 20.

Bertrand, K. 1991. "Navigating Through a Sea of Change." *Business Marketing*, (June): 17-18.

Betts, M. 1990. "Romancing the Segment of One" *ComputerWorld* (March 5): 63-65.

Caminiti, S. 1989. "A Quiet Superstar Rises in Retailing" *Fortune* (October 23): 167-174.

Close, W. 1991. "Marketing Manager Outlines Criteria for Sales Automation System." *Unisys World*, (October): 39-44.

Douglass, D. P. 1990. "Building Marketing Information Systems" *I/S Analyzer* (4): 4.

Goodchild, M.F. 1991. "Geographic Information Systems." *Journal of Retailing* (1): 3-15.

Hartman, R.E. 1990. "Streamlining and Unifying Store-Level Decisions." *Supermarket Business* (May): 19-22.

Lawler, J. 1990. "Making the Most of MCIF." *Credit Union Management* (August): 25-26.

Little, J.D.C. 1990. "Cutting Back Costly Shelf Tests." *ComputerWorld* (October 15): 100-104.

Kay, S., 1991. "Room for IS Creativity in Mail-Order Firms." *ComputerWorld* (March 18): 83.

McAllister, C. 1989. "Keeping Track of Customer Data." *Bank Systems and Technology* 26 (12): 46-48.

Malone, T.W., J. Yates, and R. I. Benjamin. 1989. "The Logic of Electronic Markets." *Harvard Business Review* (May-June): 166-171.

Mayros, V. 1990. "Have I Got a System for You." *ComputerWorld* (May 21): 97-102.

Minderman, D. 1990. "Keeping Score" *Credit Union Management* (January): 34-36.

Moffat, S. 1990. "Japan's New Personalized Production." *Fortune* (October 22): 132-135.

Molloy, M. 1991. "GEIS Rolls Out Software System for Sales Support" *Network World* (May 13): 2.

Robins, G. 1991. "Merchant System Key." *Stores* (June): 30-34.

Rothfeder, J., and M. Lewyn. 1990. "How Long Will Prodigy Be A Problem Child?" *Business Week* (September 10): 75.

Santosus, M. 1992. "Super Sonic" *CIO: The Magazine for Information Executives* 5, (7): 88.

Shanks, R., and S. Forsythe 1989. "EIS Lets Telcos Monitor Service at a Glance" *Telephone Engineer and Management* (October 15): 94-98.

Shulman, R.E. 1990. "Getting Started with Your Frequent Shopper Program." *Supermarket Business* 45 (10): 19-21.

Steinberg, D. 1989. "Life In The Food Chain" *CIO* (August): 48-50.

Taylor, T.C. 1991. "From Selling Aid to Taskmaster" *Sales and Marketing Management* (May): 69-73.

Wightman, K.R. 1990. "The Marriage of Retail Marketing and Information Systems Technology: The Zellers Club Z Experience." *MIS Quarterly* 14(4): 359-366.

Appendix follows

APPENDIX

Coverstory—Automated News Finding in Marketing

John D. Schmitz, Gordon D. Armstrong, and John D. C. Little

Abstract

Ocean Spray Cranberries, a $1 billion fruit-processing cooperative, tracks sales and assesses the effectiveness of its marketing programs with large data bases collected through bar-code scanners in supermarkets. Their level of detail is so great that it can obscure important facts and trends. Ocean Spray needed to automate as much of the analysis as possible. Working with Ocean Spray, Information Resources developed an expert system, CoverStory, to uncover the important facts and trends in the data base. Using a series of subanalyses, CoverStory reveals brands and markets that are newsworthy and identifies marketing factors that may be causing changes in these brands and markets. CoverStory is part of an overall DSS at Ocean Spray that permits a single marketing professional to manage the process of alerting all the marketing and sales managers to key problems and opportunities and to provide them with daily problem-solving information.

Introduction

Machine-readable bar codes on products in supermarkets have changed forever the way the packaged-goods industry tracks its sales and understands how its markets work. Although the codes were originally introduced and justified to save labor at checkout, the spin-off data produced provides marvelous opportunities for retailers and manufacturers to measure the effectiveness of marketing programs and to create greater efficiencies in their merchandising and promotion. Ocean Spray Cranberries, Inc. has responded to these opportunities with an innovative decision support system designed to serve marketing and sales management.

Ocean Spray

Ocean Spray Cranberries, Inc. is a grower-owned agricultural cooperative headquartered in Lakeville-Middleboro, Massachusetts with about 900 members. It produces and distributes a line of high quality juices and juice drinks with heavy emphasis on cranberry drinks but also with strong lines in grapefruit and tropical drinks. The company also has a significant business in cranberry sauces and fresh cranberries. About 80 percent of Ocean Spray products sell through supermarkets and other retail stores with lesser amounts flowing through food service and ingredient product channels. Ocean Spray is a Fortune 500 company with sales approaching $1 billion per year.

Until the mid-1980s, Ocean Spray, like most grocery manufacturers, tracked the sales and share of its products with syndicated warehouse withdrawal data and retail store data provided by such companies as SAMI and A.C. Nielsen. This data supplemented the companies' own shipments data by providing information on competitive products and the total market. Such data bases have formed the cornerstones of useful and effective decision support systems in many companies (Little, 1979; McCann, 1986). For some time, however, it has been apparent that a radically new generation is on the way. By the mid-1980s, the penetration of scanners in supermarkets was so great that data suppliers could put together valid national samples of scanning stores and provide much more detailed and comprehensive sales tracking services than previously. In 1987, Ocean Spray contracted for InfoScan data for the juice category from Information Resources, Inc. (IRI) of Chicago.

InfoScan. IRI's InfoScan is a national and local market tracking service for the consumer packaged-goods industry. InfoScan follows consumer purchases of products at the individual item level as identified by the industry's universal product code (UPC). IRI buys data from a nationally representative sample of over 2,500 scanner-equipped stores covering major metropolitan markets and many smaller cities. These provide basic volume, market share, distribution, and price information. Added to this are measures of merchandising and promotion collected in the stores and markets. These include retailer advertising in newspapers and flyers, in-store displays, and coupons. Most of the measures contain several levels of coding; for example, newspaper ads are coded A, B, or C, according to their prominence. In addition, the InfoScan service provides access to IRI's individual household purchase data collected from approximately 70,000 households across 27 markets areas.

Data Explosion. The amount of data is almost overwhelming. IRI adds about two gigabytes per week to its master data base in Chicago. Compared to the old tracking data, the InfoScan service provides its client companies with increased detail by a factor of four to six because it deals with individual weeks instead of multi-week totals, three to five because it uses UPC's instead of aggregate brands, four to five because it tracks 50 individual markets instead of broad geographic regions, two to three because it uses more tracking measures, and one to three because it includes breakouts to individual chains within a market. Multiplying out the factors reveals that 100 to 1,000 times as much data is being handled as previously.

Most packaged-goods manufacturers did not initially understand the implications of two to three orders of magnitude more data. And, in fact, this kind of change is difficult to comprehend. In terms of a management report, it means that, if a report took an hour to look through before, the corresponding report with all the possible new breakouts would take 100 hours to look through. In other words, the new detail will not be looked at.

The remarkable advances that have taken place in computing have helped conceal this issue. Today's technology certainly makes it feasible to store and retrieve all the new data and, although the hardware and software to do this are not cheap, they represent a small fraction of the sales dollars involved, so that, if using the data can lead to more effective marketing, a full-scale DSS with on-line access to the data base is certainly warranted. Indeed, it was clear in advance and even more clear after the fact that the detailed data contain much information of competitive value in running the businesses.

DSS Strategy.   Packaged goods companies today have lean staffs. Many have been restructured and lost people. This is in the face of the huge data increases just described. Although Ocean Spray has not been restructured, its roots as an agricultural cooperative have always given it an internal culture of lean self-sufficiency. It has a small IS department for the organization as a whole.

This situation led Ocean Spray naturally to a strategy of a small marketing DSS organization running a decentralized system where the users do most of their own retrieval and analysis. The marketing DSS for syndicated data currently consists of one marketing professional plus the data base administrators. The goal is to have a largely centralized data base with work stations for sales and marketing in the business units. User interfaces must be easily mastered by busy people whose main jobs are in the functional areas. The role of the DSS organization is to acquire and develop tools with which the end-users can do their own analyses. The DSS group consults with users to develop appropriate preprogrammed reports to be delivered as hard copy or on line.

An important characteristic of the system must be growth potential. Not only should retrieval of specific numbers, tables, and graphs be easy now, but the system architecture and computing power should be there for future calculations and analyses that are likely to be much more computationally intensive than simple retrieval.

Ocean Spray's InfoScan Data Base.   Ocean Spray's syndicated data base for juices is impressive, almost imposing, considering the change from the past and the level of human resources put against it. It contains about 400 million numbers covering up to 100 data measures, 10,000 products, 135 weeks, and 50 geographic markets. It grows by 10 million new numbers every four weeks. Finding the important news amid this detail and getting it to the right people in a timely fashion is a big task for a department of one.

Hardware and Software. The DSS architecture puts the data base and CPU-intensive processing on an IBM 9370 mainframe with 10 gigabytes of disk storage and puts user-interface tasks on 11 386-level work stations located in the marketing and sales areas. The basic DSS software is IRI's DataServer, which manages data and mainframe computation in the fourth generation language EXPRESS and the user interface in pcEX-PRESS. This provides menu driven access to a family of flexible, prepro-grammed reports available on the work stations.

Unlike some other solutions used by packaged-goods manufacturers, this architecture provides easy access to mainframe computing power from the work stations as is needed, for example, to run applications like the CoverStory software.

Basic Retrieval and Reporting. The basic retrieval, reporting, and ana-lytic capabilities of Ocean Spray's DSS are extensive. Any particular fact from the data base can be pulled out in a few steps with the help of pull-down menus and pick lists. Much of the use comes from standard reports: a company top line report, and four business area reports (cranberry drinks, grapefruit, aseptic packages, and tropical drinks) showing status and trends including changes in share in aggregate and in detail, and changes in merchandising and distribution against a year ago or against four weeks ago. Derived measures, such as BDI (brand development indi-ces) and CDI (category development indices), are available. Product man-agers can get a quick update of what is going on with their products. Standardized graphs can be called up, and it is easy to construct new ones. Similarly, users can readily construct measures that are ratios, differences, and other combinations of ones already in the data base. Usage has been growing steadily since DataServer and the InfoScan data base were installed.

Nevertheless, the introduction of the system has required as much learning for the DSS department as for the end users. Some people, especially in sales, made little use of the system. Within marketing, a few individuals took to the system quickly and did considerable analysis but there was a feeling that you would not want to have a reputation for spending too much time pushing numbers around. In fact, within sales, the characteristic attitude has been: "Using the computer is not my job. Give me something that is already analyzed. Give me materials that are ready to use and will help me do my job."

In response to this the DSS department has developed (and continues to develop) tools and analyses that will help solve specific user problems. There are a number of approaches; CoverStory is one of the key directions. In addition a variety of reports oriented about selected issues have been developed. Examples are reports that rank products and point out Ocean Spray strengths and identify markets where some Ocean Spray product is underdistributed relative to its inherent selling power. The intention is to let sales and marketing people identify market opportunities and product selling points.

Finding the News: CoverStory.   CoverStory is an expert system developed by IRI to tackle the problem of too much data; Ocean Spray has been a development partner and first client. CoverStory automates the creation of summary memoranda for reports extracted from large scanner data bases. The goal is to provide a cover memo, like the one a marketing analyst would write, to describe key events that are reflected in the data base— especially in its newest numbers. The project began as a teaching exercise in marketing science—"How would you summarize what is important in this data?" (Little, 1988; Stoyiannidis, 1987)—and has developed into a practical tool.

CoverStory is undergoing continuing development as we gain experience with its use in new situations. We will describe the following aspects of the system as it is now being used: (1) the role of marketing models, (2) the basic decomposition steps embodied in the search strategy, (3) the linearization and ranking processes used to decide what facts are most worth mentioning, and (4) methods for generating and publishing the output.

Marketing Models.   CoverStory is rooted in the modeling tradition. However, by design, it does not directly present model results at this stage of development, but rather reports only data-base facts, such as share, volume, price, distribution, and measures of merchandising. We want the output and underlying processes to be transparent and easy to understand as possible. The program assesses the relative importance of these facts and selects them for presentation by using weights and thresholds that come from marketing models. However, the user is able to inspect and change these values.

Furthermore, in choosing measures of marketing effort for CoverStory to consider, we select a set of marketing variables from the scanner data base that model building experience has shown to be important for driving sales and share. Measures commonly used include:

- Displays: the percent of stores (weighted by size) that displayed a brand or item;

- Features: the percent of stores (weighted by size) that ran a feature ad on a brand;
- Distribution: the size-weighted percent of stores that sold a brand;
- Price cuts: the percent of stores that sold a brand at a price reduced by more than a threshold, such as 10 percent, from the regular price; and
- Price: price can be represented by many data measures. CoverStory sometimes uses the overall average price paid at the register but often draws from a finer set of price measures that many include regular price, average merchandised price, and depth of discount. The regular price is the price of an item not undergoing special promotion; average merchandised price is the price of an item in stores where it is being promoted with feature ads or displays. Depth of discount is the difference between these two. In an InfoScan data base, we can get even finer measures of price by breaking out average merchandised price and depth of price discount by type of merchandising.

Through a marketing model, we quantify the impact of each of these marketing levers on share or on sales volume and find their relative importance. For grocery items, among the measures described above, we usually (but not always) find that distribution is most important, then price, then displays, then features, and then price cuts.

Flow of Analysis and Decomposition. The central idea in the Cover-Story analysis is that we explain the behavior of an aggregate product in an aggregate market by a series of decompositions or disaggregations. An aggregate product is a product that includes more than one UPC. The UPC (bar code on the package) is the lowest level of product detail available in a scanner data base. An example of an aggregate product is Ocean Spray cranberry juice and blends. It consists of many different sizes, package types, and flavors and blends. An example of an aggregate market is the United States, which can be disaggregated into regions or individual cities or even grocery chains within markets.

In doing decomposition, CoverStory follows a style that we have observed in the analytical marketing reports used in many companies. Analysis proceeds by answering the following series of questions: (1) What is going on overall in the aggregate product for the aggregate market? (2) What changes does this reflect in the components of the aggregate product? (3) What changes does this reflect in the components of the aggregate market? (4) What is happening to competitive products? In CoverStory, we go through each of these in turn. Within each of these sections of the analysis, the program follows a standard series of steps:

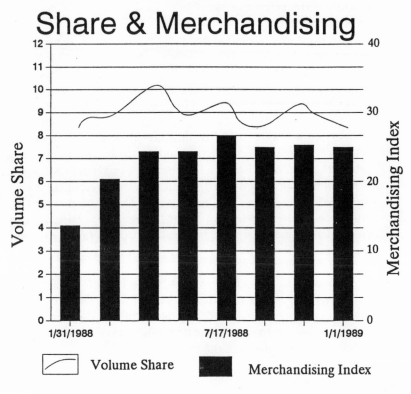

Figure 1.

- Rank the components (markets or products or market/product combinations) by some criteria.
- Select the most noteworthy for mention and for further analysis.
- Calculate causal factor changes for these top few markets, products, or combinations. Causal factor changes are distribution, price, and merchandising changes.
- Rank these causal factor changes; then select the top few causal changes to include in the report.

The need to select "the top few" items from different lists is dictated by the size of the scanner data base. The number of events that can be mentioned is enormous. Without strictly limiting the amount of information in a report, we found that the news drowned in the detail.

Ranking the Products or Markets. We nearly always rank component products or component markets by share or volume change. When we are looking at size groups within an aggregate product, for example, and we are analyzing share changes, size group ranks will be based on share changes. We have found this to be generally effective with one exception. If there has been a fundamental restructuring of the way a category is marketed, share changes may not be meaningful. This showed up when we looked at coffee sales. In late 1987 and early 1988, coffee packaging switched from packages that were multiples of a pound (1,2, and 3 pound cans) to packages that were multiples of 13 ounces (13, 26, and 39 ounces). This made it appear that a large amount of volume was switching into new products and, for a year, volume and share change calculations required special treatment.

Selecting the Top Few Products or Markets. The top few are the few that are the most noteworthy. We generally calculate which component products or markets are furthest away from average and retain these extremes for mention. Normally, this leads CoverStory to pick winners and losers. In some cases, however, when most of the products and markets are behaving in similar fashion, CoverStory will select only winners or only losers. This approach has been very effective, and it closely mimics the way that human market analysts select individual segments of a product line or individual markets for mention.

Calculating Causal Factor Changes. When we point out share or volume changes, we would like to also mention possible causes of these changes. To do so, we calculate the amount of change in marketing support in each of the marketing factors that affect the product. For example, a share change in CranApple sales in Boston may have been partially caused by activity in its distribution, price, display, features, or price cuts.

Ranking Causal Factor Changes. We can generate a large number of causal factor changes when we decompose the aggregate product and market behavior into components. If we are screening 10 product components, 50 markets, and eight causal factors, 4,000 causal changes are candidates for mention. Trimming this down to a small number for inclusion in the CoverStory report requires a ranking procedure. The procedure we have chosen is similar in spirit to the functions used in evaluating positions in game-playing programs (Barr and Feigenbaum, 1981). We calculate a score for each of the causal measure changes. The score incorporates the market in which the change occurred, which causal factor changed, and the magnitude of the change. Symbolically, Score = Change

*Factor weight*Market weight.

Change is the amount of change in the causal factor and is either a percent change or raw change depending on the factor. Factor weight is different for each of the marketing factors such as distribution, price, displays, featuring, and price cuts. These factor weights are intended, informally speaking, to make different marketing changes have the same score if their impact on sales is the same. We initialize factor weights based on analysis done outside of CoverStory based on logit models of the type described in Guadagni and Little (1983). Market weight is a term that makes it more likely that an event in a large market will be mentioned than an event in a small market. We originally used market size but found that this was too strong. Only events from New York, Chicago, and Los Angeles would be mentioned, and so we have softened the impact of market size. One approach that has proven effective is to use the square root of market size as the market weight.

In all, this scoring method yields a ranked list of causal factor changes where such a change can be described in terms of what happened (e.g., price went up by 20%); where it happened (e.g., in the southern region); and what product it happened to (e.g., the 32 ounce bottle). The events that CoverStory describes are the ones that rank highest using this scoring mechanism.

Presenting the Results

We have experimented with several methods for presenting these results. Our current style is to produce an English-language report in distribution-quality format. This has been an important piece of the overall effort and has had a dramatic effect on the acceptability of CoverStory reports to end users. The language generation is straightforward; it is based on sentence templates (Barr and Feigenbaum, 1981). We have considered but not yet implemented context and memory (Schank and Riesbeck, 1981) in our text generation. The use of some randomization of detailed wording through the use of a thesaurus keeps the CoverStory memo from sounding too mechanical. The memo is relatively short and structured so this simple language generation has not been a limitation on CoverStory.

The CoverStory results are published through a high-quality desk-top publishing package or a word-processor with desk-top publishing capabilities. Variation in typeface, use of graphic boxes, and sidebars are all intended to give the memo visual appeal and highlight the marketing facts it contains.

CoverStory is very much a decision support system rather than a decision-making system. The user can adjust all major system parameters, such as who competes with whom, what weights to use for the marketing factors, and how much information is to be reported. The final memo is published through a standard wordprocessing package so the user can edit it, although this seldom happens. Because the memo is automated and easily set up (and then left alone) to meet the needs of specific managers, the appropriate "news" can be distributed quickly throughout the organizations when new data arrives.

A CoverStory memorandum (appendix) illustrates the output. In this coded example, we present highlights about a brand called "Sizzle" in the United States. The recipient for this memorandum is the Sizzle brand manager and the brand management team. The series of decomposition in this report is:

- Break down total Sizzle volume into sales by size groups,
- Look at Sizzle's major competitors,
- Look at submarkets of the United States—cities in this data base, and
- Look at competitive activity in these submarkets.

The analysis is based on share change. A sample of a causal change shown by CoverStory is the increase of display activity to support 64 ounce bottles of Sizzle.

Benefits. Ocean Spray's DSS design strategy has successfully solved several problems. The decision to put users in charge of their own basic retrieval and analysis has generally worked well and, where it has run into problems, the DSS organization has responded by providing increasingly customized tools. The DataServer interface has been easy to learn. Usage on the 386-level work stations located in the marketing area is many hours per week and rising.

The strategy casts the DSS organization in the role of acquiring and building tools to make the users more effective. Consultation with users has led to a set of hard copy reports that are circulated regularly to marketing, sales, and top management and to customized reports that can be called up on line and printed locally on laser printers, if needed.

CoverStory is a particularly desirable development because, with very little effort, it provides users with top line summaries and analyses across a wide variety of situations. Previously this required time-consuming intervention by a skilled analyst. Furthermore the technology is an extensible platform on which to build increasingly sophisticated decentralized analysis for the user community.

The information coming out of Ocean Spray's marketing DSS is used every day in planning, fire-fighting, and updating people's mental models of what is going on in the company's markets. Typical applications include monitoring the effect of a price increase; discovering sales softness in a particular market, diagnosing its causes, and applying remedies; and following a new product introduction to alert the sales department in case of weak results in certain markets compared to others. The DSS is totally integrated into business operations, and it no longer seems possible to consider life without it.

Perhaps the easiest way to express the success of the system is that, with the help of marketing science and expert systems technology, the DSS has made it possible for a single marketing professional to manage the process of alerting all Ocean Spray marketing and sales managers to key problems with daily problem-solving information and guidance. This is being done across four business units handling scores of company products in dozens of markets representing hundreds of millions of dollars of sales.

Acknowledgments

Copyright 1990. The Institute of Management Sciences, reprinted with permission from *Interfaces* 20 (6): 29-38, November-December 1990.

References

Barr, A. and E. A. Feigenbaum (eds.). 1981. *Handbook of Artificial Intelligence*. Los Altos, Cal: William Kaufman.

Guadagni, P. M. and J. D.C. Little. 1983 "A Logit Model of Brand Choice Calibrated on Scanner Data." *Marketing Science* 2 (3): 203-38.

Little, J. D.C. 1979. "Decision Support Systems for Marketing Managers." *Journal of Marketing* 43 (3): 9-26.

Little, J. D.C. 1988. "CoverStory: An Expert System to Find the News in Scanner Data." Working paper, Sloan School of Management. MIT, Cambridge, Massachusetts.

McCann, J. M. 1986. *The Marketing Workbench*. Homewood, Ill: Dow Jones-Irwin.

Schank, R. C. and Riesbeck, C. K. (eds.). 1981. *Inside Computer Understanding*. Hillsdale, NJ: Lawrence Erlbaum Associates.

Stoyiannidis, D. 1987. "A marketing research expert system." Sloan School master's thesis, MIT. Cambridge, Massachusetts.

Appendix: The first page of a CoverStory memorandum.

To: Sizzle Brand Manager
From: CoverStory
Date: 07/05/89
Subject: Sizzle Brand Summary for Twelve Weeks Ending May 21, 1989

Sizzle's share of type in Total United States was 8.3 in the C&B Juice/Drink category for the twelve weeks ending 5/21/89. This is an increase of 0.2 points from a year earlier but down .3 from last period. This reflects volume sales of 8.2 million gallons. Category volume (currently 99.9 million gallons) declined 1.3 percent from a year earlier.

Display activity and unsupported price cuts rose over the past year — unsupported price cuts from 38 points to 46. Featuring and price remained at about the same level as a year earlier.

Components of Sizzle Share
Among components of Sizzle, the principal gainer is:
    Sizzle 64oz: up 0.5 points from last year to 3.7
and losers:
    Sizzle 48oz -0.2 to 1.9
    Sizzle 32oz -0.1 to 0.7
Sizzle 64oz's share of type increase is partly due to 11.3 pts rise in % ACV with Display vs yr ago.

Competitor Summary Among Sizzle's major competitors, the principal gainers are:
    Shakey: up 2.5 points from last year to 32.6

    Private Label +.5 to 19.9 (but down .3 since last period)

STRATEGIC INFORMATION SYSTEMS FOR FINANCIAL MANAGEMENT

Robert P. Cerveny, C. Carl Pegels, and
G. Lawrence Sanders

INTRODUCTION

The area of financial management as defined in this report includes four broad business activities related to financial resource management:

- Money and Capital Markets: This area deals primarily with banks and includes activities related to interest rate dynamics, financial instruments such as mortgages, commercial loans and personal loans, and certificates of deposits.
- Investments: This area relates to the selling and analysis of securities, and the development of security portfolios.
- Financial Management: This area deals with capital budgeting decisions, funds procurement, financial forecasting, credit administration, cash management, and merger and acquisition analysis.
- Managerial Accounting: This area relates to providing information to managers for directing and controlling internal operations.

The financial management area plays a crucial role in supporting all facets of decision making related to the allocation and monitoring of organizational resources. The development of high performance personal computers, local area networks, and special purpose software languages targeted towards financial management applications has improved both organizational efficiency and effectiveness. This improvement spans managerial levels. Managers at both the operational level as well as the strategic levels of the firm have financial information available that is more timely, more accurate, and more laden with information content than ever.

CASE STUDIES

Thirteen case studies were identified which discuss recent developments in Financial Management Systems. The primary themes that emerge in the case studies relate to improving organizational efficiency, monitoring the utilization of organizational resources, and making decisions related to resource allocations.

INFORMATION TECHNOLOGY DEVELOPMENTS IN FINANCIAL MANAGEMENT

The emphasis of the financial management function as well as of all support functions is to assist the organization in meeting its strategic objectives. We have identified three strategic thrusts and they are:

1. Operational and Strategic Oriented Activities. Information technology developments focussed on operational and strategic improvements consisting of:

   a. Improving the pricing of services and products and segmenting services in various categories or classes.
   b. Forecasting demand for products and services and also potential shortages so that steps can be taken early to avoid the shortages.
   c. Improving efficiency and effectiveness in order to position the firm in a more competitive position.
   d. Improving the flow of finished products and supplies to speed up response times and reduce customer/firm inventories.
   e. Supporting top level managerial decision making through executive information systems, decision support systems, and expert systems.

2. Operational Activities. Information technology developments focussed on organizational improvements consisting of:

    a. The integration of databases and organizational activities.
    b. Speeding and improving the quality of communication internally and externally to the firm.
    c. Centralizing the firm's activities, including a flattening of the organization chart.
    d. Distributing decision making authority to satisfy localized needs.

3. Customer/Client Service Oriented Activities. Information technology developments focussed on customer/client service oriented activities consisting of:

    a. Improving the user-friendliness and simplification of use by computer systems users.
    b. Providing tracking of such items as packages, passengers, automobiles, freight cars, projects, etc. for better management.
    c. Improving informational and functional services to customers thus assisting them in their operations.

Exhibits 1 and 2 provide an overview of the mapping of the cases to the strategic thrusts.

CASE STUDY ANALYSES

The mapping of the case studies to the strategic thrusts suggests that recently reported financial management applications support strategic, operational, and customer oriented activities.

The strategic thrust, improving organizational efficiency and effectiveness in the financial management area, is important in each one of the 16 case studies. A very interesting finding is that there is considerable emphasis on bringing the power of computing to senior level executives, as eight of the case studies were targeted towards developing computer applications to support upper-level managerial decision making. Improving pricing decisions was mentioned in four of the 16 case studies. This was of particular interest because it involved the total restructuring of the managerial cost accounting system.

In terms of supporting organizational and operational systems, there was approximately an even division among the 16 case studies. Speeding up and improving the quality of communication and transaction processing through electronic means was critical in six of the 16 case studies.

Strategic Thrusts/ Activities	FMA1	FMA2	FMA3	FMA4	FMA5	FMA6	FMA7	FMA8	FMA9
1a									x
b									
c	x	x	x	x	x	x	x	x	x
d		x							
e						x	x	x	x
2a	x	x							
b				x			x		
c	x	x							
d	x	x			x				
3a						x	x	x	
b			x			x	x	x	x
c				x					
Number	4	5	2	3	2	4	5	4	4

Firm Identifiers for Case Studies

Exhibit 1. Mapping of Case Studies on Strategic Thrusts/Activities

| | | Firm Identifiers for Case Studies | | | | | | |
Strategic Thrusts/Activities	FMA10	FMA11	FMA12	FM13	FMA14	FMA15	FMA16	TOT
1a	x	x			x			4
b					x			1
c	x	x	x	x	x	x	x	16
d								1
e	x	x			x		x	8
2a				x		x		5
b			x	x		x	x	6
c			x	x		x		6
d			x		x		x	4
3a								3
b	x	x			x	x	x	8
c					x			4
Number	4	4	4	4	7	5	5	66

Strategic Thrusts/Activities

1. Operational and Strategic Thrust Activities
   a. Improve pricing;
   b. forecast demand;
   c. improve efficiency/effectiveness;
   d. improve just in time; and
   e. supporting top level decision making.

   Note See Exhibit 10-2 for list of firms.

2. Organizational Thrust Activities
   a. Integration of databases;
   b. improve communication; and
   c. centralization.

3. Customer/Client Service Oriented Thrust Activities
   a. Improve user friendliness;
   b. provide item tracking; and
   c. improve customer services.

Exhibit 1. (Continued)

Identifier	Industry Area	Firm
FMA1	Computer Manufacturing	Digital Equipment Corporation
FMA2	Prepared Food Manufacturing	Campbell Soup Co.
FMA3	Insurance	John Hancock
FMA4	Manufacturing	Cummins Engine
FMA5	Manufacturing	Dial Corporation
FMA6	Insurance	The New England Insurance Company
FMA7	Banking	Bank of New England (1)
		Home Federal Savings and Loan (2)
FMA8	Pharmaceuticals	ICI Pharmaceuticals
FMA9	Electronic Circuit Manufacturing	CAL Electronic Circuits
FMA10	Manufacturing of Plumbing Fixtures	Firm identity not given
FMA11	Aircraft Manufacturing	Hughes Aircraft
FMA12	Computerized Trading of Stocks	National Association of Securities Dealers
FMA13	Electronic Stock Exchange Information	Telerate (subsidiary of Dow Jones & Co.)
FMA14	Expert Systems for Management	
	Accountants	Texas Instruments (2)
		Exxon (3)
		Associated Grocers (4)
		Arthur D. Little (5)
		Coopers & Lybrand (6)
		KPMG Peat Marwick (7)
FMA15	Travelers Checks and Electronic Transfer	Citicorp Global Payments Products
FMA16	Automated Financial Transactions	VeriFone Inc.

Exhibit 2.   Listing of Industry Areas and Firms for Case Studies

Centralizing the firms information systems and organizational activities was an important strategic thrust in 6 of the case studies. Integrating organizational databases are important complementary strategic thrusts in five of the 16 case studies. Four of the case studies also called for distributing decision making authority, reflecting the importance of decision making in the financial management area at the operational level of the firm.

Customer oriented applications of information technology can be found in several of the case studies. Applications such as providing information on customers, customer service, sales activity, departmental activity, product costs, inventory, and projects occurred in eight of the 16 case studies. An important recurring theme throughout the financial management case studies is in creating an environment which supports strategic level decision making as well as supporting the operational and tactical levels of the firm. A further emphasis of the financial management applications has been on improving the efficiency of processing transactions. That will be the first topic discussed in the detailed analysis of the important trends and applications in the financial management area.

IMPROVING THE EFFICIENCY OF PROCESSING TRANSACTIONS

As discussed before many firms in an attempt to reduce costs and put processing power in the hands of the end users, are considering "downsizing" their current hardware from the mainframe architecture to a network of mini and microcomputers. The Client/Server architecture— which involves networking, relational data-base technology, and distributed processing—is thought to be less expensive and very flexible because it puts processing power in the hands of the end-users.

Five firms have been particularly active in this area. For example, Digital Equipment Corporation (FMA1) has developed a decentralized financial system which reduced year-end closings by 2.5 weeks. Campbell Soup (FMA2) developed a financial management system using a LAN network which will also link to the computer integrated manufacturing systems at 39 plants. John Hancock (FMA3) has moved its system for tracking financial portfolios to a PC LAN. However, John Hancock is leaving their mission-critical 6.8 million customer policy records on a mainframe because there is simply no PC LAN that can search and retrieve records from a terrabyte of data in 6 seconds. Dial Corporation (FMA5) has recently hired Andersen Consulting to develop a distributed network involving DEC VAX computers for their financial systems. Dial is leaving so-called "commodity applications" such as accounts payable and general ledger on the mainframe. There are few companies who have such a large commitment to the network solution as VeriFone (FMA16). In addition to their CIM and financial applications, all employees are required to use the E-Mail system for internal transactions. Paper has in effect been banned.

DECISION MAKING APPLICATIONS

There are several case studies which describe systems for supporting managerial decision making for senior level executives. The New England Insurance Company (FMA6) has developed an Executive Information System (EIS) which has a user-friendly interface, permits data searching and data aggregation, and has graphical presentation capabilities. The system supports senior managers in understanding and monitoring the performance of 3600 sales agents. The Bank of New England (FMA7) has developed an EIS to monitor and analyze daily bank operations. The system also accesses information on the banking industry and supplies stock prices. Home Federal Savings and Loan (FMA7) uses similar software to review lending information, track the prime rate, and evaluate investment performance and liquidity ratios. ICI Pharmaceuticals (FMA8) has developed a sophisticated Decision Support System (DSS) to monitor R&D projects.

Expert systems (ES) applications are also finding their way into financial management. IBM (FMA14) has developed FAME for assisting customers in analyzing the financial ramifications involved in acquiring a mainframe. Texas Instruments (FMA14) has developed a system for capital budgeting decisions. Exxon (FMA14) has developed an ES to manage inventories and fixed assets on a global scale. The Associated Grocers (FMA14) has developed a system to assist in buying, pricing, and promoting their products. The system also assists in space allocation. Arthur D. Little (FMA14) has developed an ES to assist a client in variance analysis for cost control, budgeting and planning. Coopers and Lybrand (FMA14) has developed an ES to assist in the auditing process. KPMG Peat Marwick (FMA14) has developed an expert system to analyze bank loans.

SHORT-TERM FINANCIAL MANAGEMENT

The term "working capital management" has been used for numerous years to denote the management of current assets and current liabilities. The term "short-term financial management" puts emphasis on all aspects of organizational decisions involving cash flows in the short term (typically less than one year). Electronic payments and electronic data interchange have had a dramatic impact on the management of short-term cash flows. In particular this has led to:

- A redefinition of managerial responsibilities. Float management will not be a critical activity in the future and will eventually be eliminated. A treasury manager will then be able to focus on short-term financing and investigating better investment opportunities.
- Many services provided by banks for short term financing could become obsolete.
- Payment dates can be made with greater certainty. Thus borrowing and investing will rely less on uncertain forecasts.
- The typical payment terms, of net in 30 days or 2 percent discount if paid in 10 days, may be replaced with renegotiated credit terms because of the speed and precision of electronic payments.
- A smaller investment in inventory will be necessary because of just-in-time inventory replenishment (Sartoris and Hill, 1989).

Several of the case studies utilize EDI, local area networks, or electronic messages to improve communications and increase the efficiency of processing financial transactions. One particularly successful company is

Cummins Engine (FMA4). Cummins Engine is currently using EDI to facilitate funds transfers with their banks and distributors. Cummins has found that the system has improved the accuracy and timeliness of financial transactions. Citicorp Global Payments Products (FMA15) has developed an integrated database system to handle massive transactions related to travelers checks and foreign currency payments. The mainframe-based system provides the company with better customer service and better quality information on company performance.

INFORMATION SYSTEMS IN THE SECURITIES MARKETS

The stock market is very dynamic and complex, and information systems have played a crucial role in reducing uncertainty and providing the right information at the right time to investors. Some of the main advantages information systems have offered are:

1. *Speed:* Information systems have considerably reduced the lag time between transactions, information, and company reporting.
2. *Volume:* Given the huge volumes of shares traded in the stock market, information systems have helped investors in constantly monitoring important stocks.
3. *Evaluation:* Besides providing routine data, some systems also provide other pertinent information to evaluate and provide advice based on this information. At the higher end are the arbitrage buy/ sell programs. These programs automatically buy stocks when the stock index futures are more expensive than the underlying stocks and sell stocks when stocks are more expensive than the stock index futures.
4. *Integration Across Markets:* These systems constantly monitor stocks at separate locations. When the system detects a difference in price by location, it informs the trader who can profit from the information through arbitrage. Analysts believe future systems will have the ability to track information world-wide.

In spite of all the advantages, not everybody is happy with these systems. The use of these systems requires substantial capital investments, which tend to favor large investors over small investors. Many analysts have attributed the stock market crash of 1987 to the use of these systems and they question the wide spread use of these systems without human intervention.

The National Association of Securities Dealers (FMA12) has developed a computerized network for trading so-called "penny-stocks." This system has increased the accuracy and speed for trading stocks as well as creating a less corrupt market. Another example is Dow Jones and Companies with their Telerate system (FMA13). Telerate is an on-line financial information system which provides analytic and data manipulation services for financial markets.

ACTIVITY-BASED COSTING APPLICATIONS

Managerial accounting has traditionally focused on the establishment of managerial cost accounting systems. Recently, there has been an emphasis on looking towards the development of strategic cost analysis systems (Shank and Govindarajan, 1989). In strategic cost analysis the process of measuring and evaluating costs is done in the context of the corporate goals and objectives. This emphasis on linking accounting to strategy is driven by a multi-stage cycle involving strategy formulation, communicating the strategy throughout the organization, developing a plan to implement the strategy, and establishing controls to monitor activities. Establishing controls (budgets, standard costs, variances, and return on investment) to monitor organizational activities related to the strategy also relates to evaluating managerial performance and providing reward mechanisms which are linked to the corporate strategy.

There is growing awareness that traditional accounting and finance methodologies are undermining the strategic potential of new technologies because the techniques used to measure and quantify the benefits of emerging technologies are inaccurate (Noori, 1990). The traditional approach of allocating overhead costs to products and product lines according to direct labor hours is misleading, because direct labor costs are now a minor part of the total cost of producing a product. Poor strategic decisions can be made when so-called overhead and fixed costs are allocated according to direct labor costs. Product lines which are thought to be profitable can actually be losing money, and product lines which look like they are losing money can in reality be making money when traditional cost accounting systems are in place. The activity-based costs (ABC) approach attempts to attribute costs and revenues to activities throughout the product life cycle.

Before reviewing the ABC approach it should be pointed out that there are instances when it makes sense to assign overhead costs using the direct labor metric. They are when:

- Direct labor is a significant proportion of total product costs.
- The amount of direct labor hours and the amount of machine hours used to produce products does not differ greatly between products.

- The volumes and lot sizes for products do not differ greatly.
- A high statistical correlation is observed between direct labor hours and overhead costs (direct labor is thus a cost driver for overhead costs) (Garrison, 1991).

In contrast Activity-based costing (ABC) is desired where there are significant differences in product volumes and the complexity of product assemblies. The focus in an ABC environment is on identifying the *activities* for a product. For example, activities involving product design, engineering, machine set-ups, parts delivery, quality control, marketing, and distribution. Identifying activities, the cost drivers, is typically a function of the way in which the organization does business, though there are often industry similarities. The primary advantage of the ABC approach is that it improves the traceability of overhead costs, thus it provides management with more accurate unit cost data to use in assessing the viability of product lines, the benefits of automation technologies, and the effectiveness of new process technologies.

The ABC approach is slowly finding its way into the financial systems of firms. Three organizations were identified which have turned to the ABC approach to get a better handle on product costs. The first, CAL Electronic Circuits (FMA9), manufactures printed circuit boards. CAL's manufacturing process is a very capital intensive process and direct labor accounts for only 8 percent of the total production cost. At CAL materials costs are 13 percent while overhead costs are a whopping 79 percent of the total cost. The system is used to evaluate the effectiveness and efficiency of department units. SuperFaucet (FMA10), a pseudonym, manufactures numerous plumbing fixtures with literally billions of permutations of styles, finishes and substitutions. SuperFaucet turned to the activity-based costing approach as a way to reduce costs and improve profitability because their overhead was nearly 60 percent of the cost of goods sold. The introduction of ABC led to a better understanding of the relationship between manufacturing costs and volume, and ultimately led to better product line decisions.

Increased competition and governmental mandates forced Hughes Aircraft (FMA11) to turn towards activity-based costing to assist in make/buy decisions, identifying investment opportunities, and product performance evaluations. A primary goal of the system was to obtain accurate product information to support operational and strategic decisions. Hughes found that total participation by all affected parties, such as cost accountants, auditors, design engineers and the U.S government, is critical for successful implementation of an ABC system.

The individual case studies for the 16 firms included in this chapter are presented:

Number:	FMA1
Industry:	Computer Manufacturing
Area:	Interconnecting Financial Management Systems
Firm:	Digital Equipment Corporation
Location:	Maynard, Massachussets
Manager:	Bruce J. Ryan, Vice President and Corporate Controller
Size:	45,000 Employees
	Sales: $8 Billion (1988)

Summary: Digital Equipment Corporation developed a decentralized financial system. The objective of the system was to keep pace with the company's tremendous growth and to give operating units responsibility for information processing and storage. They identified common financial systems and established guidelines for how and what was stored. The systems were linked using advanced networking and interconnecting technologies. They have reduced their year end closing with this system by 2.5 weeks. They also cut 150 data-gathering jobs at the corporate level although the company is three times larger than when it started.

Source: Ryan (1989).

Number:	FMA2
Industry:	Prepared Food Manufacturing
Area:	Integrating Financial Management Systems
Firm:	Campbell Soup Co.
Location:	Worldwide
Manager:	Michael T. Moylett
Size:	55,000 Employees
	Sales: $5.7 Billion (1989)

Summary: Campbell is attempting to integrate higher level financial management applications at corporate headquarters in Camden, New Jersey with factory financial systems (including purchasing, receiving, inventories, bill payment, and payroll) at 39 plant sites. It is also trying to link the financial systems to the systems that control the automation process on the floor.

    What is ambitious about this project is that Campbell is trying to bring together the production and financial management systems into an integrated system. Through this system, higher level financial management applications at corporate headquarters will link up with the factory-level financial systems (including purchasing, receiving, inventory, bill payment, and payroll processing) at all 39 plant sites. The factory-level financial systems will in turn be linked to the local CIM systems. This integrated system also links to the systems that control the automation process on the shop floor.

To smooth the transition to a fully automated, corporate-wide CIM/financial management system and to ensure the success of implementation, Campbell is using a lab which houses a duplicate version of the standardized system. At the lab, developers use software to simulate factory conditions and production processes.

They have found that in-depth testing before releasing integrated systems into production is essential. This is particularly true when using new technology such as IBM's OS/2 which brought down the network during testing.

Source:	Sivula (1990).
Number:	FMA3
Industry:	Insurance
Area:	Rightsizing Financial Management Systems
Firm:	John Hancock
Location:	United States
Manager:	Mark Roy, Consultant for John Hancock
Size:	Sales: $115 Billion (1990)
	Assets: $1.5 Billion

Summary: John Hancock has been dealing with the various problems associated with "Rightsizing." Rightsizing is a term which describes how an organization distributes applications and data throughout a corporation. It involves the determination of the most cost-effective and efficient way of doing business. In particular, it deals with the tradeoffs between mainframe and PC LAN applications. Recently, John Hancock moved its system for tracking financial portfolios of its investment clients from a mainframe to a Novell LAN network. However, mission critical applications, such as their service policy system for their 6.8 million customers remains on a mainframe. There is simply no PC LAN that can search and retrieve records from a terrabyte of data in 6 seconds.

Source: Coale (1992).

Number: FMA4
Industry: Manufacturer of diesel engines, component systems and power systems for larger trucks
Area: EDI in Financial Management Systems
Firm: Cummins Engine
Location: Columbus, Indiana
Manager: Martha M. Heidkamp, Credit Manager for Cummins Engine
Size: Sales: $3.46 Billion (1990)
                   Assets: $2.09 Billion

Summary: The benefits of EDI include reduced cost, improved accuracy, and increased timeliness. Cummins used EDI to facilitate funds transfer and information regarding remittances with their banks and distributors. Cummins reduced the time for processing transactions, improved customer credit decisions, and improved overall company efficiency.

Source: Heidkamp (1991).

Number: FMA5
Industry: Manufacturer of personal care products, detergents, and canned meats
Area: Decentralizing MIS Systems
Firm: Dial Corporation
Location: United States
Manager: Not Applicable
Size: Sales: $133 Million (1989)

Summary: Dial Corporation went through an organizational restructuring that reduced the number of management levels and decentralized decision-making authority and accountability. As part of the assessment process, Dial also decided to decentralize and downsize the MIS function. The senior controllership and MIS managers adopted a distributed architecture utilizing a network of DEC VAX computers to replace the central IBM mainframe. Dial contracted with Andersen Consulting to maintain and operate existing mainframe applications during the conversion to distributing computing.

Dial originally decided to transfer all applications to the DEC VAX network. However, the information systems managers believe that certain common applications (e.g. accounts payable and general ledger) with little strategic potential should remain in the mainframe environment.

Source: Robinson (1991).

Number: FMA6
Industry: Insurance (1) Oil (2)
Area: Executive Information Systems Supporting Profitability Analysis.
Firm: The New England Insurance Company (1) Phillips 66 Oil (2)
Manager: (1) Vince Ficcaglia, Vice President of insurance and personal insurance services. (2) Robert G. Wallace, retired President
Size: Not Available

Summary: Executive Information Systems (EIS) have been touted as a way for senior managers to be able to access critical information to assist in top level decision making. EIS uses a combination of data searching techniques, data aggregation operations, intuitive interfaces, and graphical presentation routines to enable top level managers to "drill down" and conduct a multi-layer divisional investigation. Questions to be answered include: Why are profits lower in the West? Why are sales above average in Chicago?

At The New England Insurance Company, an EIS was developed by a group involving vice presidents and systems people to assist divisional president Robert A. Shafto in understanding sales distribution. The system improved information accuracy as well as assisted in the monitoring of 3,600 sales agents.

Phillips 66 Oil has been using an EIS in oil trading and estimates that it produces an increase in profits between $830 and $850 million a year according to retired president Robert G. Wallace.

Source: Jones (1988).

Number: FMA7
Industry: Banking
Area: Financial Management Systems
Firm: Bank of New England (1) Home Federal Savings and
                  Loan (2)
Location: United States
Manager: Jim Peck (1) Ed Nichols (2)
Size: Assets: $31 Billion and 450 branches (1)
                  Assets: $17 Million (2)

Summary: The Bank of New England (1) adopted a "Commander
                  Executive Information System." The system is
                  designed for the special information needs of top-level
                  management. The system allows executives to
                  monitor and analyze daily banking operations,
                  communicate this information to other executives and
                  provide bank industry news and stock prices through
                  the Dow Jones/Retrieval Service. The software assists
                  executives in corporate budget management, monthly
                  financial statements, monitoring strategic business
                  units, loan reports and daily statements of conditions.
                  Executives at Home Federal Savings and Loan also use
                  the software to review financial information on
                  lending activity, the prime rate, investment perfor-
                  mance, liquidity ratios, borrowing goals and the price
                  of their stock.

Source: Anonymous (1990).

Number: FMA8
Industry: Pharmaceuticals
Area: Research and Development Portfolio
Firm: ICI Pharmaceuticals
Location: United States
Manager: Not Applicable
Size: Not Available

Summary: A DSS was developed to aid senior management in
                  R&D portfolio modeling. Traditionally the senior
                  management used cost-benefit analysis to "optimize"
                  the performance of the research section. This was

found to be unsatisfactory as cost-benefit analysis does not consider the "qualitative" aspects of research projects.

Consequently, a DSS framework provided a basis for selecting the projects, monitoring the progression of the projects and thus enabling the senior manager to focus on critical developments which may require specific management attention and intervention. The system has proven to be very effective.

Source: Islei (1991).

Number: FMA9
Industry: Electronic Circuit Manufacturer (FMA)
Area: Implementation of Activity Based Accounting System
Firm: CAL Electronic Circuits
Location: United States
Manager: John Y Lee, Chair and Professor of Accounting at California State University
Size: Not Available

Summary: The article deals with implementation issues of ABC costing system at CAL Electronics Circuits Inc. (CECI), which manufacturers printed circuit boards (PCBs). PCB manufacturing is a capital intensive process and direct labor was just 8 percent of the total cost. Materials costs were about 13 percent while overhead was 79 percent of the total cost. Initially, CECI used standard costs for inventory valuation and product costing and overhead was allocated on the basis of direct labor. Since the direct labor content was less than 10 percent of the overall product cost, the cost accountants decided to discontinue the practice of allocating overhead using direct labor and to use an ABC system instead.

The ABC system was expected to identify process costs, incorporate the complexities of production in costing and identify the cost-volume-profit relationships more clearly for different products. First, 23 key processes were identified. Then, a preliminary list of cost drivers that affect costs in the manufacturing process were identified. A matrix was constructed using a spreadsheet and it was used to correlate the processes with the potential drivers. This was done by assigning weights using a five point scale, five representing maximum effect and one for minimum effect. The cost drivers had to be meaningful parameters of operating controls and also convenient bases for calculating overhead allocations for product costing purposes. Compromises had to be made in selecting cost drivers that were compatible with the operational measures used to monitor and control the manufacturing process.

As a result of adopting the ABC approach, the following changes occurred:

1. Direct labor was included as part of overhead.
2. Allocation of overhead was made across five process cost centers, based on process activity and not direct labor.
3. Work-in-process was valued on the basis of the percentage of completion.
4. Inventory valuation was made for each part number and standards were reviewed periodically.
5. Variance analysis was used to indicate those areas that needed further attention.

Accountants' involvement throughout the adoption and implementation process was key to the success. Soundness of the system was reviewed periodically and the efficiency and effectiveness of each department was evaluated with respect to the system.

Source: Lee (1990).

Number: FMA10
Industry: Manufacturer of Plumbing Fixtures
Area: Implementation of Activity Based Accounting System
Firm: Not Available (Author calls it SuperFaucet. Firm identity is not given.)
Location: Not Available
Manager: Michael O'Guin, President of Activity Costing Systems Hunting Beach, California
Size: Not Applicable

Summary: SuperFaucet manufactures plumbing fixtures with an enormous number of product permutations, extending into the billions of styles, finishes and substitutions. SuperFaucet began to lose money and therefore decided to do a manufacturing study with the assistance of a consulting firm. The objective was to reduce costs and improve profitability. The first phase of the study was aimed at recosting the client's manufacturing operations to resolve make/buy decisions. Because of the enormous number of the product permutations, overhead amounted to almost 60 percent of the cost of goods sold. Initially, the overhead costs for production control, purchasing and manufacturing engineering were allocated to each manufacturing department based on the standard direct labor hours. Tooling, utilities and maintenance costs were allocated on annual depreciation costs. These allocations were obscurely misrepresenting the true causes of these activities and hence their costs.

Accurate costs for each direct labor and overhead department were available and the major task was of redistributing the overhead. This was completed through interviews and matching the overhead to the activities. Eventually 26 cost drivers were identified. The 26 allocations were accumulated into two cost pools. One pool consisted of the overhead elements driven by volume and the other pool consisted of elements driven by transactions. For example, utilities, supplies, equipment depreciation and maintenance are all volume driven while functions such as purchasing, receiving warehousing, production control and shop floor control are transaction driven. Earned labor dollars were used to allocate overhead driven by volume. A transaction measure called the transaction rate, which equated the number of production runs for each part, was calculated and assigned to the parts based on the number of transactions on the part.

The in-place MRP system used an A, B, and C approach to classify transaction volumes for parts. Thus A parts have a high-volume of transactions and C parts have low transaction volumes.

The system resulted in the following changes:

1. The new cost system revealed that a part's manufacturing cost was inversely proportional to volume. This is contrary to the way in which the old system functioned.
2. Product lines once though to be the most profitable were found to be actually losing money.
3. The system revealed that vast improvements in profitability could be made by eliminating low-volume product lines.
4. Make/buy decisions and manufacturing decisions can be worked out in a more meaningful way.
5. The controller was assigned the job of installing an on-line activity-based system patterned after the prototype. The consultant was interested in having three overhead pools instead of two.

Source: O'Guin (1990).

Number: FMA11
Industry: Aircraft Manufacturing
Area: Implementation of Activity Based Accounting System
Firm: Hughes Aircraft
Location: Worldwide
Manager: Jack Haedicke and David Feil
Size: Not Available

Summary: Recent changes in the procurement policies of the Department of Defense has forced its contractors to aim for lowest cost with highest quality, and not necessarily highest technology. These changes along with changes in global politics have forced contractors to participate in cost wars. While manufacturing techniques have improved over the years, financial systems have remained the same over the years. Traditional systems typically focus on areas that have little to do with the real causes of production costs. These cost systems have relied on direct labor to allocate costs. With continued industry specialization and factory automation, direct labor has decreased and therefore current methodologies are irrelevant. Hughes Airfraft adopted ABC due to the various advantages it offers in make/buy decisions, investment opportunity analysis, and in making comparisons across facilities.

The ABC system was implemented over a period of five years, to allow local auditors to learn the system along with the cost accountants. The goal was to obtain accurate product information to support operations management in making operational and strategic decisions. The system was initially tested in pilot sites before it reached the level of experimentation with fully implemented activity-based costing. The implementation took place essentially in four steps. The first step was to break the cost centers into multiple burden centers or basically activities. The second step was to determine how to allocate all central services based on the activities. The next step was to decompose the activities to assure that each activity is accomplished as cost effectively as possible. In the final step, all the concepts mentioned above are pulled together to implement the final activity-based costing system.

This article stresses the involvement of all affected parties, including cost accountants, auditors, design engineers and the clientele (in this case, the government), in the implementation of the system.

Source: Haedicke (1991).

Number: FMA12
Area: Computerized Trading of Stocks
Firm: National Association of Securities Dealers
Location: Not Applicable
Manager: Not Applicable
Size: Not Applicable

Summary: NASD buys and sells stocks through a computerized network which has allowed it to rival the American Stock Exchange (AMEX) and the New York Stock Exchange (NYSE). The move to innovative technology has resulted in more listings and higher retention levels for viable firms. The market has even drawn an extensive foreign listing. NASDAQ was the first U.S. market to go towards round-the-clock trading. It opens at 3:30 a.m. and British investors can now trade directly in over 500 stocks. NASD has caused "pink sheet" listings of penny stocks to be traded more evenly and with less corruption by offering a bulletin board screen which uses an artificial-intelligence programs to track activity and prices. The system is actually making pink sheets obsolete and brokers have more accurate information on prices and stock availability. Because of these advances, NASD is now retaining big name listings, rather than losing them as companies grow and stabilize.

Source: Foust (1990).

Number: FMA13
Area: Electronic stock exchange information
Firm: Telerate (parent Dow Jones & Co.)
Location: Not Available
Manager: Not Applicable
Size: Not Available

Summary: Telerate's growth is finally slowing after huge gains in the 80's. Telerate let the good times roll too far and is now behind in financial and analytical capabilities and data manipulation functions. Telerate provides on-line financial information and transactional services to investors and brokers. Telerate has recently installed a new electronic foreign exchange system called The Trading Service (TTS). Other companies are now offering similar programs with more functionality, such as MoneyCenter by Knight-Ridder and Reuter Monitor Dealing Service by Reuters Holding, PLC. Quotron Systems Inc. also offers a similar product.

Source: Bremner (1990).

Number: FMA14
Industry: Computing
                   Computing
                   Oil
                   Wholesale & Retail
                   Consulting

Firms: IBM
                   Texas Instruments
                   EXXON

Associated Grocers
Arthur D. Little
Coopers & Lybrand
KPMG Peat Marwick

Area: Expert Systems for Management Accountants

Summary: Expert systems applications are no longer confined to universities and the research and development departments of corporations. They are now finding their way into the normal day-to-day operations of corporations. The following examples taken from Brown & Phillips illustrate the diffusion of expert systems applications. IBM has developed an expert system to assist customers with mainframe capacity and financial planning for the acquisition of mainframe computers. The system provides sensitivity, competitive, and financial analyses along with providing a justification for the recommended plans. FAME takes into account operating costs, the tax savings, software costs, and maintenance expenses. The system also assists in determining the correct accounting treatment to use for recording the asset cost. FAME is currently in the field testing stage.

Texas Instruments has developed a system called the Capital Investment System. The system is used by a 190 departments throughout the world for preparing reports related to capital investment decisions. The Capital Investment System provides payback and gives recommendations on the value of an investment decision.

EXXON has hired Andersen Consulting to customize their Integrated Capital and Operations Reporting (ICOR) system. The expert system is being developed to assist EXXON in managing and accounting for inventories and fixed assets on a worldwide basis. The system assists in determining transfer prices for inventory and equipment moved from one location to another, the sales and use taxes related to these transactions, and it prepares journal entries to record the transactions.

The Associated Grocers, a large wholesale and retail chain with more than 400 member stores located in the Pacific Northwest, has developed the Buyers's

Workbench with the assistance of Deloitte & Touche. Ultimately the Buyers's Workbench will assist buyers in a variety of ways including pricing, promotion planning, assortment selection, and retail space allocation.

Arthur D. Little has developed an expert system to assist in analyzing variances for cost control, budgeting, and planning of manufacturing operations. The system analyzes budget line variances for items as well as budget line groups. The system also identifies variances that are significant.

Arthur D. Little has also developed the BUCKS expert system. This system assists controllers and managers in analyzing the performance of division projects and consulting activities by region. The expert system takes into account a variety of factors including environmental and resource constraints by regions. BUCKS contrasts net operating revenue with budgeted revenues, business contribution margin with budgeted margin, and business contribution margin with net operating revenue.

Coopers & Lybrand developed AShell to assist in the auditing process. AShell assists in planning, executing, and the automatic generation of work papers and audit reports. The PC based system uses an intelligent questionnaire format that leads an auditor through the entire audit process. AShell can also test mainframe transaction data.

KPMG Peat Marwick has developed the Loan Probe expert system to analyze bank loans and determines the level of loan reserves needed. The 8,000 rule system was developed using the expertise of KPMG senior managers and partners. The system's knowledge base contains statistical data and projections for more than 150 industries. The output of the system is a recommendation about the adequacy of the loan loss reserve.

Source: Brown and Phillips (1991).

Number: FMA15
Industry: Travelers' checks and electronic foreign-currency payments

Area: Development of a mainframe-base transaction system

Firm: Citicorp Global Payments Products, Division of Citicorp

Location: Worldwide in 33 countries

Manager: Dave Starr

Size: 1600 Employees

Summary: Citicorp Global Payments Products division, headed by Dave Starr, developed an integrated database system to handle massive transactions related to travelers checks and foreign currency payments. There was tremendous inconsistency in the data, in fact it was not unusual to have five people with five different reports containing conflicting data. Another problem with the system is that their 9000 customers (primarily banks and corporations) could not get one-stop service. The system was exceedingly complex, with 42 different applications subsystems and 6,500 different data elements. The system ran on a variety of hardware platforms including IBM, DEC, HP, Burroughs, Perkin- Elmer, and Amdahl. The software supporting the system had poor documentation and was written in COBOL, PL/I, FORTRAN, Assembler, and APL.

The new system contains 2.2 million lines of code. Some of it is written in fourth generation languages. The database management system utilized is IDMS. The system runs on an single Amdahl 5890 model 400e in Tampa, Florida and a 3081 in Buffalo, New York. The current system cost is $12 million and that cost will eventually rise to $20 million over the next four years. There were some technical and development problems which were overcome though brainstorming and by throwing out the traditional development life cycle and replacing it with prototyping and CASE tools. They also cut down on the amount of project documentation during development. System benefits include a 2,500 element data dictionary, a complete customer profile in one place, a complete sales picture by region, and better customer service.

Source: Kelly (1991).

Number: FMA16

Industry: Automated Financial Transactions

Area: Distributed network for business transactions
Firm: VeriFone Inc.
Location: Worldwide, Headquartered in Redwood City, CA
Manager: Hatim Tyabji, CEO and President, William Pape, CIO
Size: $150 Million 1200 Employees

Summary: Verifone's primary business is producing point-of-sale hardware and software that businesses use to validate credit card transactions. Verifone has developed a network of 14 Digital Equipment Corp. VAX computers. Half of the employees use terminals and half use personal computers. The system supports computer integrated manufacturing software and financial software. A cornerstone of their business is an electronic mail system which is being utilized by approximately 35 percent of the company at any given time. Managers receive, on average, 60 messages per day. Because the corporation is worldwide, and all employees have access to the E-Mail system, they often use a cascade approach to producing proposals. In essence the work is passed to different time zones as the work day ends.

Verifone also has an official ban on all internal paper transactions and uses electronic forms for hiring, capital expenditures, and travel arrangements. The system also has financial performance data, project status, manufacturing, inventory, and order status information available to employees. They do not use the highly touted Jointed Application Design approach in requirements determination, but rather use prototyping, one-on-one interviews, and keep track of what users actually do with the systems. Mr. Tyabji claims that the ability to use information technology effectively is what gives VeriFone their greatest competitive edge.

Source: Freedman (1991).

REFERENCES

Anonymous. 1990. "Systems Review — Commander EIS: Providing Strategic Information to Bank Executive." *Banking Software Review* (Spring): 8, 11.

Bremner, B., and J. Rothfeder. 1990. "Dow Jones' 1.6 Billion Baby is Hardly a Bundle of Joy." *Business Week* (September 10): 60-62.

Brown, C.E. and M.E. Phillips. 1991. "Expert Systems for Management Accountants." *Management Accounting* (January): 18-23.

Coale, K. 1992. "Rightsizing Moves Power to Corporate Users" *InfoWorld* 20: 44.

Foust, D. and D. Zigas. 1990. "The NASD: A computerized Mouse That's Roaring." *Business Week* (September 17): 128-129.

Freedman, D. 1991. "A Virtual Company." *CIO* (September): 43-47.

Garrison, R.H. 1991. *Managerial Accounting Concepts for Planning, Control, Decision Making, 6th edition*. Homewood, IL: Irwin.

Haedicke, J. and D. Feil. 1991. "Hughes Aircraft Sets the Standard for ABC." *Management Accounting* (February): 29-33.

Heidkamp, M.M. 1991. "Reaping the Benefits of Financial EDI." *Management Accounting* (May): 39-42.

Islei, G., G. Lockett, B. Cox, and M. Stratford. 1991. "A Decision Support System Using Judgmental Modeling: A Case of R&D in the Pharmaceutical Industry." *IEEE Transactions on Engineering Management* (August): 202-209.

Jones, D.C. 1988. "GAs Tracked With Software System." *National Underwriter* (September): 23-24.

Kelly, T. 1991. "Stalking the King-Sized System." *CIO* (February): 24-34.

Lee, J.Y. 1990. "Activity-Based Costing at CAL Electronic Circuits." *Management Accounting* (4): 36-38.

Noori, H. 1990. *Managing the Dynamics of New Technology* Englewood Cliffs, NJ: Prentice Hall.

O'Guin, M.O. 1990. "Focus the Factory with Activity-Based Costing." *Management Accounting* (71 (8): 36-41.

Robinson, M.A. 1991. "Decentralize and Outsource: Dial's Approach to MIS Improvement." *Management Accounting* (September): 27-31.

Ryan, B.J. 1989. "DEC's Decentralized Financial System Puts Strategy Above Controls." *Financial Executive* 5: 42-46.

Sartoris, W.L. and N.C. Hill. 1989. "Innovations in Short-term Financial Management." *Business Horizons* (November-December): 56-64.

Shank, J.K. and V. Govindarajan. 1989. *Strategic Cost Analysis: The Evolution from Managerial to Strategic Accounting*. Homewood, IL: R.D. Irwin.

Sivula, C. 1990. "What's Cookin in Campbell's CIM Lab." *Datamation* (September): 70-82.

APPENDIX

Allocating Telecommunications Resources at L.L. Bean, Inc.

Phil Quinn, Bruce Andrews, and Henry Parsons

Abstract

We developed and implemented a model for optimizing the deployment of telemarketing resources at L.L. Bean, a large telemarketer and mail-order catalog house. The deployment levels obtained with economic optimization were significantly different from those formerly determined by service-level criteria, and the resultant cost savings were estimated as $9 to $10 million per year. To develop the economic- optimization approach, we used queuing theory, devised an expected total-cost objective function, and accounted for retrial behavior and potential caller abandonments through a regression model that related the abandonment rates to customer service levels. Management at L.L. Bean has fully accepted this approach, which now explicitly sets optimal levels for the number of telephone trunks (lines) carrying incoming traffic, the number of agents scheduled, and the maximum number of queue positions allowed for customers waiting for a telephone agent.

Introduction

We conducted a project at L.L. Bean, Inc. to develop an optimization model for their telemarketing operations. L.L. Bean is widely known for retailing high-quality outdoor goods and apparel, with more than 85 percent of sales generated through mail orders and telephone orders via 800-service, which was introduced in 1986. While 15 percent of the 600 million dollars in 1989 sales was conducted through store transactions and 20 percent was mail-ordered, about 65 percent of the total annual sales volume was generated through orders taken at two telemarketing centers located in Maine—one in Portland and the other in Lewiston.

An Overview of Telemarketing Resources Management

As is the case in most operational settings, the types of decisions made in managing a telemarketing call center depend on the time horizon and the nature of the resources involved (Figure 1).

In the long term, decisions must be made on the number of telephone lines (trunks, s_t) to install, the number of agent positions (s_a) to establish, the labor markets to use, and such capacity considerations as facilities, buildings, and acquisition of equipment (automatic call distributors [ACDs], work station, CRTs, and other support equipment).

At the opposite extreme, in the shortest term, decisions must be made to schedule staff on a half-hourly basis, 24 hours a day, seven days per week. Also included in this short-term category are decisions on queue capacity ($K - s_a$), a controllable which dictates the moment-to-moment call-waiting capacity of the switching system. The automatic call distributor at each call center has a feature that allows the queue length to be limited so that incoming calls attempting to enter a full system are issued a busy signal.

Finally, in the intermediate term, the most critical decisions for the telemarketing operation concern the number of agents to hire and train. These decisions also affect longer-term capacity questions on training

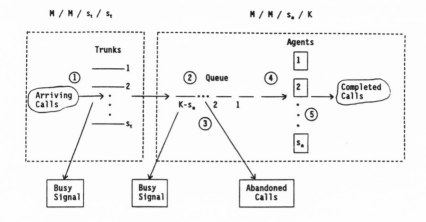

Figure 1.

KEY: s_t number of trunks installed
s_a number of agents on-duty
K system capacity for calls waiting an in service

Notes: For the L.L. Bean system, the network is characterized by the flow of calls, the points in the system where congestion occurs, and the three key controllables: number of trunks (s_t), number of agents (s_a), and queue capacity (K - s_a). Flowing cell processing is used: (1) An arriving call seizes one of s_t trunks if one is available; otherwise, it is routed to a busy signal; (2) The call arrives at an L.L. Bean switch; the switch checks the queue length; if the queue is full, call is routed to busy signal, freeing trunk; otherwise, the call enters the queue, taking up a queue position; (3) Callers may abandon (hang up) while waiting for an agent, freeing trunk and queue position; (4) When one of s_a agents is available, the call is serviced, freeing a queue position; and (5) When the call is completed, a trunk and an agent are freed.

facilities and the amount of training staff to have on hand. As would be expected, decisions at one level affect the outcomes and choices at other levels.

While these long-, intermediate-, and short-term decisions might seem quite routine—especially when sales volume remains steady—the seasonal build-up, with its big profit potential, changes the stakes dramatically. The three-week peak period just before Christmas makes or breaks the year for the company. For the peak-season build-up in 1989 for example, the number of telephone agents on payroll increased from 500 to 1,275, telephone trunks expanded from 150 to 576, and the overall operational capacity geared up to meet a full 18 percent of annual call-volume in a hectic three-week period. In this environment, management typically makes many critical decisions about schedules, the number of agents on duty, the number of temporaries to hire and train, the number of stations to have available, the number of trunks to lease and activate, and other operational capacity considerations.

Management must make these decisions in rapid succession to obtain a smooth, integrated build-up for resources within fixed budgetary constraints. Furthermore, following this rapid build-up for the peak season, management must shift its focus to the opposite extreme—the "build-down" process: the number of temporary agents must be cut back, the number of temporary work stations must be reduced, and trunk capacity must be cut back to match the drastically lower expected call volumes. Management must accomplish all this while paying attention to the long-term and short-term effects on the attendant customer-service levels, which by 1988 had become unacceptable to the company. The deterioration in customer service was due principally to suboptimal resource management (i.e., the number of telephone trunk lines installed and the number of agents scheduled into operation were suboptimal).

Problems with Telemarketing.   With annual sales of $580 million in 1988, L.L. Bean conservatively estimated that it lost $10 million of profit because it allocated telemarketing resources suboptimally. Customer-service levels had become clearly unacceptable: in some half hours, 80 percent of the calls dialed received a busy signal because the trunks were saturated; those customers who got through might have waited 10 minutes for an available agent. The extra telephone expense of keeping these customers waiting was as much as $25,000 in a single day. Worse, when large numbers of callers abandoned (hung up after waiting for an agent), this resulted not only in lost orders but also incurred queue-time connect charges for L.L. Bean. On exceptionally busy days, the total orders lost because of trunk "busies" (incoming calls not finding an idle trunk) and caller abandonment (after waiting for an agent) were estimated—based on conservative retry probabilities—to approach $500,000 in gross revenues. When annualized, based on call volume, the accumulated penalty cost of these allocations of resources amounted to $10 million in lost profits in 1988.

The Consultant Team and a Solution Approach.   In the spring of 1989, L.L. Bean's senior management decided that it needed a better allocation of resources in the telemarketing area. As a consequence, L.L. Bean initiated a project to answer the need for a more structured approach to planning for proper trunking, telephone-agent staffing, and queue management. After an exhaustive shopping expedition showed that no outside source had taken optimization in the telemarketing context to a level that met the firm's needs, L.L. Bean decided to build an economic-optimization model (EOM) in-house. They needed to apply economic optimization to the simultaneous sizing of the trunks, the agent work force, and the queue capacity.

The management science team charged with defining and implementing a model-based approach to resource management consisted of two of the authors who already had an ongoing consulting relationship with L.L. Bean, Quinn as an insider and Andrews as an outsider. This two-person consulting team was invited to follow up on suggestions they had made three years earlier that emphasized a more global form of economic optimization. Thus, the philosophical basis for EOM was actually born several years ago when economic-optimization principles were first applied to agent scheduling without regard to the other controllable resources in the telemarketing environment. We reported on the first step toward optimization in *Interfaces* (Andrews and Parsons, 1989).

As late as 1987, telemarketing was still planning for the peak-period expansion using quality-of-service measures and goals determined through experience; the sizing decisions used some quantitative methods but they were based on traditional service-level criteria rather than economic optimization. In contrast, with integration and economic optimization currently built into the process of managing telemarketing resources, the situation with the new approach is almost precisely the opposite: in the 1989 three-week peak period, customer wait times were down, operating personnel reported higher agent morale, lost-order penalties were substantially reduced, and most important, profits from the telemarketing operation were maximized (Table 1). This drastic turn in telemarketing performance resulted directly from a basic shift in philosophy, away from resourcing the traditional way—using customer-service level and productivity goals—towards an economically optimum, profitability-based orientation. These improvements were clearly attributable to the influence of EOM since the season-to-date call volumes were up only 6.5 percent for 1989 over 1988. The more profitable telemarketing operations, coupled with greatly improved quality-of-service levels for callers, have produced an unusual win-win outcome for both L.L. Bean and its telemarketing customers. From a cost/benefit standpoint, moreover, the modeling effort produced a real home run for the management science project, which was funded at a mere $40,000.

Model Description and Operation. The model sets explicit levels for the following key resources:

1. The number of trunks carrying incoming traffic to telephone agents;
2. The number of agents scheduled; and
3. The queue capacity, the maximum number of wait positions for customers who are successful in seizing a trunk but who are forced to wait for a telephone agent.

These fundamental decision variables, whose level must be tightly planned and managed, directly and indirectly affect a variety of important

Table 1.

Criterion Measured	1988 (Before)	1989 (After)	% Change
Call answered	1,260,530	1,562,457	+24.0
Orders taken	1,038,557	1,211,759	+16.7
Revenued generated	$85,367,372	$99,273,655	+16.3
Percent abandoned callers	11.2	2.1	-81.3
Percent calls spending <20 seconds in queue	25.0	77.0	+208.0
Average speed of answer	93 seconds	15 seconds	-83.9

Note: To compare three-week peak periods before and after the economic optimization approach, we took measurements for the corresponding three-week peak periods in 1988 and 1989. The significant performance improvements shown for 1989 are the result of implementing an economic optimization approach to allocating telemarketing resources in response to the projected offered load. The percent of abandoned callers was measured by the L.L. Bean automatic call distributor (ACD).

company resources and their associated costs. The required number of agents on payroll, for example—originally derived from the model's projections of optimal staffing levels—determines recruiting needs and the accompanying training commitment. In addition, since agents need work stations, the deployment level of agents also dictates the sizing of facilities. Similarly, the sizing of the trunk group determines trunk installation charges and their monthly maintenance costs.

Our approach to optimization is to minimize expected costs, which is an extension beyond the service-level approach to setting queue-resource levels implemented by numerous other researchers (Gaballa and Pearce, 1979; Holloran and Byrn, 1986; Segal, 1974; and Taylor and Huxley, 1989). Conversely, at least three previous researchers have considered the minimization of cost-based objective functions in their analyses. Mabert (1979), in analyzing a shift-scheduling problem, minimized a total cost function by including both the wages of servers and their opportunity cost. In analyzing manpower-scheduling algorithms, Tien and Kamiyama (1982) weighed agent-staffing costs against the penalty cost of undesirable schedules. Similarly, Grassmann (1988) has formulated a more comprehensive objective function, maximizing total profits, defined as the difference between sales revenues and the costs of waiting customers and active servers on duty. With EOM, however, we expand on the queuing resources still further by including the periodic installation costs and monthly leasing costs for the trunks, as well as the capacity- expansion costs associated with training new agents and furnishing them with leased work stations.

Conceptually, in EOM, the cost of resources (e.g., trunks and agents) is balanced against the sum of queuing costs and the cost of lost orders, based on the optimal point where total expected costs are minimized. Due to the complex nature of the objective function, the optimal point is identified by using a bisection search procedure (Sedgewick, 1983). The (M/M/s/s) Model (Erlang B formula) and the general finite-queue model (M/M/s/K) are used to estimate the operating characteristics for the trunks and agents, respectively (Cooper, 1989; Hillier and Lieberman, 1986; Gross and Harris, 1985). These operating characteristics are then used to assess the economic impact of blocked calls, abandoned calls, and queue times.

For optimality, the model searches for the combination of resources that minimizes the expected total cost of trunking, labor, connect time, and lost-order profits. The cost calculations are derived as follows:

1. The expected trunking costs are calculated to include average charges for both installation and monthly maintenance.
2. The expected labor costs are calculated straightforwardly as the number of agents times the fully-loaded pay rate.
3. The expected connect costs are calculated by using the expected connect time per call multiplied by the number of calls times the 800-service rate.
4. The expected cost of permanently lost orders is calculated in two steps. First, the percent of calls generating orders is multiplied by the expected number of permanently lost calls to get expected lost orders. This result is then multiplied by the average value of an order (the average order revenue, less average cost-of-goods-sold, less average variable order-fulfillment costs). The expected number of permanently lost calls is calculated in turn as the sum of three ingredients: (a) the expected lost calls due to network blockage (busy-signal overflows from trunks), (b) the expected lost calls due to switch blockage (busy-signal overflows from the agent queue), and (c) the expected lost calls due to call abandonment (callers aborting from queue).

In item (4), we derive network blockage using the Erlang B formula (blocked calls cleared) and obtain the switch blockage from the finite-queue model (M/M/s/K), where s represents the number of agents (s_a) on duty and K is the system capacity. We estimate expected caller abandonment using a simple linear regression model with the average queue time per called (average speed of answer: ASA) as the independent variable. Using 1,161 observations, this regression produced a highly significant correlation coefficient of $r = 0.901$ with p-value of 0.000.

With realistic parameter values, the model's minimization of total expected costs leads to small optimal queue capacities. This results in small average queue times (ASAs) which, in turn, yield small abandonment rates, averaging less than one percent. Thus, we regarded the impact of abandonments on the queuing assumptions underlying the M/M/s/K model as negligible.

Similarly, we also regarded the impact of queuing assumptions made by retrials from among callers who first experience a busy signal as negligible: first, only a small percentage of callers receive a busy signal while the system is optimized, and secondly, retries are typically spread over future time intervals, thus creating no significant disruptions to the underlying Poisson arrival process in the current time interval.

On the other hand, for their economic impact, permanently lost calls are not considered negligible; in absolute annual dollar terms they can represent considerable sums. For the expected total cost calculations, therefore, it is important to calculate the expected half-hourly penalty costs associated with lost calls appropriately. To account for callers who fail to retry, either after abandonment or subsequent to a busy signal, the model applies separate retry probabilities. The probability that a caller who receives a busy signal on the first attempt converts to a permanently lost order was estimated with the help of AT&T Bell Laboratories using actual L.L. Bean peak-season data. Researchers in Bell's new services performing planning group furnished L.L. Bean with an interval estimate of 19-27 percent, that is, 19 to 27 percent of blocked first-attempt phone calls never lead to an order—including all subsequent retries. These percentages were calculated by dividing the total number of blocked first-attempt callers into the number of these callers who never retried or always received busy signals on all subsequent retries.

Because Bell Laboratories was unable to determine whether or not a caller who did not receive a busy signal subsequently abandoned, it was not possible to do an empirical study of retrial probabilities for abandonments. So, in order to estimate the retrial probability, the project committee took a Delphi approach to arrive at a consensus of what should be used. The committee felt that a caller who had abandoned would be less likely to call back than one who had received a busy signal. It selected a consensus value of 35 percent for the probability that a caller who abandons on his or her first visit to the queue converts to a permanently lost order. Although the probability of retrial is likely to vary throughout the year, we justify a single, annual number by basing it conservatively on peak-season data. For additional details on caller-retrial probability estimation, see Hoffman and Harris (1986).

Figure 2 shows the model inputs, the major processing elements for the search procedure, and the outputs. The core of the objective function, which utilizes queuing-performance characteristics in its half-hourly expected total-cost computations, is included in the appendix.

In applying the queuing models, we made the traditional telephony assumptions—that statistical equilibrium was sustained during each half-hourly interval of the 24-hour day, that call arrivals were properly represented by the Poisson arrival process with rate λ, and that customer-

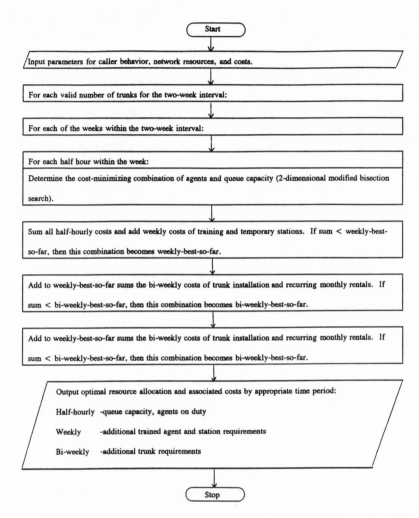

Notes: The inputs consist of the percent of calls that generate orders; *Pr* (permanently lost order/trunk blockage or queue overflow); *Pr* (permanently lost order/abandonment); average order value; average speed of answer/percent abandoned regression coefficients; low/high/step for employee stations, trunks, and queue capacity; agent-hour constraints; agents' fully-loaded wage; connect-time coast; agent-training time cost; station rental cost; trunk installation and monthly rental costs. While searching for the minimum cost combination of resources, the three-dimensional algorithm spans three time horizons—two weeks, one week, and a half hour. The search process obtains a limit for the maximum number of agents from the maximum number of work stations, and the queue capacity is constrained by the difference between the maximum number of trunks and the maximum number of stations. The queuing-based constraints are embedded in the half-hourly segment of the search procedure.

Figure 2: A model flow diagram shows inputs, major search procedures for cost minimization, and outputs.

service and trunk-service times followed the negative-exponential distribution with mean $1/\mu$. The call-counting capability of the switching equipment was not sufficient to examine the arrival process for pure randomness; we did, however, run further statistical tests on the service times observed, since the service-time assumption is the one most often questioned for its validity. Here we needed to actually consider two different overlapping times: agent time and trunk time. In the sequence of servicing a call, trunk time starts slightly earlier than agent time (due to possible caller waiting), and trunk time also ends slightly earlier than agent time (due to possible post-call processing by the agent). Consequently, the major portion of trunk time is really made up of agent time, with the portion of total trunk time not attributable to agent time amounting to less than five percent on average.

Using a sample of 1,240 observations, we conducted a chi-square goodness-of-fit test exclusively for the agent times. This yielded a very small chi-square statistic whose associated p-value was 0.5792, corroborating the validity of the negative exponential assumption for the agent service times. Although we conducted no corresponding chi-square test specifically for the trunk times—since trunk times were not available—we felt safe in assuming that the trunk times also closely followed a negative exponential distribution. We based this assumption on the fact that trunk-time composition was made up of more than 95 percent agent time, which itself fits the negative exponential distribution extremely well.

For more background on queuing assumptions—and their validation in the context of a telephone application—see, for example, Harris, Hoffman, and Saunders (1987) for their work with modeling the IRS telephone taxpayer information system.

Effects and Implementation of EOM.   As budgets were prepared for the 1989 busy season, the model software was not yet fully operational. However, prototyped model results were already showing sufficient promise to convince people of the new philosophy: the way to increase profits was to expand resource deployment. Rather than determine resource needs with productivity- based goals, such as 85 percent TSF (percent of calls answered within 20 seconds), two percent abandonment rate, or the rule-of-14 (handle, on average, 14 calls per agent per hour), the profitability-based model continues to add resources until the incremental cost of additional resources exceeds the return on that investment. One measure of the model's impact is seen in the significantly higher levels of resource allocation that resulted in 1989 (Table 2).

Clearly, the operating personnel were the ones who experienced the more tangible effects of the model. A recent comment by a telemarketing floor manager made to one of the consultants typifies the reactions to the

Table 2.

Item	1988	1989	% Change
Trunks	480	576	20.0
Training classes	31	37	19.4
Agent employed	1014	1275	25.7
Maximum number of agents taking calls	450	568	26.2

Note: In 1989, substantial increases in the allocation of telemarketing resources resulted from the impact of the economic-optimization model. These increases ranged from 19 to 26 percent. However, since at the time when resource-level decisions were made, increased call volumes amounted to only 6.5 percent, the 19 to 26 percent resource increases would not have been justified without the economic optimization model.

improved resource allocation: "Just as the customer calls start speeding up—getting the operators real busy—a new group of operators arrive and start their shifts ... and every time it looks like there aren't enough calls to keep the operators busy, suddenly a bunch of operators start to leave—it's the end of their scheduled shifts. Things sure are different now from the way it used to be. This stuff really works!" The improved quality of the resource allocation levels with EOM has clearly enhanced the performance of the call center, which is now optimally resourced to handle calls efficiently and economically.

An important aspect of our implementation process was a series of feedback and educational sessions. Immediately after the model's earliest runs, but still prior to the December peak period, we distributed some sample output to all the people on the steering committee, which consisted of the director of telemarketing, the three telemarketing managers, the customer service manager, the scheduler, and a floor supervisor. In this in-depth session, we solicited and received criticisms and reactions from the steering committee that subsequently led to several important modifications to the model. This session also served to update the members of the committee on the latest status of the model.

We also conducted an educational session exclusively for the floor supervisors, who actually manage the agents and the queue capacity on a half-hour-by-half-hour basis. By explaining the new model to their agents and in general staying close to the action on the floor, these supervisors played a crucial role in the acceptance and success of the model.

Following the 1989 peak period, we held another feedback session with the steering committee. By this time, the focus had shifted to results already achieved during the peak, giving us an opportunity to interpret committee members' views on operational procedures and outcomes after the peak period run. The most significant outcome was the decision to integrate the half-hourly optimal agent-levels electronically with the existing automated agent-scheduler.

The meetings helped us initially to understand the issues and gave others many opportunities to offer input and have their concerns and questions answered every step of the way. These meetings gave us an opportunity to provide feedback to all interested players—from floor supervisors to the senior vice-president of operations—in many forms, including tables, pictures, bits of problems, and lists of questions about the choices to be made in designing the system. As a result of our honest concern for user interests throughout the project, the system now enjoys wide acceptance at all levels of the corporation.

An Analysis of Economic Considerations

It was not feasible to conduct controlled experiments to empirically assess the financial and operational impact of the model on the telemarketing operations. That would have required running one call center by traditional methods and the other by EOM. Given the improvement in operating characteristics and profitability that was anticipated, management was understandably not keen on the idea of continuing to run one call center by traditional methods just to precisely quantify the other call center's achieved gain. However, to demonstrate the extent of profit improvement and the degree of improvement in performance measures achieved through our optimization efforts, we conducted two ex-post-facto system performance analyses. We based our analysis on the 1988 three-week peak period that occurred prior to EOM. We conducted the analysis in four phases:

1. First, we ran the model to emulate the 1988 peak-period conditions. In this first phase, we used as inputs the actual 1988 peak-period call volumes and agent work times. We then entered into the model the actual resourcing levels for agents and trunks employed in the 1988 peak period and applied the model's what-if analyzer module to cost out the three-week period. This provided a baseline for the model-calculated expected total cost, given the level of resourcing, the call volumes, and average work times that actually had occurred. Subsequently, we used this "status quo" baseline for comparison purposes.

2. Next, we took the forecasts that were available in 1988 for the 1988 peak-season call volumes and agent work times, and applied the model with its optimizer module running. This determined the optimum level of resourcing level used. The key outputs from this phase of evaluation were the optimum levels of resources that would

have been used in the 1988 peak season had the model been fully implemented at that time.

3. In this final run, we set the resourcing levels to the optimum amounts determined in paragraph 2 above and played these against the actual 1988 call volumes and average work times. These emulated operational results were then fed to the what-if analyzer module to determine the model-calculated expected total cost for the 1988-peak period that would have occurred if optimum resource levels had been used.

4. As a last step in the ex-post-facto analysis, we simply computed the difference in the expected total cost obtained in paragraph 1 with actual resourcing levels, and the expected total cost obtained in paragraph 3 using hypothetical, optimal resource levels. This difference in expected total costs is attributable to optimization and represents the expected gain in profits that would have been obtained had the model been in use for the 1988 three-week peak period (Table 3).

To sum up, we computed the model's expected total cost of providing optimal service for the 1988 peak period by costing trunks and agents at the optimal levels. We also ran the analyzer module with actual 1988 resource levels to compute a comparable model-based expected total cost for operations as they actually existed during the 1988 peak season. The difference between these two we attribute to optimization. Finally, since this difference in the calculated expected total costs applies only to the three-week peak period, the total impact on the company on a yearly basis is quite significant. Given that 12 to 13 percent of annual call volume occurs during this three-week peak period, multiplying the three- week profit improvement of $1.25 million by eight yields an expected annual increase in profits of $10 million.

Of additional interest is the fact that if the 1989 three-week peak period (the most recent peak period for which data were available) was resourced in the economic optimization model, as was the actual case—then the expected total cost would have been $1.64 million more than it actually was with optimization. Annualizing this amount conservatively, using relative call-volume data, yields a yearly profit gain of $9.2 million for 1989. Table 4 summarizes the 1989 ex-post-facto analysis.

Decision Support and Other Benefits

Although the ex-post-facto analysis indicates conservatively-estimated annual profit gains with the model of approximately $10 and $9.2 million for 1988 and 1989, respectively, the intangible, long-term benefits to L.L.

Table 3.

Item	1988 Actual	1989 Optimal	Difference
Trunks	480	600	120
Connect time (hours)	98,604	94,804	-3,800
Trunk costs	$1,280,000	$1,470,000	$190,000
Agents employed	911	1,131	200
Labor hours	95,531	111,000	15,469
Labor costs	860,000	1,000	140,000
Resource costs			
(trunks and labor)	$2,140,000	$2,470,000	$440,000
Lost orders	187,044	116,571	-70,473
Lost orders cost	$4,640,000	$3,060,000	-$1,580,000
Total Costs	$6,780,000	$5,530,000	-$125,000

Note: These figures provide a comparison of the actual versus the optimal resourcing costs calculated ex-port-facto for the 1988 three-week period—the last peak period managed without benefit of EOM. Labor costs include wages, benefits, training costs, and temporary station costs; trunk costs include connect-time charges, trunk installation costs, and monthly rental fees. Using call-volume data to annualize the three-week peak period, the $1.25 million total-cost reduction yields $10.0 million per year in net profit.

Table 4.

Item	1989 Traditional	1989 Actual	Difference
Trunks	504	675	72
Connect time (hours)	105,304	104,484	-820
Trunk costs	$1,369,000	$1,427,000	$58,000
Agents employed	1,119	1,255	136
Labor hours	102,671	122,687	20,016
Resource costs			
(trunks and labor)	$2,354,000	$2,608,000	$254,000
Lost orders	181,524	106,665	-74,859
Lost orders cost	$4,647,000	$2,749,000	-$1,989,000
Total Costs	$7,001,000	$5,357,000	-$1,644,000

Note: This ex-post-facto analysis for 1989 compares traditional vs. actual resourcing for the three-week peak period. Based on annual call-volume data, the $1.64 million reduction in total cost due to optimization yields a projected gain in profits of $9.2 million for the year (1989). All costs are defined as they were in Table 3.

Bean may well outweigh these tangible profit gains. As a result of our management science project, estimated to have cost only $40,000, telemarketing management now has a tool that allows it to simultaneously optimize all of the queuing resources over which it has control. Not only does this allow for fully-integrated planning, but each alternative plan can also be immediately evaluated by the analyzer module that performs what-if analyses. Given that forecasts will always miss their targets to some extent, the analyzer module allows the evaluation of potential risks: If the stock in inventory drops, for example, talk time with callers goes up, orders as a percent of calls go down, and the cost of a lost order goes down. How do all these changes affect the total cost? Similarly, what would have happened if we had dropped 24 trunks and not hired 60 agents? Or, what would the costs have been if we allocated resources by traditional methods last December? By allowing us to quantify the expected costs and benefits for each plan considered, the what-if analyzer makes it practical to conduct sensitivity analysis, which in turn enhances the overall quality of planning.

Managers also report benefits in operations, indicating that L.L. Bean's reputation in the eyes of calling customers has improved and that the number of problems that agents now experience with callers has been drastically reduced. Where customers before grew irritable with long waits and subsequently vented their frustrations on our agents, this situation has been alleviated. Now, more customers are served immediately; those who do not get immediate service either experience a shorter delay or receive a busy signal promptly.

Perhaps the most important benefit is that the usefulness of management science has been so successfully demonstrated at L.L. Bean. Our current project and its optimal agent-scheduling predecessor suggests a shift in outlook at L.L. Bean. A similar shift in managerial outlook was reported at QANTAS Airlines at the time of their telephone-sales manpower-planning study (Gaballa and Pearce, 1979).

It was only three years ago at L.L. Bean that queuing-based results— inherently nonlinear and, therefore, not always intuitively obvious—were first accepted as a viable alternative to the "14-rule." Today, the acceptance of queuing-based teletraffic-engineering concepts seems almost a matter of course. Furthermore, not only has there been acceptance of the MS approach at L.L. Bean in the area of quantitative decision making and optimization, but the present model's high degree of integration could very well serve as a prototype example for other potential integrated systems, thus fostering the evolution of another way of thinking about problem solving, while creating a whole new philosophy within the company.

This project's findings have already had a major influence on strategic thinking at L.L. Bean by raising management's service-level perspective on resource allocation. Historically, the company philosophy was that customers would come back, even if service at times was not the best—L.L. Bean relied on high customer loyalty as a prime market force. Recently, this thinking has been dramatically changed, especially since the three measured customer retry probabilities used in the model were discovered to be lower than previously assumed—customer loyalty was lower than expected. As a result, now very much at issue in telemarketing is the question of what constitutes an appropriate level of customer service. The philosophy on resourcing at L.L. Bean appears to have turned around; the new rationale calls for higher levels of resource deployment, as long as the cost of these additional resources continues to be offset by savings obtained from reducing lost orders and queuing costs. This, of course, requires more trunks and agents, which affects in turn the recruiting practices and training capacity for agents and ultimately leads to a general expansion. Interestingly, both call centers in 1989 were used to their maximum limit during the peak seasons; the company has made preliminary plans to increase space, add equipment, and hire more agents. In short, an important managerial outcome is that the short-term optimizer results will ultimately lead to the development of long-term strategy on facilities planning and human-resource planning. Moreover, in the long-run, a broader scope for integration of the model appears possible when one considers the overall effectiveness of the model from a systems viewpoint. Since the economic optimization of telemarketing resources leads to a general increase in business for L.L. Bean, its overall effect on other parts of the organization—beyond its impact on just telemarketing resources—will also be significant. It is tempting to envision a future version of the model that would include in its optimization calculations the cost of inventories (stockouts vs. safety-stock levels) and other marginal downstream production costs due to the new volume.

To sum up, the acceptance of management science at L.L. Bean—as evidenced by EOM and other MS undertakings now underway, such as drop-shipping optimization, total-quality management, modeling the effects of customer identification numbers of the length of telephone calls, and quantitative forecasting of telemarketing call volumes—gives concrete evidence of an enriched corporate culture that is conscious of quantitative analysis. We believe that this new corporate culture, embedded into the decision-making process at all levels of the company, in the long run offers L.L. Bean the greatest benefit.

Appendix

At the heart of the model's algorithm to minimize the expected total cost over a full two-week horizon are three half-hourly expected cost ingredients (labor, connect time, and lost orders), which are combined to create the expected total cost per half hour. For a specific half hour, the expected total cost for a given number of agents s_a, a given agent queuing-system capacity (K), and a given number of installed trunks s_t is represented as follows:

E(total cost)
   = E(labor cost)

+ E(connect-time cost)
+ E(lost-order cost).

where,

E(labor cost)

= (number of agents on duty)
$\times$ (average queue time + average agent-service time)

E(lost-order cost)

= [{trunk arrivals per half hour}
$\times$ {average fraction of calls which generate orders}]
$\times$ {average value of a permanently lost order}]
$\times$ [{Pr(caller blocked because all st trunks are busy)
+ (1 − Pr (caller blocked because all st trunks are busy))
$\times$ Pr (caller blocked because queue for agents is full)}
$\times$ Pr (order is permanently lost caller blocked on first attempt)
+ (1 − Pr (caller blocked because all st trunks are busy))
$\times$ (1 − Pr (caller blocked because queue for agents is full))
$\times$ Pr (caller abandons average queue time)
$\times$ Pr (order is permanently lost caller abandons)].

Steady-state results for the well-known M/M/s/K model are used to estimate three of the elements in the half-hourly E (total cost) equation. The probability of blocking at the trunks is computed using the Erlang B formula to determine the probability that all s_t are busy:

Pr (caller blocked because queue for agents is full) = p_k, average queue = W_q.
Here, K = s = s_t in the M/M/s/K model.

The probability of blocking at the agent queue and the average amount of time a caller spends in this finite queue waiting for one of the s_a agents are determined by the following expressions:

Pr (caller blocked because queue for agents is full) = p_k, average queue = W_q.
Here, s = s_a and K = s_a + Q_{max} where Q_{max} refers to the adjustable queue capacity which regulates the maximum number of callers admitted to the waiting line for agents.

Callers who are blocked when all trunks are busy or blocked when the agent queue is full receive the same busy signal. Thus, the likelihood that their orders are permanently lost when they are unable to get through is the same in either case. Occasionally, callers who are admitted to the queue grow impatient and abandon. However, under optimal resourcing, this happens to less than one percent of the callers because sufficient capacity has been provided to ensure a high quality of service. When callers do abandon, the likelihood that their orders are permanently lost is different than that associated with callers who receive a busy signal.

Acknowledgments

Copyright 1991. The Institute of Management Sciences, reprinted with permission from Interfaces, Vol. 21, No. 1, pp. 75-91, January-February 1991.

References

Andrews, B. H. and H. L. Parsons. 1989. "L.L. Bean Chooses a Telephone Agent Scheduling System." *Interfaces* 19 (6): 1-9.

Cooper, R. B. 1989. "Queuing Theory." *Handbool of Operations Research and Management Science, Vol. 2, Stochastic Model*, edited by Daniel P. Heyman and Matthew J. Sobel. NY: Elsevier.

Gaballa, A. and W. Pearce. 1979. "Telephone sales manpower planning at Qantas." *Interfaces* 9 (3): 1-9.

Grassmann, W. K. 1988. "Finding the right number of servers in real-world queuing systems." *Interfaces* 18 (2): 94-104/

Gross, D. and C. M. Harris. 1985. *Fundamentals of Queuing Theory*. New York: John Wiley and Sons.

Harris, C. M., Hoffman, K. L., and P. B. Saunders. 1987. "Modeling the IRS Telephone Taxpayer Information System." *Operations Research* 35 (4): 504-523.

Hillier, F. S. and G. J. Lieberman. 1986. *Introduction to Operations Research*. Oakland, Cal: Holden-Day.

Hoffman, K. L. and C. M. Harris. 1986. "Estimation of a Caller Retrial Rate for a Relephone Information System." *European Journal of Operations Research* 27 (2): 207-214.

Holloran, T. J. and J. E. Byrn, 1986. "United Airlines station manpower planning system." *Interfaces* 16 (1): 39-50.

Mabert, V. A. 1979. "A Case Study of Encoder Shift Scheduling Under Uncertainty." *Management Science* 25 (7): 623-631.

Sedgewick, R. 1983. *Algorithm* Reading, Ma: Addison-Wesley.

Segal, M. 1974. "The Operator-Scheduling Problem: A Network Flow Approach." *Operations Research* 22 (4): 808-823.

Taylor, P. E. and S. J. Huxley. 1989. "A Break From Tradition for the San Francisco Police: Patrol Officer Scheduling Using an Optimization-Based Decision Support System." *Interfaces* 19 (1): 4-24.

Tien, J. M. and A. Kamiyama. 1982. "On Manpower Scheduling Algorithms." *SIAM Review* 24 (3): 275-287.

STRATEGIC INFORMATION SYSTEMS FOR HUMAN RESOURCE MANAGEMENT

Robert P. Cerveny, C. Carl Pegels, and

G. Lawrence Sanders

INTRODUCTION

Human Resources Information Systems (HRIS) is an umbrella term used to describe the portfolio of applications for supporting the human resources (HR) function in organizations. An HRIS is defined as:

> *The information system used to support the organization in effective and efficient employee recruiting, staffing and planning, employee training and development, employee compensation, and employee performance and appraisal. The system should also provide reporting mechanisms related to how well human resources are being utilized.*

Exhibit 1 presents an overview of how the human resources systems are related to other organizational systems and the external organizational environment.

The human resource function has been slower than other areas to computerize. The major reason that human resources have not received

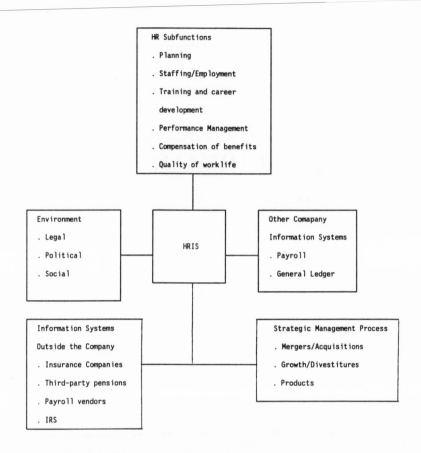

Source Adapted from Kavanagh, Gueutal, and Tannenbaum, (1990, p. 31).

Exhibit 1.   How HRIS Interfaces with Other Systems

the attention of top-level managers and the Information Systems department is that the financial accounting, operations, and marketing functions typically dominate the assignment of corporate resources. In many organizations employees were considered as simply an input into the production process.

Three developments have caused organizations to reevaluate the HR function. First and foremost, employees are now being viewed as a strategic resource because employees represents a vast pool of skills and knowledge distributed throughout the organization. Organizations can cultivate and draw on this pool of expertise to match skills to organizational tasks and to locate individuals with unique and specialized skills. Secondly, hardware and software—particularly relational data base systems, fourth generation languages, and local area networks—have made tremendous technological advances in the past ten years. Thirdly, HR employees are becoming not just computer literate, but rather computer proficient, as HR departments have invested in education programs for HR employees and new management school graduates with computing backgrounds have joined HR departments. Several management schools have in fact developed a major course of study in Human Resource Information Systems.

CASE STUDIES

Eleven case studies were identified which discuss recent developments in Human Resource Information Systems. One of the most interesting aspects of the HRIS cases is their diversity. The HRIS applications have a significant impact on how organizations deal with their most critical resource. HRIS applications will undoubtedly provide organizations which implement them with the leverage to compete effectively in this decade.

INFORMATION TECHNOLOGY DEVELOPMENTS IN HUMAN RESOURCES

The emphasis of the human resources function is on assisting the organization in meeting its strategic objectives. In that context it is viewed as a support function with the primary emphasis being on improving operational efficiency in respect to employee staffing. The three strategic thrusts we shall focus on are:

3. *Operational and Strategic Oriented Activities. Information technology developments focussed on operational and strategic improvements consisting of:*

   a. Improving efficiency and effectiveness in order to position the firm in a more competitive position.

2. *Organizational Activities. Information technology developments focussed on organizational improvements consisting of:*

   a. The integration of databases and organizational activities.
   b. Speeding and improving the quality of communication internally and externally to the firm.
   c. Centralizing the firm's activities, including a flattening of the organization chart.

      d.   Distributing decision making authority to satisfy localized needs.

3.   *Customer/Client Service Oriented Activities. Information technology developments focussed on customer/client service oriented activities consisting of:*

      a.   Improving the user-friendliness and simplification of use by computer systems users.

      b.   Providing tracking of such items as packages, passengers, automobiles, freight cars, projects, and so on, for better management.

Exhibits 2 and 3 provide an overview of the mapping of the case studies to the 11 strategic thrust activities.

CASE ANALYSES

Several themes emerge from reviewing the Human Resource Information Systems applications. First of all, as expected, the primary focus of HRIS applications has been on increasing organizational efficiency and effectiveness by improving internal organizational activities as reflected by strategic thrust 1c. The integration of organizational databases (strategic thrust 2a), improving organizational communication (strategic thrust 2b), the centralization of certain activities (stratetic thrust 2c), and the distribution of decision making authority and discretion (stratetic thrust 2d) are important internal strategies in nearly all of the cases. For example, all of the above strategies appear to work at 3M (HRM2) where they have integrated human resources, finance, engineering project management, and CAD/CAM. 3M asserts that integrating common systems has reduced the time it takes to bring a product from the laboratory to the marketplace from two years to six months. Interestingly enough, the 3M culture also emphasizes decentralization and flexibility and 3M has apparently found a way to decentralize decision making as well as integrate certain common applications.

It may appear unusual that organizations want to centralize databases and distribute decision making discretion, but on further inspection this strategy makes sense. Organizations want employee data to be accurate and widely available, and the easiest way to accomplish this task is through a centralized employee database. At the same time organizations want some level of computing available for specialized processing and reporting needs. Relational database management systems with fourth generation languages can support standardization and centralization as well as provide the flexibility to develop local applications.

Strategic Thrusts/Activities

Strategic Thrusts/ Activities	Firm Identifiers for Case Studies											
	HRM1	HRM2	HRM3	HRM4	HRM5	HRM6	HRM7	HRM8	HRM9	HRM10	HRM11	TOTAL
1a	x	x	x	x	x	x	x	x	x	x	x	11
2a	x	x		x	x		x	x	x		x	8
b	x	x	x	x	x	x			x	x	x	9
c	x	x		x	x		x	x	x			7
d	x	x	x	x	x	x			x	x		8
3a										x		1
b	x		x	x	x	x	x	x	x	x	x	10
Number	6	5	4	6	6	4	4	4	6	5	4	54

Strategic Thrusts/Activities

1. Operational and Strategic Thrust Activities
   a. Improve efficiency/effectiveness.

2. Organizational Thrust Activities
   a. Integration of databases;
   b. improve communication;
   c. centralization; and
   d. distributing decision making authority.

3. Customer/Client Service Oriented Thrust Activities
   a. Improve user friendliness; and
   b. provide item tracking.

Exhibit 2. Mapping of Case Studies to Strategic Thrusts/Activities

249

Identifier	Industry Area	Firm
HRM1	Electronics Manufacturing	Motorola
HRM2	Manufacturing	Minnesota Mining and Manufacturing (3M)
HRM3	Airline Transportation	America West
HRM4	Healthcare, Manufacturing and Tobacco	Toledo Hospital in Ohi, Rothmans Benson & Hedges in Toronto, Inland Steel in Chicago, Turner Corporation in New York City, and Whirlpool Financial in Benton Harbor in Michigan
HRM5	Manufacturing Homecare Products	SC Johnson Wax
HRM6	High Technology	Compaq Computer Corporation
HRM7	Mining	Newmont Mining Corporation
HRM8	Cable Television	Home Box Office Inc.
HRM9	Financial and Chemical	Sovran Financial Corporation, Rohm and Haas
HRM10	Clothing	Levi Strauss & Co.
HRM11	Petroleum	Chevron Corporation

Exhibit 3.   Listing of Industry Areas and Firms for Case Studies

Integration has been a productivity booster at Newmont Mining Corp. (HRM7). Newmont implemented an integrated HR package and found that the real savings are not simply in terms of labor costs but rather in being able to concentrate on making the human resources function more effective.

The rapid growth and increasing importance of HR has prompted some companies to actually form special groups to support the HR function. For example, Rohm and Haas (HRM9) established a human resource information center and they are migrating and integrating their human resource applications to a DB2 relational database platform.

Chevron's (HRM11) approach to HR integration has been systematic and global. An important consideration in the development of the integrated EPIC (Emphasizing People in Chevron) system was the currency of the core HR databases. Another benefit of the EPIC system is that paperwork is reduced because fewer forms have to be filled out, mailed and filed.

The distribution of paper, and particularly reports, is of utmost importance in HR systems. Integration can also help in this area. Compaq Computer's (HRM6) HRIS department spent so much time in dealing with report distribution and processing that there was no time left for new development. The CARD (Corporate Automated Report Distribution) System assisted the HR group in delivering 200 reports to 150 individuals. Before CARD was implemented 50 reports were distributed to 150 individuals. It is estimated that the system saves Compaq $47,000 per year.

MATCHING SKILLS TO JOBS AND PROJECTS

Matching employees with certain skills to jobs is an excellent example of an application which requires a centralized human resource data base and a fourth generation language. In fact, tracking and matching employees can readily be identified as thrust 3b in the service oriented activities in four of the five cases.

Matching skills to projects and providing the ability to search for expertise looms as a very critical, albeit strategic HR application in the next decade and it will require some type of centralized database. Employee-owned America West (HRM3) has developed a system which tracks employee expertise and background experience. Motorola (HRM1) has taken an additional step and developed a system to assemble interdisciplinary project teams and the system is also sensitive to employee preferences.

Johnson Wax (HRM5) is probably one of the most progressive companies in terms of developing employees as a corporate resource. Selecting and keeping qualified staff has become a major issue and they have chosen to develop internal expertise rather than rely on consultants and outsourcing. The company has developed a system which contains a skills inventory database application for matching an individual's expertise to projects. The system also assists in forecasting future skills requirements and it has reduced professional development investment by 20 percent.

From this review and the author's past experience the ability to match skills to projects and to send out electronic requests for assistance is becoming a very important information systems application to high technology firms, large business consulting firms and systems integrators.

BENEFITS MANAGEMENT

One area in which there is a significant amount of pressure for applications development is in the benefits management area. The arrival of so-called "cafeteria benefits" plans places significant stress on existing HR systems. In a cafeteria benefit plans employees are given a fixed dollar amount which they can use to select from a variety of benefits options. Thus an employee can select the level of benefits such as hospital coverage, dental coverage, death benefits, disability insurance, and so on, desired. These systems require more processing power and additional reporting mechanisms than traditional benefits systems. In an ideal setting a cafeteria benefit plan would also have some sort of on-line interaction available for employees to check on their current level of coverage and to assist them in sensitivity analysis.

Levi Strauss (HRM10) has developed a very sophisticated on-line system, OLIVER (On-Line Interactive Visual Employee Resource System), which gives their employees access, through personal computers, to information on compensation, disability, health care, pension status, investments, and other human resource benefits. The system also assists employees with financial planning, training and development.

Performance evaluation is a necessary and complex aspect of the HR function. Home Box Office Inc. (HRM8) links bonus pay to performance and uses a variety of computer generated tools to support the evaluation process including calculation worksheets and reports. The merit planning process also involves a number of HBO economic variables as well as industry variables in determining merit.

THE ROLE OF NETWORKS AND
DOWNSIZING IN HRIS

In an attempt to reduce costs and put processing power in the hands of the human resources function there has been a trend towards "downsizing" from mainframes to minicomputers and microcomputers and to invest in Local Area Networks (LANs) and Wide Area Networks (WANs). The Client/Server architecture which involves networking, relational technology, and distributed processing is thought to be less expensive. It also puts processing power in the hands of the end- user. Whirlpool Financial (HRM4), Inland Steel (HRM4), and Turner Corporation (HRM4) have converted many of their HRIS applications over to the client/server architecture, Toledo Hospital (HRM4) is in the process of converting to the clients/server architecture, and Rothmans, Benson & Hedges (HRM4) is investigating the possibility of migrating to the client/server architecture.

It should be pointed out that the client/server architecture can still use a mainframe as a repository for human resource data. In fact companies are finding that there are fewer technical problems when the mainframe is used as the data repository. In addition, in many instances minicomputer and microcomputer file servers simply cannot handle high transaction rates. LaPlante (1992) cautions organizations, that downsizing and the client/server architecture may not be a viable solution for many companies because:

- The client/server architecture is not stable enough for critical business applications.
- There are not enough qualified systems personnel both within companies and in consulting to assist in the implementation of downsized applications.
- There are not enough off-the-shelf applications for a distributed environment.

- IS development and operations need to be redesigned for the distributed environment.
- Distributed applications require a significant investment in resources up-front for hardware, software, and systems development.

A major problem with the client/server mix involves compatibility. Compatibility between the development language, the network architecture, the operating systems, and the hardware is difficult to achieve. System crashes are an inevitable part of many distributed environments.

Another critical problem with personal computer-based LANs is that they are more vulnerable to security risks than their larger mainframe counterparts. There is in fact no way to prevent someone with the technical know-how and motivation from breaking into a DOS machine. For, example anyone who is a trained Certified NetWare Engineer has the knowledge to go into a Novell NetWare server running NetWare 2.1 and change the supervisor password and erase the audit trail. It has been estimate that there are 25,000 people who have this knowledge to enter through the backdoor of this LAN operating system (LaPlante, 1991). Security is an important issue in the human resources area because of the sensitive nature of the data that is maintained in the HRIS.

But there are benefits to a PC-based LAN, currently a PC MIP (millions of instructions per second) costs $1,000 while a mainframe MIP costs $100,000. The appropriate mix of microcomputer-based LANs versus the centralized mainframe architecture looms as an important decsion for the human resources department.

FUTURE DIRECTIONS OF HRIS

As information technology becomes more advanced and professionals in the human resources departments become more computer-oriented, the applications in HRIS will become increasingly sophisticated. A theme that is repeated throughout the HRIS literature relates to integration of data resources and the distribution of computing power to satisfy localized information processing requirements. But there are additional decision support and expert systems applications that are emerging. The appendix provides illustrations of a variety of mathematical modeling tools can be used to facilitate the decision making from the operational level of the firm up through the highest levels of the firm, including the levels where strategic decisions are being made.

The human resources function and the ensuing computer-based applications are now beginning to have a positive impact on firm performance as management begins to realize that employees are a valuable resource.

It has been estimated that billions per year can be saved in the United States by only making minor improvements to the employee selection process. There are tremendous monetary and competitive benefits that organizations can realize when HR and HRIS applications are viewed as a strategic resource.

Summaries of the eleven case studies in the Human Resource Management area follow below:

Number:	HRM1
Industry:	Electronics Manufacturing
Area:	Human Resources/Manufacturing System
Firm:	Motorola
Location:	Schaumburg, IL
Manager:	Peggy Eastwood
Size:	Sales: $10.8 Billion (1990)

Summary: In 1989, a manufacturing system department was created to accelerate manufacturing automation and computer integration. The department uses several strategies to ensure system quality and minimize development and implementation time. The key aspect was the "personal networking." The department acts as matchmaker between one group that needs a particular technology or application, and another group that has successfully implemented that technology. To that end, the department compiled an information base that tracks various projects at Motorola. The department also compiled a database of different people around the company who are technical experts in a topic. Thus, the department was able to create a forum that brings together cross-functional teams typically composed of people from engineering, manufacturing, financial and human resources. This process has ensured the identification and resolution of conflicting priorities which resulted in minimizing manufacturing costs.

Source: Horwitt. (1990).

Number:	HRM2
Industry:	Manufacturing
Area:	Integrating Human Resources and other common systems.
Firm:	Minnesota Mining and Manufacturing (3M)

Location:	Worldwide
Manager:	Carl A. Kuhrmeyer, Chief Information Officer
Size:	Sales: $12 Billion (1990)

Summary: 3M has several key company-wide systems such as financial, human resources, engineering project management, and CAD/CAM in which data can be swapped between units located anywhere in the world and then consolidated at headquarters. Information sharing has given them the ability to bring a product from the laboratory in three to six months rather than two years. Integration has also assisted marketing in sharing information related to separate units which have the same customers such as GM or Toyota.

However, many of the key applications in business units are developed locally. The 3M culture emphasizes decentralization and flexibility. Idea sharing and decentralized decision making are supported by the integrated applications.

Source: Freedman (1990).

Number:	HRM3
Industry:	Airlines
Area:	Human Resources Management
Firm:	America West
Location:	Tempe, Arizona
Manager:	Jorge France, Sr.
Size:	Not Available

Summary: The company's business services technology services division is developing a human resources system for "employee tracking." The company needs to keep track of the 'currency' of individuals—their expertise and background experience. The need for employee tracking is greater at America West than most other airlines because it is employee-owned, and that twist on ownership changes the way the things are done. For instance, in systems development, an employee might find it useful to have a particular development tool. The management evaluates this proposal and if found feasible the employee's idea is implemented.

Source: Savage (1990).

Number:	HRM4
Industry:	Health Care, Manufacturing, Tobacco
Area:	Down sizing Human Resource Management Systems
Firms:	(1) Toledo Hospital in Ohio
	(2) Rothmans Benson & Hedges in Toronto
	(3) Inland Steel in Chicago
	(4) Turner Corporation in New York City
	(5) Whirlpool Financial in Benton Harbor, Michigan
Managers:	(1) Miriam Ward, Manager at Human Resources Systems
	(2) Jan MacRae, Compensation Analyst
	(3) Nate Soles, Human Resources, Information Manager
	(4) Richard Schell, Director of Information Systems
	(5) Denise Clark, Systems Engineer
Size:	Not Applicable

Summary: Human resource managers are looking towards the client/server architecture which involves networking, relational technology, and distributed processing, to provide easier data access, to reduce costs, and to put processing power in the hands of the end-user. At the Turner Corporation the process of converting from the mainframe to a local area network based on a microcomputer is almost complete. Toledo Hospital is investigating the client/server architecture, but as yet HR applications are running on an IBM 3090 mainframe. Rothmans, Benson & Hedges is anxious to migrate to the client/server architecture but is still running payroll and HR applications on an IBM 3800 mainframe. They find the mainframe too slow, cumbersome and too technical for casual users. Inland Steel uses an HRIS which utilizes a PC LAN and incorporates the Windows 3.1 graphical interface, with an IBM LAN Server, Microsoft's LAN manager and Novell's NetWare. Nate Soles, the project manager for Inland Steel's HRIS feels that "when the information tools are readily available you tend to be more creative and innovative." Inland Steel has an IBM 3090 that is used as a file server and data repository which can be accessed by PC users. Whirlpool

Financial uses a Novell Network, with OS/2 and a relational data base as the basis for their HRIS system. There was some resistance and problems with installation but the HRIS system is currently being used.

Software vendors estimate that demand for client/server applications is still in its infancy. The decision to go towards the client/server architecture is typically an enterprise decision.

Source:	Frye (1991).
Number:	HRM5
Industry:	Manufacturing and Distribution of Homecare Products
Area:	Human Resource Systems
Firm:	SC Johnson Wax
Location:	United States
Manager:	Laurance Burden
Size:	Sales: $2.5 Billion
	13,000 Employees

Summary: Traditionally, the strategic role of IS has meant providing users in such functional areas as sales, marketing and manufacturing with quick access to corporate resources that allow them to make better decisions faster. However, Johnson Wax has decided that IS employees themselves are strategic resources. Finding and keeping qualified staff has become a major IS issue, and Johnson has chosen to invest in developing internal expertise rather than turning to consultants and outsourcing for "quick fixes." The company developed a system called PROFICERE. The system contains a "skills inventory" database application to match an individual's expertise with projects that suit them. In addition, PROFICERE compares available expertise with the skills required for upcoming projects so IS can determine its educational needs. PROFICERE has actually saved the company money. The company says it has decreased its annual professional development investment by 20 percent. The company also developed another system called Computer Integrated Customer Service System which reduced the customer order turnaround time from 14 days to approximately five.

Source: Wexler (1990).

Number: HRM6
Industry: High Technology
Area: Report Distribution System
Firm: Compaq Computer Corporation
Location: Worldwide
Manager: Greg Bergin and Kathy Seesing
Size: 12,000 Employees

Summary: Compaq Computer Corporation's human resource information system department (HRIS) experienced some growing pains in dealing with report distribution. The department spent more time managing the production report distribution process rather than developing new systems. To correct this, Compaq designed a system to document programs and distribute reports. More importantly, it enabled employees to devote time to non- maintenance tasks. The Corporate Automated Report Distribution (CARD) system has been in place for one year and has resulted in significant time reductions. Before the system was implemented, the HRIS staff distributed about 50 reports to 150 recipients each month. Currently, 200 reports are distributed to 600 recipients per month. It only takes about 52 hours — a 46 percent decrease in time to distribute 4 times as many reports. The new system saves the company approximately $47,000 a year.

Source: Bergin and Seesing (1991).

Number: HRM7
Industry: Mining
Area: Integrated Human Resource Systems
Firm: Newmont Mining Corporation
Location: Denver, Colorado
Manager: Donald Costine
Size: Not Available

Summary: At Newmont Mining Corporation the personnel staff was having difficulty keeping up with daily employee record-keeping and payroll applications, and the human resources systems needed to be integrated. The company built one central database on the corporate mainframe, a Unisys Corporation A17 operating under Unisys' MCP operating system and running Unisys' DMS2 database management system. Although there is potential for labor savings, the biggest benefit of the new system is that the HR people concentrate on doing other things. Productivity in personnel, in management information systems, and at the executive level is the number one factor driving the integration of HR applications.

Source: Davis (1991).

Number: HRM8
Industry: Cable Television
Area: Human Resource Information Services
Firm: Home Box Office Inc.
Location: United States
Manager: Maryanne Coleman-Carlone
Size: Not Available

Summary: Home Box Office Inc. (HBO), a subsidiary of Time Inc., believes in pay based on performance. The process begins with goals being set for each employee at the beginning of the year, followed by an interim review at midyear. Toward the end of each year, the department head meets with an employee and goes through a process of performance review relative to these goals. There are a number of tools that the human resources information systems staff provides for the bonus administration process, including calculation worksheets, data entry, and reports for review. Through the use of these tools, HBO has developed a solid program to reward its employees' superior performance. The merit planning process uses a budgeting tool that is based on the percentage of the company's total base salary at the first of each year. The firm's financial and strategic performance, expected growth in the new year, the current national inflation rates, and national average pay increases in the entertainment industry also figure into the process. Senior management then uses the economic factors to assist in determining the total merit pool and allocating merit increases.

Source: Coleman-Carlone (1990).

Number: HRM9
Industry: Financial and Chemical
Area: Human Resource Systems
Firm: Rohm and Haas
Location: Philadelphia
Manager: Doug Perry
Size: 12,000 employees

Summary: International Data Corporation expects the annual market for human resources (HR) software to nearly double from $398 million in 1989 to $730 million by 1993, not including the sizable HR information system (HRIS) consulting market. Many firms have formed special information systems groups solely dedicated to supporting HR. Rohm and Haas was using a 16-year old batch system running on mainframe database. The company then established a human resource information center which plans to migrate to IBM's DB2 relational database. Technically and architecturally the direction of the new HRIS follows two established trends in the larger IS arena: (1) the move to distribute processing across a variety of computing platforms, and (2) the use of relational databases.

Source: Stamps (1990).

Number: HRM10
Industry: Clothing
Area: On-Line Interactive Visual Employee Resource System
Firm: Levi Strauss & Co.
Location: Worldwide
Manager: Reese Smith
Size: 2,500 employees

Summary: OLIVER (On-Line Interactive Visual Employees Resource) is an interactive computer network that enables all 2,500 employees at Levi Strauss & Co. to log on to the clothing manufacturer's mainframe through their personal computers and look at as many as 500 screens of personal data. Using OLIVER, Levi Strauss employees can review such items as total compensation, disability, health care, pension, employee investment plan, survivor information. After OLIVER leads users into one of the main menus, they can stray off the beaten path to view more details. Once on the health care menu road, users can turn off on such paths of information as coverage details, covered dependents, or a quick facts menu. To access OLIVER, employees simply type in their names, identification numbers, passwords, and their social security numbers. What makes the software unique is that it covers not only benefits, but also such areas as financial planning and training and development.

Source:	Leabs (1991).
Number:	HRM11
Industry:	Petroleum
Area:	Human Resources Management System
Firm:	Chevron Corporation
Location:	Worldwide
Manager:	Lou Fernandez
Size:	300,000 employees

Summary: Chevron Corporation's human resource management system (HRMS), called EPIC (Emphasizing People in Chevron), is a flexible, integrated, worldwide system. Integration promised several advantages, including minimized paperwork. A smaller number of forms need to be filled out, mailed and filed. This will save both employee time and company resources. Integration also will keep the core database current, which will aid managers at all levels in making personnel, organizational, and other business decisions. Chevron implemented EPIC in four phases: (1) Business Development, (2) Software Purchase, (3) Software Adaptation, and (4) Rollout. To ensure acceptance, Chevron attempted to make EPIC as easy to use and learn as possible. At all human resources field offices where EPIC is being introduced, EPIC client services has trained representatives, which includes 60 site coordinators from field offices and 70 trainers in the online and reporting environments. Chevron has also developed an internal marketing program for EPIC.

Source: Straight (1990).

REFERENCES

Bergin, G. and K. Seesing. 1991. "CARD Deals with Report Distribution." *Personnel Journal (November): 109-113.*

Coleman-Carlone, M. *1990. "HBO's Program for Merit Pay." Personnel Journal* (May): 86-90.

Davis, L. 1991. "On the Fast Track to HR Integration." *Datamation* (September): 61- 65.

Freedman, D. 1990. "The Company that Innovation Built." *CIO* (August): 23-30.

Frye, C. 1991. "MIS Eyes. HRMS Applications for Experimental Downsizing" *Software Magazine* (June): 110-115.

Horwitt, E. (1990). "Matchmakers in Manufacturing." *ComputerWorld* (September): 47, 52.

Kavanagh, M.J., H.G. Gueutal, and Tannenbaum, F.S. 1990. *Human Resource Information Systems: Development and Application.* Boston, MA: PWS-Kent Publishing Company.

LaPlante, A. 1992. "Chipping Away at the Corporate Mainframe." *InfoWorld* (January): 40-42.

LaPlante, A. 1991. "Guarding Their Turf." *Infoworld* (September): S59-S64.

Leabs, J.J. 1991. "OLIVER: A Twist on Communication." *Personnel Journal* (September): 79-82.

Savage, J.A. 1990. "America West Airlines Clears 3090 for Takeoff." *ComputerWorld* (July 2): 28.

Stamps, D. 1990. "Human Resources: A Strategic Partner Or IS Burden?" *Datamation* (June): 47-52.

Straight, J.F. Jr. 1990. "Creating Chevron's HRMS: An EPIC Tale." *Personnel Journal* (June): 72-81.

Wexler, J.M. 1990. "Playing 'Skill Connection' with IS" *ComputerWorld* (December 17): 1, 63.

APPENDIX

Human Resource Decision Support Systems (HRDSS): Integrating Decision Support and Human Resource Information Systems

David B. Meinert, Donald L. Davis

Abstract

Human resource information systems (HRIS) have vastly improved structured human resource management decision making while failing to improve semi- or unstructured decision making. This paper describes a human resource decision support system (HRDSS) which integrates DSS capabilities with those of HRIS to overcome the limitations inherent in the design of HRIS.

1. increased organizational size and complexity;
2. geographical dispersion of firms;
3. government regulation and reporting requirements; and
4. an increase in white collar work which demands a greater variety of skills for any given job (DeSanctis, 1986, p. 16).

A concise definition of HRIS is provided by Mathys and LaVan (1982), who described them as "management information systems designed specifically to provide managers and others with information necessary to improve human resource decisions" (p. 83). Unfortunately, empirical research suggests that HRIS are not perceived by managers outside of the human resource areas as contributing significantly to improved decision making (DeSanctis, 1986; Mathys and LaVan, 1982; Moore and Clavadetscher, 1985). This common misperception that HRIS offers only limited support to decision making, particularly to managers outside of the human resource organizational unit, can partially be attributed to the approach taken by system designers in developing an HRIS. An observation by Magnus and Grossman (1985, p. 43) that "automation in the personnel department to date has focused on the bread and butter issues of human resources management: employee records, payroll, and compensation and benefits administration" is representative of other studies. DeSanctis (1986), Moore and Clavadetscher (1985), and Mathys and LaVan (1982) all reported similar findings, indicating that a majority of the HRIS applications are administrative (i.e., recordkeeping) in nature.

Particularly disturbing are the findings by Verdin (1987) which suggest that HRIS may also be of limited or questionable value to decision makers in the human resources organizational unit. Verdin (1987) found that computer applications had failed to reduce the amount of time spent on decision making for a majority of human resource managers studied, and that over 50 percent of the respondents reported low quality for decisions made using the HRIS. Moore and Clavadetscher (1985) found that over 40 percent of the respondents in the human resources unit reported only moderate to low utility for computerized HRIS systems. Recent reviews of commercially available HRIS software further substantiate these findings (Frantzreb, 1986; Magnus and Thomsen, 1986).

HRIS have not been totally unsuccessful. On the contrary the systems have improved the efficiency of the human resources area in accomplishing routine, structured tasks (Verdin, 1987). HRIS, by their design, are well suited for generating the voluminous routine reports associated with the human resource management areas previously mentioned. Their major limitation is in their inability to offer support for decision makers facing non-routine and/or semi-structured or unstructured problems throughout the organization.

Thus, the stage is set for the development of a Human Resource Decision Support System. The HRDSS should be designed to assist decision makers throughout the organization and viewed as complementing rather than replacing an existing HRIS, an integration of the two systems.

Benefits of Decision Support Systems

To fully appreciate the contributions that a HRDSS will offer, one needs to consider the differences between a DSS and MIS (in this particular case, HRIS). Decision Support Systems are characterized "as interactive computer-based systems that help decision makers utilize data and models to solve unstructured problems" (Sprague and Carlson, 1982, p. 4). MIS are designed to provide periodic and exception reports primarily for structured problems (Kroeber and Watson, 1987). The differences between the major types of Human Resource Information Systems are summarized in Figure 1.

Clearly, managers or decision makers confronted with human resource management decisions, typically semi- or unstructured in nature, would gain little support from the HRIS. The contribution of traditional HRIS is in the area of structured tasks, that is in improving the recordkeeping and routine reporting functions of the human resources areas. The HRDSS by design will support the decision maker with appropriate data and models in their decision making process. Thus, a HRDSS should be viewed as a tool to aid decision makers in the utilization of existing human resources information in their analyses of problems and opportunities.

As shown in Figure 2, an HRIS consists of a database, database management system, an application program base, and an application base manager. The transactions are recorded, maintained, and retrieved through the database management system. Other recordkeeping activities and reports are generated by the application programs maintained in the application program base manager. Usually there is some inquiry capability via the database management system. Depending on the type of system, however, that inquiry capability may be very user unfriendly. Thus, the HRIS satisfies a design requirement to provide only recordkeeping and report generation capabilities.

An HRDSS illustrated in Figure 3 consists of a model base with an appropriate management system and a sophisticated, interactive, user interface and dialogue system which is integrated with the HRIS database. The model base contains analytic, heuristic, and statistical models which use the information in the HRIS data base to provide support in the decision-making process for the user. The models may vary from simple statistical means to multiple regression, linear and nonlinear programming, and sophisticated simulation models of organizational tasks.

HUMAN RESOURCE TRANSACTION PROCESSING SYSTEMS (TPS)

Acquire data from various HR sub-units and functional line units to provide a consolidated data base. These systems capture fundamental data and make it available to the other HR information systems. Only highly structured problems, such as payroll, and processed within these types of systems. Data acquired would include:

- Individual Employee Data
    - -name, address, employee #, position, date of hire, department
- Recruitment and Selection Data
    - -number of applicants, interviews, job offers
    - -AA/EEO data
- Compensation Data
    - -salary, benefit options
- Performance Appraisal
- Training and Development

HUMAN RESOURCE REPORT GENERATING SYSTEMS (RGS OR TRADITIONAL MIS)

Provide HR information to managers, in the form of periodic, exception, and ad hoc reports, to support operations and decision making. Generally, systems of this nature address structured problem solving or decision making. Reports provided would include:

- Date of hire reports
- Salary comparisons
- Turnover reports
- Absenteeism reports
- AA/EEO reports
- Overtime reports
- Budget reports

HUMAN RESOURCE DECISION SUPPORT SYSTEMS (DSS)

Assist decision makers in using data and models to solve un- or semi-structured problems. Systems are generally interactive in nature, and are designed with user-friendly interfaces to facilitate use by non-MIS professionals. Examples of HR decision support systems can be found in Table 2.

HUMAN RESOURCE EXPERT SYSTEMS (ES)

Allow users to generate solutions to problems approximating those at which "experts" would arrive. Expert system software attempts to capture the knowledge and inferences procedures of experts to provide solutions to such tasks as interpretation, diagnosis, prediction, and planning. Explanation subsystems allow users to query the system concerning data required and inferences generated. Examples of expert system applications could include:

- Termination programs (designed to consider the myriad of legal implications)
- Selection programs (aimed at reducing selector bias)
- Skill Assessment programs (appraise skill levels)

Figure 1.   Hierarchy of Human Resource Information Systems

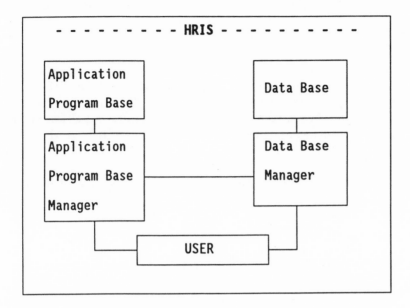

Figure 2. Model of Human Resource Information System (HRIS)

An overriding concern of systems designers is the ability to communicate with the user of the system in the most effective and efficient manner possible. That concern is addressed in the design of the HRDSS. The user

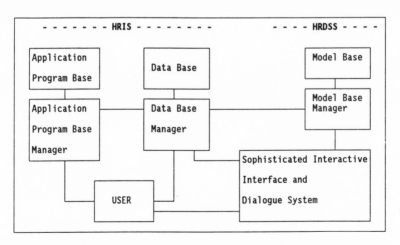

Figure 3. Model of Integrated Human Resource Information system (HRIS) and Human Resource Decision Support System (HRDSS)

interface and dialogue system provides user friendly communication with the overall system, and in conjunction with the model base a means to ask "what if" questions as well as the ability to develop simulated scenarios of alternative solutions to problems.

Anthony's (1965) classification of management decision making is a useful tool for the illustration of the various levels at which HRDSS could support human resource decision making. According to Anthony's classification scheme, there are three distinct levels of decision making: operational, managerial, and strategic. These levels were defined by Anthony (1965) as:

1. Operational level decisions focus on the execution of day-to-day activities, and are highly influenced by the direction established at the managerial level;
2. Managerial level decisions are concerned with establishing policies, procedures, and programs to provide necessary and sufficient resources to accomplish goals established at the strategic level; and
3. Strategic level decisions are generally more long-term, concerned with goal setting and policy formulation (pp. 16-18).

Human resource decision making can be further classified according to the types of human resource problems or decisions facing managers at each of the decision making levels described by Anthony. The majority of human resource decisions could be classified as: (1) staffing, (2) training and development, (3) performance review/appraisal, or (4) compensation administration. Figure 4 contains examples of HRDSS applications (models) for these four areas of human resource decisions across Anthony's decision making classification.

It should be noted that the applications described in Figure 4, and similar applications/models, could be utilized by both human resource professionals and managers external to that functional area. The paucity of analytic models specific to the human resource area can be attributed to its "qualitative" reputation. The accessibility to human resource data provided by HRIS, and the growing interest in more quantitative human resource decision-making, should provide the necessary impetus for further advancements in this area.

While the contributions of DSS and HRIS, are somewhat dependent upon one another, they are distinctly different and yet very complementary. Keen (1980) described DSS as efforts to synthesize MIS and Management Science. The following descriptions of the potential benefits of HRDSS are presented with this relationship in mind.

Staffing	Training/Development	Performance Review and Appraisal	Compensation Administration
		STRATEGIC	
Manpower Planning Models Labor force Tracking (Forecasting, Decision Trees)	Succession Planning Models (Simulations, Markov Analysis)		Contract Costing Models Salary Forecasting Models
		MANAGERIAL	
Budget Analysis Models Turnover Analysis Models Turnover Cost Models Absenteeism/ Performance Models	Training Effectiveness Models Career Match Models (Goal programming)	Correlation Model (performance/ training)	Compensation Effectiveness Model (relative to performance) Benefit Preference Models (Conjoint Measurement)
		OPERATIONS	
Recruiting Models Structured Interview/ Assessment Models Workforce Planning Models Scheduling Models (Cost Minimization) Selection Models (Bayesian, LP)	Skill Assessment Models	Computer-Based Evaluation Programs and Models	Compensation Equality (evaluation factors relative to compensation)

Figure 4. DSS Applications for Human Resource Areas Across Decision Making Levels

Competitive Advantage. The development of HRDSS to augment the information provided to managers by existing HRIS should be viewed by organizations as an opportunity to develop a competitive advantage (Rynes and Milkovich, 1986). According to Rynes and Milkovich (1986):

> The consequences of employer hiring decisions are both substantial and far reaching. For organizations, the quality of selection procedures determines the willingness and ability of workers to master immediate job requirements, as well as to adapt and contribute to future organizational changes (p. 154).

Based on this observation, the authors concluded that more effective selection procedures can provide organizations with a competitive advantage not unlike those provided by advances or improvements in other functional areas (e.g., revolutionary technological improvements in production processes).

The utilization of information systems such as HRDSS to develop a competitive advantage is not a unique concept. Brancheau and Wetherbe (1987) reported that a recent survey of information system professionals indicated that the use of such systems for competitive advantage was the second most critical issue facing information system executives over the next three to five years. Recent interest in the need for close alignment of strategic planning and human resource planning for the achievement of organizational goals also supports this position (Golden and Ramanujam, 1985; Lavin, 1981; Scarpello and Ledvinka, 1988).

The most important issue identified by IS executives in Brancheau and Wetherbe's 1987 survey was improved strategic planning. Those responsible for HRIS administration, regardless of whether they are aligned with a centralized MIS function or operate as a separate entity (MIS subsystem) within the human resources area, should recognize the potential for HRDSS to support strategic planning. The contribution that HRDSS can make to strategic planning was stressed by Golden and Ramanujam (1985), who reported that a survey of senior human resource executives indicated that HRDSS would increase their contribution to strategic planning.

More Efficient and Effective Utilization of Information. The utilization of HRDSS in the human resources area would provide a means for more efficient and effective management and utilization of the massive amounts of generated information. The variety, magnitude, and complexity of information required for efficient and effective human resource decision making was highlighted by Bassett (1979) who enumerated 149 types of information pertinent to this area. This complexity, which increases the demands placed on HRIS, is compounded by the need for much of the information to be shared with managers throughout the organization at different times for widely divergent types of human resource management issues. Traditional MIS, after which the majority of HRIS are patterned, were not designed to efficiently or effectively accommodate unusual requests for reports, nor do they provide user-accessible capacities for the analysis or manipulation of information. As noted above, the strength of MIS lies in the area of structured or routine tasks. DSS, as noted previously, allow managers the flexibility to address semistructured and unstructured problems through inquiry and analysis capabilities.

Many managers external to the human resource area face semistructured or unstructured decisions, as the needs of the organization and the availability or quality of applicants and employees are changing. For most managers external to the human resource area, recruitment, selection, training, and development issues are typically non-routine, performed on an as needed or ad hoc basis. The situation specific nature of these types of decisions makes them all the more difficult for human resources personnel to provide assistance, and all but impossible for HRIS to adequately support.

HRDSS would allow individual managers the opportunity to identify, access, and analyze relevant information with models designed for specific applications. The DSS capacity for interfacing data and model bases, combined with its sophisticated graphic/report generators, should provide managers with a means for augmenting the information presently made available through HRIS generated routine and exception reports.

Increased Productivity. In keeping with Keen's (1980) observation that "benefits of a DSS can be hard to quantify, but not necessarily to recognize ..." (p. 34), the following discussion of potential gains in productivity is general in nature. The intent of this section is to illustrate the promise of improved human resource decisions through the use of HRDSS. Improved human resource management decisions resulting from the use of HRDSS could potentially result in substantial productivity gains.

Hunter and Schmidt (1983), in an effort to quantify the economic impact of improved employee selection, calculated that the potential increase in productivity achieved across the economy from improved selection criteria would result in an increase of the gross national product of from $89 to $100 billion per year. Although Hunter and Schmidt suggest that this figure is conservative, based upon only relatively minor improvements in selection, an examination of their efforts suggests that even a modest improvement in selection would lead to significant gains in productivity.

A specific DSS proposed by Davis and Steen (1983) for contract administration provides one example of the potential benefits to be derived from an HRDSS. The proposed DSS supported the administration of a collective bargaining agreement involving employee absenteeism and tardiness, grievance analysis and response, layoff and recall, overtime and job assignment.

A more detailed appraisal of the benefits afforded by HRDSS would require knowledge of existing hardware and software, the level of sophistication of data and model bases needed, and the diligence and commitment with which management would apply the new decision aid.

Implications

The following areas merit consideration in the development of HRDSS and should be of interest to HRIS administrators, Human Resource specialists, MIS/DSS designers, and MS/OR researchers.

First, types or classes of human resource decisions to be supported by HRDSS need to be identified. The classification matrix presented in Figure 4 should provide some direction in this area. Human resource specialists must carefully assess the needs of decision makers in terms of required information and presentation format. Caution should be exercised to ensure that end user needs and desired are addressed both within and external to the human resource area. This process will assist in the identification of the capabilities, including models that should be incorporated in HRDSS.

Second, models specifically designed to assist managers involved in human resource decisions must be developed. Efforts in this regard are unlikely to produce models approaching optimality, however, even modest improvements in decisions involving personnel have been shown to be capable of producing significant benefits. A synthesis of MS/OR techniques and existing knowledge of employee performance with respect to various variables, combined with the information available through existing HRIS should serve as a starting point in this venture.

Third, future HRIS designs must necessarily support complementary HRDSS capabilities. This relationship holds implications for both commercial analysts and designers, as organizations are presently utilizing a variety of inhouse, purchased, and external or timesharing HRIS software (Magnus and Grossman, 1985). The successful integration of DSS capabilities, through the customized development or commercially available software packages will naturally be dependent upon the degree of compatibility with HRIS.

Finally, managers must be educated as to the availability and utilization of HRDSS capabilities. Managers only recently introduced to the DSS concept and technology may hesitate to utilize the formalized decision tool, HRDSS.

Conclusion

An integration of Human Resource Information System (HRIS) with Decision Support Systems (DSS) technology will support decision makers throughout an organization. The development of Human Resource Decision Support Systems (HRDSS) will complement the capabilities of existing HRIS, and provide a means for a more complete utilization of the massive amounts of information available.

HRDSS will extend the capabilities of the HRIS from its present task of recordkeeping and generating routine reports. Through the Model Base and sophisticated Interactive User Interface of the HRDSS, along with the database of the HRIS, managers will be able to gain support in making their human resource decisions, thereby providing gains in organizational productivity, competitive advantage, and managerial effectiveness.

Acknowledgment

Copyright. Information Resources Management Journal, pp. 41-49, Winter 1989, reprinted with permission.

References

Anthony, R.N. 1965. *Planning and Control Systems: A framework for analysis.* Cambridge Ma: Harvard University Press.

Bassett, G.A. 1979. "PAIR Records and Information Systems." In *ASPA Handbook of Personnel and Industrial Relations* edited by D. Yoder and M. B. Heneman, Jr. Washington, D.C.: Bureau of National Affairs: 1-56-2-90.

Brancheau, J.C. and J.C. Wetherbe, 1987. "Key Issues in Information Systems Management." *MIS Quarterly* 11(1): 23-39.

Burack, E.H. and N.J. Mathys, 1980. *Human Resource Planning: A Pragmatic Approach to Management Staffing and Development.* Lake Forest, IL: Brace-Park Press.

Darany, T.S. 1987. "Computer Applications to Personnel (Releasing the Genie-Harnessing the Dragon)." *Public Personnel Management Journal* 13(9): 451-473.

Davis, D.L. and J.E. Steen. 1983. "Computing the Advantages of Detailed Data Systems." *Personnel Journal* 62(1): 888-892.

DeSanctis, G. 1986. "Human Resource Information Systems: A Current Assessment." *MIS Quarterly* 10(1): 15-27.

Enderle, R.D. 1987. "HRIS Models for Staffing. *Personnel Journal* 66(11): 73-79.

Frantzreb, R.D. 1986. "The Microcomputer-Based HRIS: A Directory. *Personnel Administrator* 31(9): 71-98.

Golden, K.A. and V. Ramanujam, 1985. Between a Dream and a Nightmare: On the Integration of the Human Resource Management and Strategic Business Planning Processes. *Human Resources Management* 24(4): 429-452.

Harris, D. 1986. "Beyond the Basics: New HRIS Developments." *Personnel* 63(1): 49-56.

Hunter, J.E. and Schmidt. 1983. "Interventions on Employee Job Performance and Workforce Productivity." *American Psychologist* 38(3): 473-478.

Johnson B.H., G., Moorhead, and R.W. Griffin. 1983. Human Resource Information Systems and Job Design." *Human Resources Planning* 6(1): 35-40.

Keen, P.G.W. 1980. "Decision Support Systems: Translating Analytic Techniques into Useful Tools." *Sloan Management Review* 21(3): 33-45.

Kroeber, D.W. and H.J. Watson. 1987. *Computer-Based Information Systems: A Management Approach.* New York: Macmillan Publishing Company.

Lavin, M.J. 1981. "HRDSS: A Computerized Human Resource Development Information System." *Human Resource Planning* 9(1): 25-35.

LaPointe, J. and J.A. Verdin. 1988. "How to Calculate the Cost of Human Resources." *Personnel Journal* 67(1): 39-45.

Magnus, M. and M. Grossman. 1985. Personnel Journal Reports: Computers and the Personnel Department." *Personnel Journal* 64(4): 42-48.

Magnus, M. and D.J. Thomsen. 1986. "Microcomputer Software Guide." *Personnel Journal* 65(2): 49-70.

Mathys, N. and LaVan, H. 1982. "A Survey of the Human Resource Information Systems (HRIS) of Major Companies." *Human Resource Planning* 5(2): 83-90.

Moore, L.L. and C.J. Clavadetscher. 1985. "Computerized HRIS: Still Simmering on the Back Burner. *Personnel* 62(8): 8-11.

Murdick, R.G. and F. Schuster. 1983. "Computerized Information Support for the Human

Resource Function." *Human Resource Planning* 6(1): 25-33.

Nardoni, R. 1985. "The Building Blocks of a Successful Microcomputer System." *Personnel Journal* 64(1): 28-34.

Rynes, S.L. and G.T. Milkovich. 1986. *Current Issues in Human Resource Management: Commentary and Readings.* Plano, TX: Business Publications, Inc.

Scarpello, V.G. and J. Ledvinka. 1988. *Personnel/Human Resource Management: Environments and Functions.* Boston: PWS-Kent Publishing Company.

Schultz, C.B. 1984. "Saving Millions Through Judicious Selection of Employees." *Public Personnel Management Journal* 13(4): 409-415.

Sprague, R.G., Jr. and E.D. Carlson. 1982. *Building Effective Decision Support Systems.* Englewood Cliffs, NJ: Prentice Hall.

Sprague, R.H., Jr. and B. Konsynski. 1986. "Future Research Directions in Model Management." *Decision Support Systems: The International Journal* 2(1): 103-109.

Tomeski, E.A., M.B. Yoon, and G. Stephenson. 1976. "Computer-Related Challenges for Personnel Administrators." *Personnel Journal* 55(6): 300-302.

Verdin, J.A. 1987. "The HRIS and Managerial Performance." *Personnel Administrator* 32(6): 24-28.

MODELING STRATEGIC DECISION MAKING AND PERFORMANCE MEASUREMENTS AT ICI PHARMACEUTICALS

Gerd Islei, Geoff Lockett, Barry Cox,
Steve Gisbourne, and Mike Stratford

This chapter consists of a paper describing the development of a decision support system [DSS] used for strategic decision making at ICI Pharmaceuticals in the United Kingdom. The system was developed over a period of ten years with the purposes of selecting research projects, monitoring research portfolios, and assisting in the decision to terminate projects. It is based on judgmental modeling concepts that have been incorporated into a modern computer-based information system. The system provides a unified analysis and reporting format that helps communication and decision-making among a team of research managers. Although the strategic support system described in this chapter is largely confined to the research and development area of pharmaceuticals, the system has migrated to a number of other areas in the ICI organization. Specifically, it is being used in the Chemical and Polymers area and also in the marketing department of two other branches of ICI. Hence, the strategic support system is not just applicable to a specific area but has strong generalizability.

ABSTRACT

Over 10 years, we have developed a DSS that is used for R&D strategic decision making at ICI for selecting research projects, monitoring portfolios, allocating resources, and terminating projects. It is based on judgmental modeling concepts that have been incorporated into a modern computer-based information system. Our DSS provides a unified analysis and reporting format that helps communication and decision making among a team of research managers. Because of its flexibility, other parts of the organization have successflly adopted it.

INTRODUCTION

Since the 1970s, decision support systems have emerged as a way to apply information technology to help managers make decisions. Such systems have been characterized as "interactive computer based systems, which help decision makers utilize data and models to solve unstructured problems" (Sprague, 1989). Even though this definition has guided much of the research in this area, its realization in the business environment has not been recognized. Nevertheless several cases have been reported of systems that meet these objectives and were successfully implemented in organizations (Alter, 1980; Gray, King, McLean, and Watson, 1989; Keen and Scott Morton, 1978; Turban, 1990). They:

- Facilitate decision-making processes,
- support rather than replace managerial decision making, and
- respond to the changing needs of decision makers.

However, many applications testify to a number of important barriers to the wider use of decision support systems in the business environment (Gray et al., 1989; PA Consulting Group, 1990). These have included:

- Incompatible, multi-vendor environments,
- hierarchical and proprietary networks,
- high costs of ownership,
- inability to transfer data between applications and data bases, and
- unfriendly user interfaces.

Most DSSs are either large-scale systems built to facilitate well-defined and repetitive decision tasks, or else they are small PC-based products offering quick and economic routines to support one-time decisions. Even though the impact of such systems on individual decision making may be substantial, they have not been adopted by organizations to any degree commensurate with their potential. A major reason seems to be that large systems are not flexible enough to aid unstructured decision tasks (and thus top-level decision making), whereas small (flexible) systems, which are useful for a specific decision making process, are difficult to translate into useable prototypes for different scenarios. Their narrow design also makes them largely incompatible with open system architectures.

Recent advances in computer technology embracing powerful local area networks, compatible PC environments, and a move towards connectability and transferability of models and data could hold the key to bringing flexible decision support to organizations. New systems should emerge that are capable of handling large volumes of data, and can interpret, develop and communicate these data to suit changing organizational requirements. In addition, they will be flexible and manageable and remain relevant to their users (i.e., able to support a diversity of models and management styles). To achieve this, systems developers must address the whole spectrum of decision making; in particular, they need to develop systems able to accommodate the interdependencies of managerial decision making.

So far computer systems have had little impact in supporting strategic decision making, an area in which managers face very unstructured tasks and cope with a high degree of uncertainty (Gray, et al., 1989; Sprague, 1989). Decision makers often rely on their own judgments and experience. We must improve our understanding of the type of support they need for unstructured decision making and examine the models appropriate for tackling such tasks. To do this, we have to monitor the progress of suitable systems over extended periods of time and match that progress with appropriate resources.

We used a series of judgmental models to develop a decision support system in a research and development (R&D) environment. The purpose of the system is to help management choose a portfolio of research projects, monitor project development, and change the allocation of resources if necessary. The system evolved as a result of several years of collaboration between managers at ICI Pharmaceuticals, consultants at ICI Corporate Management Services, and researchers at the Manchester Business School.

THE DSS ENVIRONMENT

In the pharmaceutical industry over the past decades, research has become increasingly competitive. In response to this increased competition, the research- based pharmaceutical companies have tried to develop effective strategies to ensure success. Different organizational structures have been designed to achieve this, ranging from relatively free association of scientists to tightly controlled research environments. The challenge to research management is to create an environment that favors and is conducive to innovative research but that, when an innovative discovery is made, permits the company to act efficiently to capitalize on it (Cox, 1989).

Typical aims of a research-based pharmaceutical company are (DeStevens, 1986; Cox, 1989):

- To discover and produce drugs that make worthwhile contributions to human health by means of research and development,
- to improve or maintain high efficiency to achieve a good competitive position,
- to optimize creativity and scientific debate, and
- to identify and develop creative young scientists.

In attempting to fulfill these aims, pharmaceutical firms must decide what therapeutic areas to work in and how much of their effort and resources to place in each. The enormous costs of pharmaceutical research and increased development times make decisions concerning research portfolios crucial for maintaining a competitive position. While developing a new drug cost less than $10 million in 1950, it now costs over $120 million. The times consumed in the various stages of developing and marketing a drug are also enormous: five to 10 years of research, two to four years in early development, and three to seven years in late development and launch.

Research management faces some key issues:

- To maintain and build on the past reputation of certain drugs and to pursue research in new therapeutic areas,
- to take advantage of existing and experienced research expertise and to explore new cultures for developing research initiatives, and
- to pursue structured research and exploit serendipity.

All these factors and many more, influence the selection of a research portfolio and thus determine the organizational design needed to support innovative research activities.

ICI Pharmaceuticals is an international producer of pharmaceutical products. It is part of a much larger group that also produces bulk and fine chemicals and fiber and nutrition products. Our application affects the cardiovascular pharmacology section of ICI, the largest of the pharmaceutical research groupings. The company has always placed great importance on managing its R&D and has often taken innovative approaches. ICI is not an organization that follows every management fashion, but constantly strives for excellence and investigates new methods and ideas.

The company has explored various ways to improve its management of research portfolios. For example, it provides consultants from a special management services unit to help senior managers develop new approaches. In many cases, they designed methods that measure the success of current research. Since typical research projects last over five years, instantaneous decisions are usually not required. However, the competitive position of the company depends on its ability to produce new drugs on a regular basis: assessing the state of research projects is vital. Of all management functions, R&D is notoriously the most difficult to manage. Reliable information is in short supply, and the stochastic nature of the process is evident. The research section has therefore used a variety of approaches to assess project worth with varying degrees of success, keeping one method until a better one is proven.

In the past, ICI used methods based on linear programming (Bell and Read, 1970; Gear and Lockett, 1973) to assess the state of the research portfolio and, although they provided valuable insights, for this environment they have not proved sustainable in the long term. They assume project selection as a one-time process; in fact it is part of a series of interdependent decisions. However, the data collection exercise was considered of value.

Another method that has been used successfully is cost/benefit analysis (Gear, Lockett, and Muhlemann, 1982; Islei, Lockett, Cox and Stratford 1991). This approach also points to a key prerequisite for such decision problems: measurement without the constraint of intricate model development. Even though cost/benefit analysis was considered unsatisfactory for appraising research projects, some of its concepts are valuable and have been incorporated in later developments.

Finally, ICI explored the approach of the Boston Consulting Group (Lockett, et al., 1986) throughout the organization but found it not entirely appropriate for this research environment. The data demands were seen as the biggest impediment, and therefore it was not fully implemented.

However, the problem remained, and the senior management group continued to look for a system that would support its management of a portfolio of research projects. The managers regularly asked their internal consulting team for advice and thus kept abreast of the developments in the MS/OR literature. They were the driving force for change; they had used several models before, but they were not looking to be part of an academic exercise. Any decision support developed that would have to offer greater benefits than the system in current use.

PROJECT EVALUATION

A senior manager of the cardiovascular section initiated the first systematic examination of procedures to support the process of managing pharmaceutical research at ICI. He had cooperated with external consultants in assessing how the organization and its methods for evaluating and selecting research topics could be improved. At about the same time he attended a management course at the Manchester Business School in which various MCDM (multicriteria decision-making) approaches were discussed as frameworks for supporting project management in R&D environments. He realized the potential of judgmental models that use computer support for capturing and evaluating basic data, and he though that such a tool might offer a more transparent and effective method for product profiling than the current means (Lockett, Hetherington, Yallup, Stratford, and Cox, 1986).

When the project with the external consultants was completed, the section manager decided to evaluate the research projects in his area using a more sophisticated computerized technique. He could also compare its outcome with the recommendations from the consultancy project.

After some initial discussions among the senior manager, the internal consulting team, and researchers from the Manchester Business School, we decided to involve the project managers from the cardiovascular section in building a project selection model. Over a period of weeks and several meetings, the group explored the modeling task and clarified the various factors it considered most relevant for assessing project worth. The group members pooled their experience and thoroughly discussed their different assumptions. At all stages, they checked the progress of the model carefully by screening the various options. Finally, they adopted a hierarchy of eight attributes for formally evaluating projects. (Lockett, et al. [1986] gives a full description of this process.)

In total, they intended to assess 10 projects (abbreviated IH, AR, CA, RI, AT, CS, FA, RS, II, CC). They used a computer package based on the analytic hierarchy process (AHP) (Saaty, 1980) to obtain data. However, before participating in this structured evaluation, each team member ranked the research projects using a simplified version of the Kepner-Tregoe method (Kepner and Tregoe, 1965). We later compared the initial expectations of the participants with the results of the computer supported assessments (Figure 1) (Lockett, et al., 1986; Islei and Lockett, 1991). As a result of this exercise, we changed the project portfolio.

Because of the differences between the intuitive and the final results, we had a very thorough discussion of the merits of the decision support system. We felt that the computer-supported judgmental model allowed a depth of analysis that would otherwise have been difficult to achieve. The computer-assisted evaluation facilitated the process of quantifying individual preferences and gave scope to an easy exchange and comparison of information. This approach, together with some simple statistical routines, enabled the participants to highlight commonalities in their evaluations, and equally important, to trace crucial differences (Islei and Lockett, 1991.

Project Managers													
Rank	**1**		**2**		**3**		**4**		**5**		**6**		**Sr. Mgr.**	
Position	**Bef**	**Aft**	**Bef**	**Aft**	**Bef**	**Aft**	**Bef**	**Aft**	**Bef**	**Aft**	**Bef**	**Aft**	**Bef**	**Aft**
1	CA	CA	RI	IH	AT	AT	AR	AR	RI	RI	RI	IH	CA	CA
2	CC	CS	IH	CA	CA	IH	RS	CA	CA	CA	II	CS	CS	RI
3	II	AT	AR	RI	RI	RI	AT	AT	II	IH	IH	AT	II	IH
4	RI	II	CS	AT	CC	CA	FA	II	IH	CC	CA	RI	RI	CC
5	IH → IH		CC	CC	IH	CC	CC	RI	AT	II	FA	CA	IH	CS
6	AR	CC	CA	AR	RS	II	CA	IH	FA	AT	CS	II	CC	AR
7	CS	AR	RS	CS	FA	CS	IH	CC	AR	RS	AR	AR	RS	II
8	AT	RI	II	RS	AR	AR	CS	RS	CC	AR	CC	CC	AT	AT
9	RS → RS		AT	FA	II	FA	RI	FA	CS	FA	RS	FA	FA	RS
10	FA	FA	FA	II	CS	RS	II	CS	RS	CS	AT	RS	AR	FA

Figure 1. In this comparison of intuitive ranks (Bef) with final choice ranks (Aft), the arrows indicate two changes in rank positions that the team of managers discussed.

In other words, it made it possible for group members to examine their concepts in the broader context that derived from their colleagues. During the discussion, we realized that the structured evaluation was a valuable aid to justifying preferences and associated decisions. In the end, we agreed on the selection of a research portfolio.

Apart from selecting the portfolio, our aims in this initial exercise had been:

- To develop a model that could be used to appraise research projects,
- to involve the team of project managers in formulating and evaluating the model, and
- to use this exercise to pull the team together.

Overall we saw this fairly simple technique as successful and worth more detailed investigation. In particular, the senior manager thought that on the basis of this experiment a computerized system could be developed to help him monitor the progress of research projects.

However, we had several issues to address. First the software used in the original exercise lacked flexibility and adaptability and needed changes to improve its user interface. Secondly, although we considered the basic judgmental modeling approach valuable, we were critical of some aspects of the analytic hierarchy process. We thought its data requirements were excessive, and the participants did not feel at ease with the pairwise comparison procedure (Islei, 1986; Lockett and Stratford, 1987).

Because of this and trials in several other organizations on different decision problems, we developed a computer package based on geometric least squares (Islei and Lockett, 1988). This technique avoids several of the shortcomings of Saaty's AHP methodology while retaining its adaptive format using a hierarchical decomposition. The software (called Judgmental Analysis System—JAS for short) is flexible and user-friendly and has been applied very successfully in a variety of settings (Liddell, 1988; Lockett, Naude, and Gisbourne, 1991; Islei and Lockett, 1991).

The management team at ICI used this software on a number of occasions to appraise research projects. It also had access to other software packages based on different MCDM methods that were coming onto the market for PC use. We finally decided to use JAS as a core element in developing one system. It would support the process of assessing attribute weights since it allows users to examine their preferences and inconsistencies in great detail. Therefore, this component of data collection could be carried out thoroughly.

For evaluating project scores, the team at ICI were encouraged by the results of their experiments (Lockett and Stratford, 1987) with a version of Edwards' swing weight technique (Von Winterfeld and Edwards, 1986). On the basis of this, they wrote a simple computer program internally to study project evaluation but finally decided on a commercial package called VISA (Belton and Vickers, 1989), which could be modified to suit their requirements. The systems development was guided by the habitual decision processing of practicing managers and reflected the learning of the management team.

As the users gained experience with the DSS, they developed confidence in the model and its associated output. In consequence, we gradually refined the original attribute structure (Figure 2).

Although we changed the primary attributes very little, we disaggregated them into several layers of subattributes. Figure 3 shows the current structure of the four most important attributes (technical feasibility, product champion, staff competence, and competitive position).

To facilitate scoring the various projects in terms of these subattributes, we established detailed word-models. Figure 4 gives a typical example.

Word-models are simply standard reference frames with explicit anchor points. The user is faced with a series of discrete and well-defined ratings rather than a continuum of choices. Because the data requirements increased considerably as we differentiated the attribute structure, we regarded the use

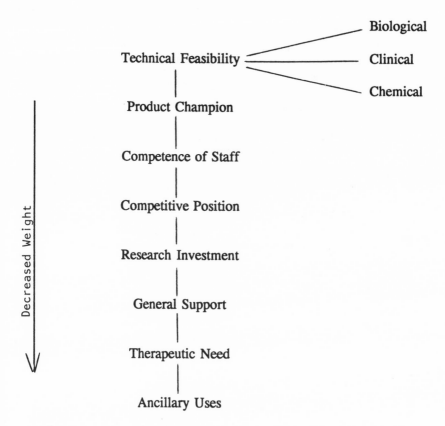

Figure 2. The original attribute structure had eight attributes of decreasing importance.

of such word-models as a necessary simplification of the DSS. We also saw it as making assessments more transparent and easier to communicate.

We made another major modification to the model concerning the attribute Technical Feasibility. We replaced the original subdivision of this important attribute (Figure 2) with a supplementary structure (Figure 3) that contains estimates of risk and time as separate components; the current model differentiates between assessing the achievement of technical goals and the time necessary for attaining these goals. To do this, we adopted a distinctive scoring procedure based on the work of Boschi, Balthasar, and Menke (1979) using probability-time curves (Figure 5).

We examined a series of simple judgmental models and implemented them as part of the DSS. Each component can be used separately, but the major benefit comes from their accessibility from within a common shell.

Introduction

Although Human Resource Information Systems (HRIS) have been addressed in terms of their implementation and availability (Frantzreb, 1986; Magnus and Thomesen, 1986), purpose (Johnson, Moorhead, and Griffin, 1983; Nardoni, 1985), and current status (DeSanctis, 1986; Magnus and Grossman, 1985; Moore and Clavadetscher, 1985) future directions for such systems have for the most part been ignored. HRIS are relatively new subsystems of organizational Management Information Systems (MIS). Their development has been similar to that of information systems of other functional areas although slower to develop. The most apparent difference between HRIS and the information subsystems maintained by other functional areas is the relatively recent interest in the development of such systems (Tomeski, Yoon, and Stephenson, 1976).

At present, HRIS provide the traditional transactional data operations and reports for personnel/human resource management administration (e.g., payroll, benefits administration, compensation administration, etc.), but are not designed to support managerial decision making (DeSanctis, 1986). Moore and Clavadetscher (1985) conclude that organizations will need to be firmly convinced that HRIS will save money and improve decision making before they pursue the acquisition of state-of-the-art systems.

That observation suggests that the allocation of additional resources to, and higher priority for, future HRIS development will require very persuasive justification. The human resource area will need to develop HRIS which extend their effect from the traditional transaction/report generating function to that of explicitly providing support for organizational decision making. This paper develops the integration of HRIS with Decision Support Systems capabilities to formulate a Human Resource Decision Support System (HRDSS) as a means to accomplish that goal.

Current Status of Human Resource Information Systems

As mentioned above, HRIS developed much later than information systems in other functional areas. Compared to other areas, researchers have shown relatively little interest in decision support systems for the human resource area. Articles proposing specific systems have been few in number (Davis and Steen, 1983; Enderle, 1987; Harris, 1986; LaPointe and Verdin, 1988). It appears that a very limited number of current HRIS have incorporated decision support features despite their enormous potential.

DeSanctis (1986) suggested that increasing demands by government agencies for human resource information, coupled with decreasing computing costs led to the initial interest in HRIS. Some factors now stimulating interest in HRIS include:

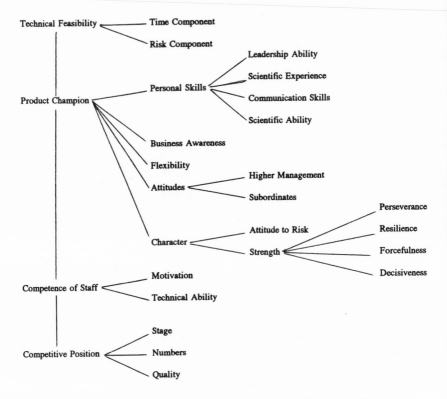

Figure 3. The current structure emphasizes the four most important attributes (technical feasibility, product champion, competence of staff, and competitive position), which are further broken down into subattributes.

Users can store and retrieve data easily and exchange and compare information. Because they share a common shell, the systems components can be used to arbitrate between differing goals or valuations. In the initial exercise, participants found that the DSS helped them to make decisions and enabled them to defend their assessments. The structured evaluation increased the credibility of their judgments.

PROJECT IMPLEMENTATION

The management team found the initial modeling process extremely valuable: it enabled them to identify and appreciate the differences and commonalities of their judgments. In fact, developing a judgmental model

LEADERSHIP ABILITY

Subattribute of Product Champion/Personal Skills/

100 Sapiential authority, instills enthusiasm and confidence, has drive, initiative plus all positives from below

80 No sapiential authority but instills enthusiasm and confidence, has drive and initiative

60 Encourages team to participate in discussions and has any two of the above at 80

40 Authoritarian, but operates his people as a group rather than on a 1:1 basis

20 Authoritarian, operates on a 1:1 basis, does not engender a team spirit

0 "Wally," only issues instructions which may be wrong/confused, inconsistent

Figure 4. The word model used to assess the subattribute Leadership Ability.

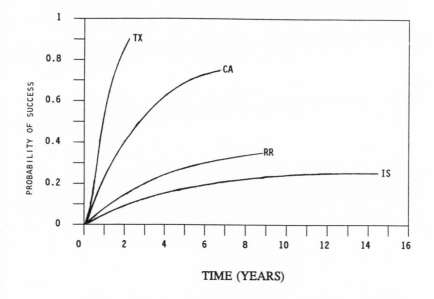

TIME (YEARS)

Figure 5. The early state of the combined-probability-versus-time curves: IS is seen as a new, risky project whereas TX is near completion.

as a group was the basis for their commitment. The structured approach helped to clarify critical issues and provided a basis for informed negotiations. The members felt that using the DSS improved their efficiency and facilitated communication and that it offered access to judgmental data that had either been unavailable or in unusable form.

Our investigation of the actual decision-making process provided the basis for developing several components of the DSS. We have gradually implemented them by prototyping and then refined them until an agreed procedure evolved. Each component reflects some critical part of the judgmental modeling frame that:

- Incorporates important characteristics of the management problem, for example, probability-time curves,
- facilitates data capture, for example, word-models, and
- offers flexibility to allow users to develop their preferences.

We designed the system in such a way that (1) it was compatible with the way the management team approached its unstructured decision task, and (2) it could be sustained by the team largely unassisted.

Even though the systems shell can be used to handle single decision tasks, its main benefit accrues from its ability to support longitudinal decision making. Unlike most decision-making scenarios that are difficult to replicate, the present case does not concern a one-time problem but affects a process that occurs over a long-time horizon with judgmental data serving as the main source of information. In this instance, we could study the impact of computerized decision support on managerial decision making quite extensively.

Although, the system changed and evolved, we have enhanced its underlying principles within the largest research section of ICI Pharmaceuticals, which uses it regularly to update and monitor the performance of the various research projects (Figure 6). By monitoring the progress of research projects, the managers are able to determine whether they must change the allocation of effort or take a more decisive action, for example terminate a project. The integrated system provides decision support whenever they need to adjust the base data, reallocate resources, or alter the portfolio. Since previous assessments are stored, they can easily monitor change.

The managers assess the various projects every three months and if they note problems, they can examine the alternatives by simulating appropriate actions: under certain conditions they discontinue research projects. (Currently we are developing an expert system that can help managers decide when to terminate a project (Wilkinson, 1991).

Each time they use the system, the managers generate new information on the state of the projects. They can do this in a variety of ways across a local area network. The results and estimates, however, can be accessed

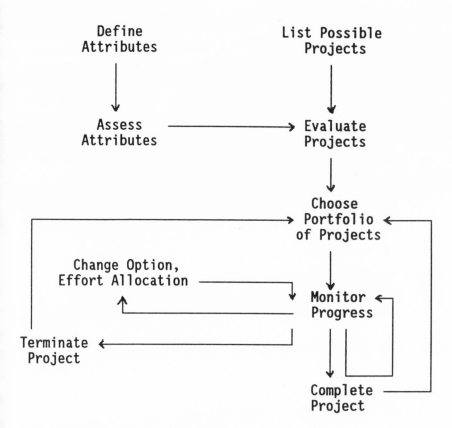

Figure 6. A flow chart of the decision-making procedures supported by our DSS shows the entire process from listing possible projects to completing projects.

by all concerned and compared with previous analyses. Because of its flexibility and accessibility, the system has helped to promote a participative and open management culture that favors innovative research. Gradually, ICI has built up a "data base" of the managers' judgments that it uses to great effect in making decisions. We will describe two simple examples to show different uses of the decision support components.

BALANCING THE PORTFOLIO

In any industrial research environment, managers must anticipate with reasonable accuracy the productivity of the research section. Using those estimates, senior managers can determine the probability of getting successful development candidates in important areas within specified time horizons. The company wants to be able, by monitoring and controlling projects, to hold its research strategy on target. One element in an effective research strategy is maintaining a balanced portfolio of research projects to ensure that projects are completed at an even rate.

We developed a model component for this problem (Islei, Lockett, and Stratford, 1991) that uses judgmental data to produce risk and time profiles (probability-time curves) for the research projects. By comparing these curves with desirable profiles the decision maker can monitor the progress of individual projects and also assess the viability of the overall portfolio. If certain indicators signal a need for a corrective action, the manager can simulate the effects of such changes in the portfolio balance.

\ The probability-time curves of an early project portfolio (Figure 5) showed the profiles of four projects, TX, CA, RR, and IS. Both RR and IS were weak options, and ICI needed a more balanced portfolio. Over time, it altered the research portfolio; Figure 7 shows the associated probability-time curves two years later.

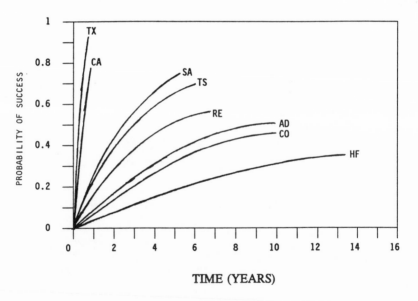

Figure 7.   The advanced state of the combined-probability-versus-time curves.

Some projects were discontinued (RR and IS), several new projects were introduced) SA, TS, RE, AD, CO. HF), and the probability-time curves of others changed (TX and CA). Both TX and CA are nearing successful completion. Clearly the project portfolio in Figure 7 is better balanced, and this balance made it possible for the research section to complete projects much more evenly.

Gradually, through careful monitoring of projects that passed successfully through the various research stages, the manager built up a data base that enables him to improve the accuracy of his forecasts. He was able to enhance the underlying model by including information about actual completion rates.

ATTRIBUTE PROFILES

Managers also appraise the performance of research projects with respect to other attributes. In each of these cases, capturing data generally involves the use of word models. By monitoring such information over time, managers become aware of trends that could signal the need for attention. In addition, all these separate assessments can be aggregated, for example, by using a simple additive weighted model, to obtain an overall preference structure (Figure 8). Most project scores are fairly stable.

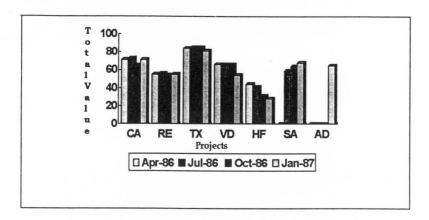

Figure 8. Overall project values change over time. Most project scores are relatively stable, with the exception of project HF. It not only underperforms but deteriorates rapidly.

When a project is not stable, looking at the disaggregate data allows us to track down the underlying causes. Figure 9 shows the scores of project HF for the four most important attributes (technical feasibility, product champion, staff competence, and competitive position) over approximately the same time horizon.

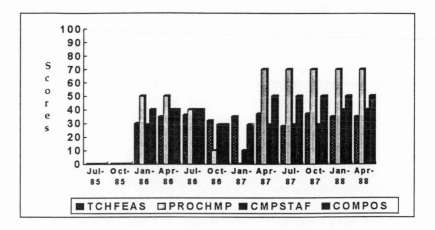

Figure 9. Attribute scores for research project HF (TCHFEAS: technical feasibility, PROCHMP: product champion, CMPSTAF: competence of staff, and COMPOS: competitive position).

The manager in charge of the project lacked the personality, skills, and attitude needed to champion a research project to successful completion. Apparently his performance had a detrimental effect on the research staff working under him. Eventually he was replaced (April 1987) by a different project manager whose performance restored the achievements of the team and improved the competitive position of ICI's product.

These two examples show the potential of the DSS and its influence on decision making. By maintaining a knowledge base of subjective data it provides an effective tool for monitoring the perceived progress of research projects and facilitates changes in resource allocation if required.

The Present DSS-User Views

So far, we have paid little attention to the most important constituent of the system, the user.

Manager A is a senior R&D manager and a visiting professor of pharmacology at a polytechnic institute. He finds that R&D managers typically take on a variety of research projects that have low probabilities of success and hold them for too long; they also often eliminate them for a single, possibly inappropriate reason. He considers the following to be the main benefits of the computer assisted process:

1. It formalizes the manager's monitoring process and permits the process to be checked by an outside expert.

2. It encourages the manager to look at the whole group of projects regularly to determine the progress of individual projects and the status of the research portfolio.
3. It improves the forecasts of project and stage completion times and information on the factors affecting these times.
4. It helps to plan resource needs and to detect problems.
5. It helps identify the types of programs that are successful and unsuccessful.

One manager who reports to Manager A has worked on developing several components of the system. Although at a different level in the organization, his views are complementary. He observed the following advantages:

1. It identifies key areas to work on to take a project from the idea to the implementation stage.
2. It provides a framework with which to determine whether new ideas are gaining or losing in the early stages of examining potential new projects.
3. It clarifies the technical feasibility of new programs and their impact on resources.
4. It offers a structured approach to selling the concept of a new program and preparing an analysis of the critical issues to be tackled in an ongoing program.
5. It helps to build a team and helps the team to see why one or two programs are selected from a broad range of potential projects.

The senior consultant from the management services unit, who has been instrumental in producing most of the systems development and has also advised other sections on implementing management support systems, offers his views. He has been invaluable in searching for new methods and bringing them to the attention of senior management. He recognized that:

1. Both the hierarchical structure of attributes and the word-model definitions helped to reduce ambiguity,
2. JAS has been an excellent tool for weighing attributes,
3. Managers have found little difficulty with VISA in scoring projects on each attribute utility scale with the aid of the word-model definitions,
4. The systems development has benefitted greatly from the use of simple models and our evolutionary approach.

These comments help to put the models in perspective and give a clear idea of their usefulness. With simple hardware and software tools, we created a DSS that has had a fundamental impact on the management of the research department. It is versatile and user friendly (using graphical interfaces that run under Microsoft Windows) and can be accessed easily by the management team for a variety of purposes. It has enabled the team to gradually build up a data base that facilitates diagnosis and control of the research portfolio.

The managers have instigated most of the developments, and therefore they have a high degree of ownership. The system is now largely stand-alone and does not require facilitation by a decision analyst. By using a judgmental model, we gave enough structure to the problem to permit transparent decision making without burdening the decision maker with excessive data requirements. Our analysis of the way the system has been used suggests that the quality of the decisions has improved.

ORGANIZATIONAL LEARNING

It is difficult to be precise about the critical factors that have led to this successful application. Quite clearly, effective implementation did not happen overnight but was a long and involved process; confidence in the models had to be earned. One special factor that was very important was top management support. In much of the literature, the involvement and support of senior management is cited as necessary for successful information technology developments. In our case it was of major importance.

Also the initial exercise, which ran over several weeks, has been very positively received by the whole group of managers. The results gave the participants some idea of the power of this approach that did not require sophisticated and time-consuming techniques. By defining a series of simple attributes, which can be used to measure the various research projects, the managers were able to clarify and improve their process of project appraisal. All the other developments centered around this concept. However, developing a structured model together was essential; all participants were interested in the effort.

Inevitably senior management realized that to optimize the likelihood of making worthwhile discoveries, it has to address several issues simultaneously: it must provide the right research environment, it must find technically feasible projects, it must engage competent staff, and it must give capable leaders (product champions) their heads in working on the projects (Cox, 1989). In other words, even though senior management defines the overall target, project leaders have to be left to achieve it their way (Islei and Lockett, 1991). All these factors were constituents of the core model, and putting values to such characteristics gave them a reality that otherwise was elusive. Ultimately it helped management to move project selection from a narrow cost efficiency concept to a more balanced approach, emphasizing the overall effectiveness of the R&D performance appraisal.

Like most innovations, these ideas met with some resistance; however, by using an evolutionary prototyping approach, we gradually overcame that resistance. We did not achieve this with pressure, but by involving the people concerned. They quickly realized the benefits of using an agreed format for evaluating projects. Decision making became more transparent, and therefore managers could focus their attention on critical factors much more easily.

Only after several data-collection exercises did the value of the DSS as a monitoring tool become apparent. With increasing user confidence, the credibility and appropriateness of the judgmental data manifested itself, and the knowledge base of the system could be progressively enhanced. The simple software and data structure enabled us to improve the system as the decision makers' understanding and needs developed. This gradually led to many enhancements of the basic model.

Similarly, the systems design was guided by the habitual decision making of the managers involved and thus underwent various modifications. The present system can be interrogated in an interactive manner and supports attractive dialogue features. Most components of the DSS also enable the user to print the essential results of a dialogue session in a standard format (Figures 10a, 10b, and 10c).

Similar standard formats are used to compare the performance of projects with respect to other attributes, and to assess the overall research portfolio. As users familiarized themselves with the available information and the possible formats, we modified the reporting procedure to reflect the organizational learning. Previously the process of providing information on the progress of research projects was lengthy and fragmented. Usually it was done under time pressure and was generally unreliable. With the present DSS, that problem has been largely overcome. The DSS has imposed a discipline on the research staff that gives them more time for their research and yet enables them to be more confident in their predictions.

ORGANIZATIONAL DIFFUSION

The system has now been used for several years, and its implementation enabled senior management to pursue a research strategy that proved effective and successful. The resultant changes created an open and informative environment that favors innovative research but that, when a discovery is made, permits ICI to act efficiently to capitalize on it. Other departments of the company have shown interest in the system and emulated several components.

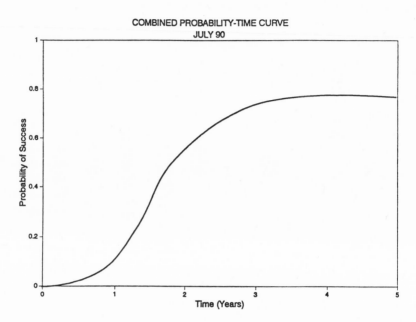

Figure 10a.   A quarterly update by senior management shows the probability-time profile for project AD as of July 1990.

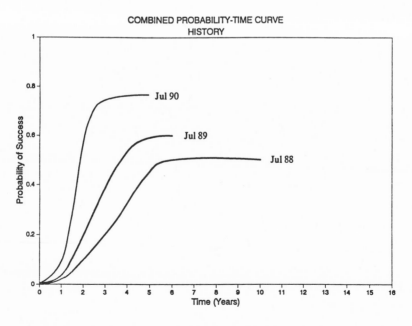

Figure 10b.   A diagram of the history of the probability-time curve.

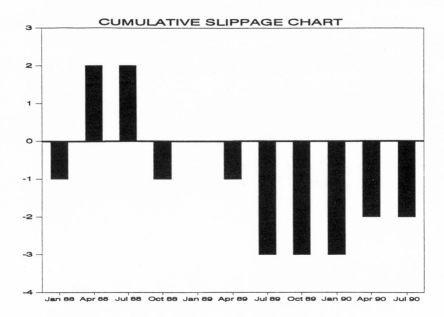

Figure 10c. A slippage chart shows how the project performed when compared to standard time estimates; it did well in April '88 and July '88 but fell behind in July '89 and is recovering only slowly.

One application took place in a research laboratory producing fine chemicals. Life cycles are much shorter, and research projects take about two years to complete instead of seven to 10 years, as they do in the pharmaceutical area. The laboratory did not adopt all of the model's characteristics, but it took the core elements of judgmental modeling together with the scoring procedures for quantifying preferences. The attribute structure and the word models looked very different, reflecting a distinct management problem. In this case, the risk-time assessments proved to be the most effective component for improving performance appraisal. Because the original system was already available, and the time scale was shorter, the lab could see evidence of benefits much more rapidly than in the pharmaceutical case.

The system components have also been used to great effect by the managers of a newly formed division. Chemicals and Polymers, who had to formulate a new research strategy. Previously, the constituent sections had used a variety of techniques to assess project worth. They believed one unified approach would:

- Provide a means for bringing section heads together to formulate and adopt an organizational structure conducive to research and development,
- make decisions more transparent, and
- facilitate communication of judgments and preferences.

The original model shell provided them with a framework for communicating differing viewpoints effectively and defusing confrontation. They could include judgments and personal values openly and explicitly in the discussion. For this group, the informative application of several system components both stimulated and stabilized organizational changes. They finally adopted the DSS in a slightly modified form, and they have now used it for more than two years (Islei, Lockett, and Stratford, 1990).

A further major application involved the marketing departments of two other branches of the company (Islei, Lockett, and Gisbourne, 1990). In both cases, the managers wanted to establish suitable strategies for marketing various products. They used the judgmental modeling framework to examine how their products performed compared to those of their major competitors. First, using the DSS, they established product profiles internally to assess their competitive positions. Then they employed a researcher to interview major customers throughout Europe using the same procedure to collect comparative data (Lockett, et al., 1991). Simple analyses of the data showed how their products were perceived in relation to competing products. The managers could then explore the strengths and weaknesses of their products and their marketing strategies. Senior management was most impressed with "the speed and uniformity with which strategically relevant data could be collected" (Lockett, Naude, and Gisbourne, 1991). The results, although unexpected, have been well received within the organization, and the methodology is finding general acceptance. Another major marketing study is underway.

These cases illustrate how computer-supported judgmental models are being diffused across the organization. Building on the success within one part of the company and incorporating managers' experiences has enabled other applications to be achieved within shorter learning cycles. The decision support system is owned by the users and is not seen as a technical black box. Managers no longer need decision analysts for day-to-day support; they seek advice only for key developments.

CONCLUSION

Our DSS has had major impact in supporting strategic decision making at ICI Pharmaceuticals. It helps to diagnose problem areas and communicate critical developments. Gradually a knowledge base of judgmental data has been built up. Reasons for its successful implementation were:

- Extensive user involvement,
- evolutionary approach to systems development,
- flexibility and simplicity of systems architecture,
- clarity of insights by using judgmental models, and
- accessibility and transferability of models and data.

Managers have aided the diffusion of ideas to other divisions of the company. They presented the judgmental approach to managing a research portfolio at group meetings, leading to a number of successful applications elsewhere. The company's experience with the original system greatly facilitated the implementation of computerized management support for similar tasks. There has been organizational learning.

This case highlights the advantages of an evolutionary approach that benefitted from a close collaboration between practicing managers and researchers. It shows how a DSS can be developed that does more than support well-defined management tasks. Our DSS helps managers to form and communicate perceptions, and to manage organizational change.

ACKNOWLEDGMENTS

Copyright 1991. The Institute of Management Sciences, reprinted with permission from Interfaces, Vol. 21, No. 6, pp. 4-22, November-December 1991.

REFERENCES

Alter, S.L. 1980. *Decision Support Systems—Current Practice and Continuing Challenges.* Reading, MA: Addison-Wesley.

Belton, V. and S.P. Vickers. 1989. "V I S A — VIM for MCDA." Pp. 287-304 in *Improving Decision Making in Organizations,* edited by A.G. Lockett and G. Islei. Heidelberg, Germany: Springer Verlag.

Bell, D.C. and A.W. Read. 1970. "The Application of a Research Project Selection Method." *R & D Management* 1(1): 35-42.

Boschi, R.A.A., H.E., Balthasar, and M.M. Menke. 1979. "Quantifying and Forecasting Exploratory Research Success." *Research Management* 22(5): 14-21.

Cox, B. 1989. "Strategies for Drug Discovery: Structuring Serendipity." *Pharmaceutical Journal* 243(6551): 329-338.

DeStevens, G. 1986. "Serendipity and Structured Research in Drug Discovery." *Progress in Drug Research* 30(5): 189-203.

Gear, A.E. and A.G. Lockett. 1973. "A Dynamic Model of Some Multi-Stage Aspects of Research and Development Portfolios." *IEEE Transactions on Engineering Management.* 20(1): 22-29.

Gear, A.E., A.G., Lockett, and A.P. Muhlemann. 1982. "A Unified Approach to the Acquisition and Subjective Data in R&D." *IEEE Transactions on Engineering Management* 29(1): 11-19.

Gray, P., W.R. King, E.R. McLean, and H.J. Watson, eds. 1989. *The Management of Information Systems.* Chicago, IL: Dryden Press.

Islei, G. 1986. "An Approach to Measuring Consistency of Preference Vector Derivations Using Least Square Distance." Pp. 265-284 in *Recent Advances and Historical Development of Vector Optimization* edited by J. Jahn and W. Krabs. Heidelberg, Germany: Springer Verlag.

Islei, G. and A.G. Lockett. 1988. "Judgmental Modelling Based on Geometric Least Squares." *European Journal of Operational Research* 36(1): 27-35.

Islei, G. and A.G. Lockett. 1991. "Group Decision Making: Suppositions and Practice." *Socio-Economic Planning Science* 25(1): 67-81.

Islei, G., A.G. Lockett, B. Cox, and M. Stratford. 1991. "A Decision Support System Using Judgmental Modeling: A Case of R&D in the Pharmaceutical Industry." *IEEE Transactions on Engineering Management* 38(3): 202-209.

Islei, G., A.G. Lockett, and S. Gisbourne. 1990. "Judgmental Modelling: An Organizational Perspective." Paper presented at ninth International Conference on Multiple Criteria Decision Making, *At the Interface of Needs in Industry, Business, and Government.* Fairfax, Virginia.

Islei, G., A.G. Lockett, and M. Stratford. 1990. "Resource Management and Strategic Decision Making in Industrial R&D Departments." *Engineering Costs and Production Economics* 20(2): 219-229.

Keen, P.G.W. and M.S. Scott Morton. 1978. *Decision Support Systems.* Reading, Mas: Addison-Wesley Publishing Company.

Kepner, C.H. and B. Tregoe. 1965. *The Rational Manager.* New York: McGraw-Hill.

Liddell, J. 1988. "Decision, Decisions ...." *Management Topics.* United Kingdom Ltd.: IBM.

Lockett, A.G., B. Hetherington, P. Yallup, M. Stratford, and B. Cox. 1986. "Modelling a Research Portfolio Using AHP: A Group Decision Process." *R&D Management* 16(2): 151-160.

Lockett, A.G., P. Naude, and S. Gisbourne. 1991. "An Application of Judgmental Modelling to the Vendor Selection Process." Working Paper 203, Manchester Business School, Manchester, England.

Lockett, A.G. and M. Stratford. 1987. "Ranking of Research Projects: Experiments with Two Methods." *OMEGA* 15(5): 395-400.

PA Consulting Group. 1990. *Information Technology: The Catalyst for Change* London, England: W.H. Allen & Co.

Saaty, T.L. 1980. *The Analytic Hierarchy Process.* New York: McGraw-Hill.

Sprague, R.H. 1989. "A Framework for the Development of Decision Support Systems." Pg. 19-48 in *The Management of Information Systems,* edited by P. Gray, W.R. King, E.R. McLean, and H.J. Watson. Chicago, IL: Dryden Press.

Turban, E. 1990. *Decision Support and Expert Systems: Management Support Systems.* New York: Macmillan Publishing Company.

Von Winterfeld, D. and W. Edwards. 1986. *Decision Analysis and Behavioral Research.* Cambridge, England: Cambridge University Press.

Wilkinson, A. 1991. "Developing an Expert System on Project Evaluation." *R&D Management* 21(1): 19-23.

THE FUTURE OF SIS APPLICATIONS

Robert P. Cerveny, C. Carl Pegels, and
G. Lawrence Sanders

INTRODUCTION

In a 1972 article in the Harvard Business Review John Dearden expressed serious dissatisfaction with the as then emerging concept of a management information system.

> Some years ago I expressed the opinion that "of all the ridiculous things that have been foisted on the long-suffering executive in the name of science and progress, the real-time management system is the silliest." I no longer believe this statement is true. We now have something even sillier: the current fad for "*the* management information system," whether it is called the Total System, the Total Management System, the management information system , or simply MIS.

The concept of a *totally integrated information system* is back with renewed vitality and perhaps with greater imperative than ever before. The next generation of strategic information systems will not necessarily be in a particular part of the firm, but will rather emerge from the synergy of integration. Global competition and global markets, the geographic dispersion of corporate functions, and increased sensitivities to customer demands for new products are putting tremendous pressure on the infrastructure for transmitting and processing information.

299

Dearden was right in 1972. At that time the hardware and software technology was not sophisticated, the concepts of competitive strategy were not well developed, and database design was very immature. We are in a new era. Telecommunications and networks have improved dramatically, and relational database management systems and the structured query language (SQL) are becoming the standard mechanisms for modeling and accessing information. Also, data modelling has given structure and formalism to the database design process, and strategic management is the centerpiece of contemporary management thought. Until now most organizations were not capable of integrating the numerous functional and support systems. The confluence of advances in hardware and software technology, information engineering, and strategic management now provide the tools for integrating organizational systems.

INTEGRATION: THE NEXT CRITICAL SIS APPLICATION

What can be said about the current state of information technology can also be said about the organizations in which they reside. Turbulence and ambiguity are the hallmarks of the organizational and competitive environments. Profit margins are lower, product development cycles are shorter, and market encroachment from competitors with what appear to be unrelated products is the norm. In spite of this many organizations concentrate on short run returns rather than on long term benefits. There is very little integration of key business sub-systems and information cannot be readily retrieved from organizational data repositories. The results have often been troublesome, resulting in weak decisions, right decisions at the wrong time, and a lack of organizational vision and direction. Mergers and acquisitions, the development of strategic partnerships, and the proliferation of new technological strategies have put additional stress on organizational processes. It is becoming increasingly difficult to know where an organization begins and where it ends. Stationary organizational boundaries have been replaced with virtual boundaries which require new approaches to systems integration. What are the symptoms of a lack of integration, particularly of poorly integrated databases? Below we shall explore a number of these symptoms. If a company answers yes to any of the following statements, it is likely that there are problems with the level of systems integration.

- We can not retrieve data from organizational databases. We know that the data exists in the computer but it cannot be combined or retrieved in a suitable manner without significant effort on the part of our systems people.

- Management reports are provided one or two weeks after end-of-month, end-of-quarter, or end-of-year closing.
- Employees are engaged in a lot of intermediate data reentry, summarizing, reorganizing, and recalculation before reports are issued.
- Some departments and employees have difficulty obtaining data in a desired format.
- Some departments and employees cannot do their job effectively because the data is simply not available anywhere.
- Some departments are doing things with their data that is making it hard for other departments to do their job effectively.
- Sometimes customers receive two bills, we loose track of what we have in inventory, and we loose track of our customers or vendors. Employees, customers, and vendors sometimes receive letters at the wrong address.
- We do not know where a product is in the production process, our equipment is improperly maintained because we do not know what equipment has or has not been maintained, and we have trouble matching employees to jobs.
- End-users from functional areas (marketing, finance, production etc.) are always complaining about their inability to obtain data.

Many organizations exhibit these symptoms to varying degrees and most of these organizations could benefit from the strategic advantages obtained from information systems integration. Organizations do not have to continue wallowing in the data quagmire. Organizations can take steps to improve their integration index, by simply recognizing that the basic transaction databases are the foundation and future of strategic information systems.

Based on the above problems and deficiencies, a strategy for pursuing information integration should include the following sequence:

- Apply approaches to developing strategic information discussed in previous chapters to derive the strategic information systems plan. (It is assumed that the information systems planning process is aligned with the corporate planning process.)
- Use the output from the information systems plan to develop an enterprise-wide data model which will be used to identify the key data elements for the core organizational databases.
- Implement core organizational systems and databases on a distributed relational database platform.

The cost of integration and the subsequent conversion of existing systems (order entry, shipping, receiving, scheduling, purchasing, etc.) can be in the millions of dollars. However, the benefits of integration—knowledge and efficiency—provide a strategic edge based on synergy. Further, if integration is conducted in a modular and consistent fashion system modifications will also be facilitated. This is particulalry important with the development of strategic partnerships. The success and failure of a merger, an acquisition, or a partnership can hinge on the compatibility of the information systems of the respective parties.

Integrating existing applications can also involve substantial reengineering and redesign. Organizations often engage in activities which, though appropriate at one time, have outlived their usefulness; they may even be detrimental to the organizational mission. The question is why automate inappropriate and inefficient processes? Some have actually called for drastic measures, including obliterating and redesigning organizational systems with outdated rules and assumptions, rather than automating them (Hammer, 1990).

The next section discusses several subsystem areas which could evolve into strategic information systems.

DEVELOPING AND EVOLVING STRATEGIC APPLICATIONS

Information systems integration is an ambitious undertaking requiring a level of investment that most organizations are either unwilling to expend or they cannot afford. In lieu of integration, there are several subsystem areas that might have strategic potential. Below we describe a variety of subsystem applications which could evolve into stratetic applications of information technology.

In the retail sector, Datatec Industries has created the ShopperTrak system which records when every shopper enters and exits a store, the direction that a shopper walks and how fast people are moving through specific departments (Miller, 1991). The system output can be used to measure the performance of in-store personnel, determine staffing levels, measure the impact of visual merchandising and in-store promotions, and assist in configuring new store layouts. The ShopperTrak system has the potential to yield significant insight into consumer buying activities, because it is in an area in which data collection has historically been difficult.

HUMAN RESOURCE MANAGEMENT

As organizations increase in size and complexity there is also a concomitant need to access and develop the knowledge and skills distributed throughout the corporation. Organizations which can draw upon the vast resources of knowledge from within the organization and organizations which develop their human resources through training and education will be a competitive force in the next decade. These systems will assist in matching skills to tasks, will permit locating individuals with unique and specialized skills, will assist in tracking and scheduling education and training programs, and will provide the typical human resource functions of payroll and benefits management.

MANAGERIAL ACCOUNTING

The traditional approach of allocating costs to products and product lines according to direct labor hours and similar schemes is rapidly changing because direct labor costs are now a minor part of the total cost of producing a product. Poor strategic decisions can be made when so-called overhead and fixed costs are allocated according to direct labor costs. Product lines which are thought to be profitable can actually be losing money, and product lines which appear to be losing money can, in reality, be making money when traditional cost accounting systems are in place. Assigning costs using the activity based costs (ABC) approach, attempting to identify costs and revenues throughout the product life cycle, and identifying non-value added costs are just a few of the major revisions to the managerial cost accounting systems that are under way (see Noori [1990] and Cooper and Kaplan [1988] for a review of the approaches].

LINE MANAGEMENT

There is increasing awareness that line managers should be responsible for leveraging and exploiting information technology in the manufacturing and operations area because people have a unique and insightful perspective on the production process. In the future line managers will be held increasingly accountable for planning and managing the business use of information technology (Dixon and Darwin, 1989). Because line managers will be responsible for identifying problem areas and opportunities where information technology can be applied, it will also be necessary to train these individuals in how to apply information technology to the production process.

STRATEGIC PARTNERSHIPS

Rather than merge, companies can join forces to take advantage of respective strengths (Konsynski and McFarlan, 1990). Typically one company has a comparative advantage in terms of a customer database and the other company has a value added service. The relationship between VISA and MCI, where MCI charges can be billed to VISA, is an attempt to develop a synergistic partnership to counter AT&Ts entry into the credit card business.

SYSTEMS DEVELOPMENT

CASE tools (Computer Aided Software Engineering) at this point in time are still in the developmental stage. CASE tools should dramatically decrease the amount of time it takes between conceptualizing a system and implementing a system. Further, CASE tools in the future will not only automate program coding, but they will also assist systems analysts in identifying strategic opportunities because they will be integrated with the strategic planning process.

ELECTRONIC DATA INTERCHANGE

At this time EDI can be viewed as a strategic opportunity. However, in the future organizations which do not have the ability to communicate with their customers and suppliers through EDI will be at a competitive disadvantage. Investment in hardware, software, and people to facilitate intra- and interorganizational communication will be required for organizations competing in the global marketplace.

Future strategic applications of information technology are hard to predict. There are some people who are of the opinion that strategic information systems simply emerge from the organizational context and competitive environment. They further note that explicit planning will not assist in identifying SIS applications. This is in contrast to the school of thought which declares that strategic applications of information technology can be identified, and they can be used to guide the firm. We ascribe to the latter notion that information technology can indeed be used as a helm to steer the organization towards new opportunities.

The secret of identifying strategic applications of information technology is actually a simple process. First of all organizations need to be constantly aware of new developments in information technology. Second organizations need to look internally and externally for potential areas in which to learn about and exploit new technology. Though the process is quite simple, the difficulty lies in cultivating an organizational environment in which employees from the line level all the way to top level management are committed to an environment of change and innovation. If an information systems planning approach is to be successful it must support and facilitate an environment of innovation and change.

INFLUENCE OF ENVIRONMENT AND DECISION PROCESSES ON STRATEGIC INFORMATION SYSTEMS DEVELOPMENT

The question of the driving forces behind strategic information systems is an interesting one. It is also of considerable interest to those managers who are wondering how strategic information systems affect their operations, and whether they should be actively involved in developing them.

A recent paper (Sabherwal and King, 1992) sheds considerable light on the above subject. It reports a study which intended to find out how environmental factors and internal decision processes affected the evolution of strategic information systems within firms.

The study found that the extent of management plans for strategic information systems is not related to the maturity of the information system within the firm. This result is particularly interesting because information system maturity is measured in terms of the existence of sophisticated information system planning processes in the organization. This result was also found earlier in a study by Runge (1988). Runge found that in the telecommunications industry, formal information systems planning activities are commonly avoided during the development of strategic information systems applications.

The findings by Sabherwal and King (1992) also indicate that the organization structure seems to be less important than the external environment and the maturity of the information systems function within the firm. In a relatively static industry environment there is an association with analytical decision making. On the other hand, a hostile industry environment is associated with more political decision making. Hence, the nature of the external environment seems to influence whether a rational (analytical decision making) or a political process is used to decide on strategic information system applications.

A limitation of the study centers on the use of information system executives to obtain data for the study. Although the senior information systems executive was found to be the most informed about the technical and operational aspects of strategic information systems and their development within the firm, he or she may not be well informed how strategic information systems are used and what benefits they generate. The study generated 81 responses, providing a reasonable sample from which to derive general conclusions. Exhibit 1 provides a listing of a sample of strategic information systems applications culled from the 81 respondents.

No.	Description	Benefits
1.	Replaced the manual system of stocking shelves with a pre-packaged system which uses input collected by the route representatives through portable computer terminals.	Enables a 90% reduction in the number of warehouse locations. Reduces the number of route personnel needed. Enables the replacement of large trucks with fuel-efficient vans. Eliminated data-entry positions.
2.	Provides on-site PC based support to plant managers for production and scheduling of work orders. Reports performance according to various work categories.	Reduces costs for customers. Makes tangible benefits more easily identified by customer. Locks customer into system dependency especially for equipment history.
3.	Provides on-line information on merchandise availability, permits immediate reservations and shipping commitments.	Greatly improves customer service through more timely, reliable and accurate information. This, in turn improves sales.
4.	A computerized system to record customers' requests. To minimize trouble calls and associate those calls with the company's internal computer-based network to identify the cause of service interruption.	Reduces service interruptions and restores service as quickly as possible when interruptions do occur.
5.	A communication network between headquarters and all distributors.	Eliminates delays of mailing orders and warranty claims. Provides up to the minute information to distributors. Improves turnaround time of truck orders and warranty claims. Helps correct errors faster.
6.	Customer service system provided by the company to retail customers. Consists of hand-held entry device for customer to enter order using wholesalers' item numbers provided via retail shelf labels as well as other data such as retail prices.	Makes it convenient for customer to place orders. Ties customer to the company by shelf labels, retail price profile, and monthly reports showing movement and profitability data to customer for items ordered through the company.
7.	Paperless item processing system to serve both clients (manufacturers) and customers (retailer) for factoring and collecting large sums of money-several billion dollars each month. Serves 250 clients and 300,000 retailers.	Allows immediate credit approval/funds transfer for clients with good credit standing. Allows electronic purchasing of these invoices and collection status reporting without a single paper changing hands.
8.	Electronic parts catalog system for the dealers. The information resource used here is the parts database (alphanumeric and drawings) which the company has great familiarity with.	Presenting the information in electronic form reduces search time, reduces ordering and billing errors, increases mechanics' production time, and increases sales for the dealers.

Note: The strategic IS applications and the resulting benefits have been presented in somewhat less specific terms than the original responses to maintain confidentiality of responses.

Source: Sabherwal and King (1992, pp. 917-943).

Exhibit 1.   A Sample of Strategic IS Applications

CONCLUSION

The current competitive environment can be characterized as being turbulent and ambiguous. Profit margins are lower, product development cycles are shorter, and competitors emerge from industries which appear unrelated. Organizations have thus turned towards information technology as a means to improve their competitiveness. More specifically, organizations have looked towards Strategic Information Systems as a way to deliver unique products and services and to deliver those products and services at a lower cost. It is the role of the SIS manager to facilitate the development of SIS applications. This book has identified the broad range of knowledge necessary for the SIS manager to successfully carry out this task. The skill requirements are extensive, but they must be accompanied by experience and vision. Experience which is developed over several years of attending to the day-to-day organizational tasks. The vision is a product of top level management's commitment to the development of Strategic Information Systems. The foundation for SIS lies in the knowledge areas outlined in the report. The eventual implementation is a function of organizational experience and vision.

REFERENCES

Cooper, R. and R. S. Kaplan. 1988. "Measure Costs Right: Make The Right Decision." *Harvard Business Review* 66(5): 96-103.

Dixon, P. J. and A. J. Darwin. 1989. "Technology Issues Facing Corporate Management in the 1990s." *MIS Quarterly* 13(3): 247-255.

Dearden, J. 1992. "MIS is a Mirage." *Harvard Business Review* 50(1): 90-99.

Hammer, M. 1990. "Re-engineering Work: Don't Automate, Obliterate." *Harvard Business Review* 68(4): 104-112.

Konsynski, B. R. and F. W. McFarlan. 1990. "Information Partnerships — Shared Data, Shared Scale." *Harvard Business Review* 68(5): 114-120.

Miller, C. 1991. "Retail System Keeps Track of Shoppers." *Marketing News* (April): 22.

Noori, H. 1990. *Managing the Dynamics of New Technology.* Englewoods Cliffs, NJ: Prentice Hall.

Runge, D. A. 1988. *Winning with Telecommunications: An Approach for Corporate Strategists.* Washington, DC: International Center for Information Technology Press

Sabherwal, R. and W.R. King. 1992. "Decision Processes for Developing Strategic Applications of Information Systems: A Contingency Approach." *Decision Sciences* 23(4): 917-943.

TERM INDEX

COMPANY INDEX

A. C. Nielsen, 189
A.T. and T. Technologies, 128
AI Corporation, 63
Aion, Inc., 63
Air Cargo Industry, 55-58
Airborne Express, 57
Allied Pilot Association, 156
America West, 251, 255
American Airlines, 1, 10, 118, 136,
144, 145
American Cyanamid, 134
American Express, 33
American Hospital Supply, 8, 108
American President Lines, 136
Anderson Consulting, 63
Andreas Stihl, 128
Apple Computer, 65
Arby's, Inc., 180
Arthur D. Little, 208, 223
Associated Grocers, 208, 223
AT&T, 167, 168, 173, 178, 180
Avis, 11, 139

B.M. Products, 132
Bank of America, 180
Bank of New England, 207, 216
Baxter Credit Union, 167, 171, 172
Baxter International, 171
Bellcore, 65
BellSouth, 167, 168, 176
Bi State Transit, 138

Boeing, 64
BRK Electronics, 141

Cabela's, Inc., 181
CAL Electronics Circuits, 211, 217
Campbell Soup, 174, 207,212
Carnegie Group, 63
Chevron, 250, 261
Cincinnati Bell Telephone, 167,
172
Citicorp Global Payments, 209, 225
Coca-Cola, 53
Coldwell-Banker, 14
Compaq Computer Corp., 258
Comshare, Inc., 172
Consolidated Freightways, 55
Control Data, 111, 140
Coopers and Lybrand, 208, 223
Corning Asahi, 135
CSX Transportation, 137
Cummins Engine Company, 131,
209, 214

Data General, 172
Dean Witter Reynolds, 10
Dial Corporation, 207, 214
Digital Equipment Corporation, 7,
61, 65, 63, 68, 71, 207, 212
Dillard's, 166, 167, 183, 168
DuPont, 67
Dylex, 139

315